Closeness

Closeness
An Ethics

Edited by
Harald Jodalen and Arne Johan Vetlesen

SCANDINAVIAN UNIVERSITY PRESS

Oslo – Stockholm – Copenhagen – Oxford – Boston

Scandinavian University Press (Universitetsforlaget AS)
P.O. Box 2959 Tøyen, N-0608 Oslo, Norway
Fax +47 22 57 53 53
URL: http://www.scup.no

Stockholm office
SCUP, Scandinavian University Press
P.O. Box 3255, S-103 65 Stockholm, Sweden

Copenhagen office
Scandinavian University Press AS
P.O. Box 54, DK-1002 København K, Denmark

Oxford office
Scandinavian University Press (UK) Ltd.
60 St. Aldates, Oxford OX1 1ST, England

Boston office
Scandinavian University Press North America
875 Massachusetts Ave., Ste. 84, Cambridge MA 02139, USA
Fax +1 617 354 6875

© Scandinavian University Press (Universitetsforlaget AS), Oslo 1997

ISBN 82-00-22563-1 ✓

Chapters 3 and 4 are reprinted from *Outside the Subject*, by Emmanuel Levinas, translated by Michael B. Smith with permission of the publishers, Stanford University Press and The Athlone Press. English translation © 1993 by The Athlone Press.
Chapter 7 is reprinted from *The Ethical Demand*, by Knud Ejler Løgstrup © 1966, with permission of the publishers, The University of Notre Dame Press.
Chapter 8 is reprinted from *Love's Knowledge: Essays on Philosophy and Literature*, by Martha C. Nussbaum. Copyright © 1992 by Martha C. Nussbaum. Used by permission of Oxford University Press, Inc.

Design: Astrid Elisabeth Jørgensen
Cover illustration: NPS/nonstøck/Jason Beck
Typeset in 9.25 on 13 point Photina by Formatvisual Ltd
Printed on Munken Golden 90gms by Østfold Trykkeri, Norway

Contents

Preface

The first step toward this anthology was our interview with Emmanuel Levinas in Paris in the summer of 1993. For some time, we had been searching for academic literature on what we came to term an ethics of proximity. We didn't find much.

Having met Levinas, we conceived the idea of collecting a number of essays dealing with the topic of our fancy. What we wanted was a combination of classical texts and papers written especially for this volume. We are very happy that this ambition is borne out in the book as now completed.

Along the way, we have benefited from the support and advice given by several friends and colleagues. We especially wish to thank Asbjørn Aarnes, Zygmunt Bauman, Robin Downie and Alastair Hannay, not only for their contributions to the present volume but also for the interest taken in the project since its inception. We also wish to thank Joel Anderson, Ole Berg, Milada Blekastad, Peder Inge Furseth and Marc J. Roberts.

H.J. & A.J.V.
Oslo, April 1997

Chapter 1
Introducing an Ethics of Proximity

Arne Johan Vetlesen

The meeting of the Other face to face defies reduction. How can this irreducible quality be conveyed into an ethics?

This question is not answered in the ethical theories most prominent today; indeed they fail to address it properly in the first place. Influential theorists such as Rawls and Habermas share a puristic conception of morality. The requirements of impartiality and procedural rationality, and the Kant-inspired criterion of universalizability, combine to set up the acid test that issues must pass to qualify as having truly moral import. As defined in the recent work of Habermas, the moral point of view requires an abstraction from context under three aspects: (1) an abstraction from given motivations, (2) an abstraction from the particular situation, and (3) an abstraction from an established mode of life. Thus conceived, the moral point of view shifts the emphasis from the question, What is good for me or us? to the question, What ought one to do? It imposes a categorical distinction between what is *good* for me or us to do and what is the *right* thing to do. Moral reasoning in the implied deontological sense is confined to interpersonal obligations. By contrast, all questions concerning the good life – how one should live, personally and as a member of a particular community – are termed evaluative and addressed in the "ethical-existential" discourse where they are settled not in terms of their normative rightness but in terms of their authenticity.

Following Habermas, practical reason in *moral* discourse proper instead of a faculty of prudential deliberation (Aristotle's *phronesis*), employed within the context of an established mode of life, becomes a faculty of principles of pure, context-independent reason. This context-independence is reflected in the aforementioned abstractions. Participants in a moral discourse are required to adopt a hypothetical attitude toward the givenness of motivation, situation, and mode of life. Having barred all evaluative questions concerning the good life, moral discourse exclusively pursues questions of normative justification, and it does so in accordance with a procedure that demands that everything – that is to say, all normative validity claims built into our lifeworld and rooted in our daily practices – counts as a hypothesis until it regains its validity from the authority of good reasons, and from them alone.[1]

What happens here is that morality is reduced to matters of justice and conflicts of rights open to argumentative resolution. We find that this conception narrows the moral universe in a way that simply will not do. The modern deontological notion of moral reason defended in Habermasian discourse ethics and Rawlsian political liberalism may be good news for rationality; but it greatly impoverishes morality.

To be sure, Habermas does not see practical rationality as in any way exhausted in his definition of moral discourse as given above. The evaluative questions barred from moral discourse and handed over to ethical-existential discourse are in principle no less open to the argumentation based on reasons than are normative questions. However, in so far as questions concerning what is good for a person are inescapably bound up with that particular person's quest for identity and self-understanding, such questions do not allow for an answer that can be valid for everybody; the interpretation called for here is self-related and intrapersonal in that it elucidates a particular (existentialists would say unique) individual's life project, thereby raising a descriptive question Who am I? – as well as an evaluative one – Who would I like to be?

Since these latter questions are raised by a particular individual, the suitable responses to them will have to conform to that individual's notion of self-realization, with regard to which there are no universally valid notions. Indeed, in political terms it is because questions of the good life are unsuitable to universalization that there exists – and rightly so – a rich plurality of individual life-styles and a corresponding diversity of ideals of a good life.

This distinction between two distinct discourses means they must be conducted within different spheres. Moral discourse is public; questions of normative rightness demand that all parties concerned have an equal say. By contrast, ethical or evaluative discourse assumes the form of the concerned individual's on-going conversation with, and examination of, her- or himself. The extent to which others may have a say here is obscure, as are the criteria by which the individual is to assess their judgements as distinguished from his own. This being so, the impression is inescapable that while Habermas seeks to work out a comprehensive notion of practical reason, the distinction he draws between different discourses ends up privileging the reason at work in moral discourse: it is here that reason is truly universal and comprises *everybody*, as opposed to the always particular somebody. Hence reason as operative in the individual's quest for meaning, identity, and authentic self-realization comes forward as impoverished when compared with reason as it works in settling moral disputes within a nonrestrictive, truly universal public domain.

Today, restriction of questions of the "good" to the sphere of the particular individual by and for whom such questions are said to be raised is met with profound dissatisfaction in many philosophical camps, in particular the neo-Aristotelian one. The priority given to the right over the good in deontological theories is vigorously contested. In a significant sense, the dispute between present-day Kantians such as Rawls and Habermas and Aristotelians such as MacIntyre and Taylor is political as well as philosophical. Modern deontology of the Habermasian kind we have focused on here has increasingly entered into what now appears almost a symbiotic relationship with political liberalism, Western style. The former offers a conception of morality and rationality nearly tailormade for the self-image cultivated by Western liberal democracy. Indeed, pointing this out would not upset Rawls or annoy Habermas; it is simply a matter of our having got their political message right.

As for the contributions in the present volume, their common worry is not chiefly the Aristotelian one just alluded to. The warrant or lack of such for privileging the right over the good will not be debated, meaning that it will be neither affirmed nor rejected. Rather, this volume is more closely concerned with the tendency to a privatization of the question of the good, hinted at above. Morality is dramatically impoverished the moment What is good? What is worth striving for? What makes life meaningful? are taken to belong exclusively within the sphere of the "one" individual posing them. To deny that these questions are properly rational (i.e., suited to *inter*subjective agreement), and on that basis declare them no longer part of what *morality* is all about, is an eminently disputable move. For one thing, it seems now a routinely taken for granted premise (a *petitio principii*) that the philosophical understanding

4 ARNE JOHAN VETLESEN

of rationality (its powers, procedural mode of operation, and criteria for adjudication) prejudge, even help *define* what is to count as being moral and having moral import. Rationality presides and reigns over morality to the point of recognizing as moral only what conforms to the requirements of rationality as formally conceived of. Morality is made to bow before the court of reason. But this amounts to a confusion. Whether moral disputes shall be settled by means of reason is of course not at issue. This ambition holds for Aristotle no less than for Kant. In Kant, universalizability was meant to be a criterion by which maxims of actions could be scrutinized for their conformity with the moral law. For a proposed maxim of action, passing the test of universalization meant that it was to count both as *rationally* grounded and as *morally* justified. Having been vindicated in this twofold sense, the maxim would in effect be acceptable to all parties concerned.

Returning again to Habermas, a shift of emphasis may be observed. In discourse ethics, form is privileged to such a degree as to determine content. Universalizability, impartiality, and impersonality – the formal criteria instrumental in defining "the moral point of view" – now function as the features a given item must possess in order to qualify as actually having moral content. In other words, only issues, questions, problems, and dilemmas lending themselves to adjudication and consensual resolution by means of the formal criteria mentioned are allowed to qualify as "moral" in content.

Such a formalistic understanding of morality – grossly anti-Aristotelian as it is, and more due to Habermas than to Kant – implausibly narrows our moral universe. Failing to satisfy the criteria referred to, a large number of concerns we experience as being moral are instead said to be merely personal or private, and so beyond the scope of moral discourse. Rawls' and Habermas' reduction of morality to the principles of distributive justice and the validity claim of normative rightness, respectively, erects a boundary between issues of genuine moral import and "personal" issues. Feminist theorists in particular have questioned the basis and implications of this boundary. In the words of Seyla Benhabib, "the moral issues which preoccupy us most and which touch us most deeply derive not from problems of justice in the economy and the polity, but precisely from the quality of our relations with others in the 'spheres of kinship, love, friendship, and sex'".[2] The claim that justice defines the core of morality and that justice is trump applies first and foremost to the arrangement of social and political institutions (to allude to Rawls); it does not capture the boundaries of morality *per se*.

To challenge the restricted fashion in which morality is theorized today, no single tradition of moral thought offers itself as a readily available alternative. However, a host of thinkers can be seen to share a common, though differently articulated, dissatisfaction with the view of morality sketched above.

Vital differences aside, thinkers such as Kierkegaard, Scheler, Buber, Heidegger, Sartre, Levinas, and Løgstrup all oppose impersonality and universalizability as characteristics of the moral point of view. These thinkers hold that moral orientation springs from a unique and, as it turns out, eminently precarious *experiential* basis: they see the human dyad (the I–thou relationship) as the fundamental locus of concern and responsibility. This being so, the cognitive and emotional abilities indispensable for adopting a moral point of view are fostered in a setting of proximity, in interaction with close and, as one might say, irreplaceable others.

How, then, should the dyadic relationship be theorized?

Moral philosophy offers two replies: one holds that the relation to the human other be understood as a relation of knowledge; the other, that it be understood as a relation of being. The first reply faces the task of specifying how knowledge of human others differs from knowledge of, say, physical objects in the world. Here the approach taken by Husserl's phenomenological theory of intersubjectivity has been particularly influential: our intuitive grasp of the other depicts him or her as a centre of intentionality and hence as *alter ego*, as a sensuous–conscious subject sharing our own repertoire of specifically human agency. By way of analogy we are in principle capable of understanding in the other what we know in and from ourselves.

The second reply faces the task of specifying how being with human others differs from sharing the simple fact of (co)existence with everything else in the world. Advocates of this reply often see connection to the human Other through being instead of through knowledge as in some sense a "deeper" kind of connectedness. A famous case in point is Sartre. In his discussion of the existence of others in *Being and Nothingness*, Sartre contends that "if we are to refute solipsism, then my relation to the Other is first and fundamentally a relation of being to being, not of knowledge to knowledge".[3] In identifying knowledge and being, Hegel allegedly fails to reach this insight; so does Husserl, since he measures being by knowledge. However, Sartre thinks that Heidegger takes a step in the right direction in his account of *Mitsein* in *Being and Time*. From Heidegger we learn that the relation between "human-realities" must be a relation of being. The upshot is that being-with is recognized as a fundamental characteristic of *Dasein*. The thesis in Heidegger endorsed by Sartre is that my being-in-the-world is partly constituted by and thus inextricably linked with my being-with-others.

In a word, the move undertaken here is to posit the relation to the other as ontological not epistemic. But why is this thought to be such an important shift of emphasis?

A first answer is the indicated one that a connectedness on the level of being is deeper than that of knowing. We come to realize that our coexistence with others is nothing less than definitive of what it means to be human.

A second answer is that what bears on our very being *qua* humans is less of an option for us than our various undertakings as subjects seeking knowledge about entities encountered in the world. Properly speaking, what involves who and what we are seems not at all an option, whereas what we *know* seems in some vague sense to be more up to us, and as individuals at that.

Though evidently correct, this difference doesn't take us very far. For there is also a strong case for seeing ontology and epistemology as twins. The totality of entities making up the world, marking the domain of what is, by the same token delineates the totality of objects of human cognition. The ambition of thought, said Hegel, is to catch up with being.

We observed that for Heidegger the knowledge we may have of the other fundamentally rests upon our sharing the peculiar mode of human *Dasein*'s being-in-the-world. Cognition enjoys privileged access to that peculiar entity – the other – who shares the mode of existence of the knowing subject. Knowledge is eminently secured insofar as knowing subject and known object are one of a kind ontologically speaking.

The question is whether Heidegger's "step forward" really is such as far as ethics is concerned. Granted that "being-with" precedes and helps facilitate understanding the other – what follows for an ethics? Is the property of being-with *already* ethical? Does the sheer fact *that* we exist as human only through being with others carry some more-closely-to-be-defined ethical import? Is responsibility for the other something we are landed in, as opposed to something open to choice? In a word, is ethical relationship prior to intentionality, as opposed to counting as one of its many products?

The philosophers discussed in this volume all wrestle with the latter question; differences notwithstanding, they – tentatively, or less so – put the case for answering it in the affirmative.

Grounding ethical relationship in being, hence in what is conceived of as non-optional, may at first sight appear a rather odd approach for ethics. All the more so since the current predominance of deontology has socialized us into expecting that what is and what ought to be represent two vastly distinct realms, epistemically no less than ontologically. Likewise the separation between fact and value has become something of a commonplace. Hume's warning against the fallacy of inferring from what is to what ought to be has helped erect what today seems an irremovable boundary between the two realms. In fact Habermas, otherwise a non-Humean, takes for granted, and thus helps perpetuate, this split when he insists that everything ontolologically given – in particular, existing structures of social interaction – be abstracted from in a threefold sense to win the morally justified consent of reasoning subjects.

So the sheer fact that something is is not an argument, least of all a normative or moral one. Social reality, the affairs of and between humans, is to be subjected to critical scrutiny so that the powers working behind the backs of agents be seen for what they potentially effect, namely systematically distorted communication. To perform this critical task Habermas proposes that we distinguish between the *social* validity of a given norm of action, that is, the fact that such a norm is observed by members of a particular society, and a norm's *rational* validity, by which Habermas means its *justified* claim to be observed. Without this distinction, Habermas contends, *ethos*-transcending critique would be impossible.

Against such a background, any claim to the effect that there is a normative, ethically non-neutral core in being-with, in the bare givenness of intersubjectivity, must appear utterly naive and so meet with disapproval if not downright denial. However, caution is called for. If my being-with an Other does not land me in an ethical relation, what does? But to grant this does not amount to making much headway. For the next question is: Where does normativity come from? Is there an ought residing *in* being-with cast as a dyad? Is normativity intrinsic or extrinsic to intersubjectivity? Is ethical conduct a matter of acting from a normative pull inherent in the relation (doing justice to a property – an ought – already there), or is it a matter of producing an ought in the face of what merely is (authoring an ought by means of one's powers of intentionality)?

These are metaphysical questions, not ontological or epistemological ones. Much in the manner of moral realism, they urge us to enquire into the furniture of the world, so as to discover and disclose normativity instead of inventing it. Though sharing this perspective, some of the philosophers discussed – and discussing – here feel that being-with in the style of the early Heidegger is too poor an ethical category. They propose instead the category of *being-for*. Whereas the sheer fact of being-with an Other allows the ethically neutral mode of existing alongside him or her, as it were, being-for is *sui generis* ethical. I can be with the Other without being for him or her. For the sake of argument, there may even be an ought – in terms of having respect and showing concern for the Other I am with – without my doing any justice to this ought in my subsequent conduct. As Sartre famously showed, being-with is compatible with indifferences as well as with love – or hatred, for that matter. There is no non-negatable ethical property residing in the structure of being-with the Other. Consequently, according to Sartre, being-for the Other is a choice I make; it is a positive way of approaching and acting out my being-with the Other; but seen simply as a structure, being-with permits the negative stance of hatred no less than the deeply affirmative one of love or sympathy.[4]

As brought out in the contributions to this anthology, it belongs to the originality (or should we say radicalness?) of Levinas and Løgstrup that they see being-for as present in every being-with. Present in what way?

Once again the categories at hand under the auspices of philosophical ontology and epistemology are ill-suited to offer explanation. To put it bluntly: What imposes limits on our ways in the world and our knowledge of entitites encountered there, is the Other. The limits meant here are not subject-relative ones; they are not of the kind exposed to the knowing subject who exercises his powers of introspection in order to ascertain the precise nature of how his interior capacities of sense, feeling, and cognition allow him to experience what is exterior to him (the task undertaken in Western epistemology at least since Descartes, only subsequently to be taken to very different conclusions by Hume and Kant). Rather, what imposes limits to our being and knowing is something not in ourselves but in the world. This something is precisely not a thing; it is the human Other. With the entry of the Other upon the scene, our existence and our understanding are not simply presented with a novel object unlike all others. To point this out, of course, is old hat. But, as we shall see in the course of this volume, Levinas and Løgstrup depart radically also from the stories about being-with and being-for familiar to us from thinkers such as Kierkegaard, Heidegger, Sartre, and Buber.

Being-for is ethical. It is ethical, yet it is so neither in the sense of highlighting the right nor in that of highlighting the good. The ethical import of being-for has nothing to do with the primacy of the right over the good. It is not a matter of legitimizing norms of interpersonal conduct or of vindicating principles of justice. But neither does being-for as understood by Levinas and Løgstrup have anything in common with virtue ethics, ancient or recent. Articulating the latter, Julia Annas describes the moral point of view as that of "a reflective person who realizes that all her various aims and values do hang together in a pattern in her life"; accordingly, "ethical theory arises from the need, for each person, to reflect on his final end, and of the place and role of virtue in his current conception of happiness".[5] Being-for, we should be clear, is not a vehicle for the agent's notions of the good and happiness – even be it the good and happiness of others.

We are trying here to stake out a third way. The core of being-for is neither right nor rights, neither the happiness nor the good of those concerned. Its core is responsibility. Responsibility not as freely assumed, not as socially or politically or legally sanctioned; and yet as coming from outside rather than inside, as originating from what is exterior not interior to the agent. Responsibility means to respond, to respond to the call for responsibility issued wordlessly from the Other and received prevoluntarily by the subject, the addressed I constituted as ethical, as uniquely responsible for the Other by that equally unique Other.

So what about justice, goodness, happiness? They all matter; but they come later. They are all issues to be solved, matters to be settled. For all that, they do not – taken together or singly – define morality the phenomenon, responsibility the task. Morality as understood here is not for the sake of anything – happiness, utility, security. Morality is not at the service of our wants, desires, needs. And yet morality defines us: responsibility does. Our humanness resides in our responsibility. We are the responsible species; but responsibility is nothing collective. It is the opposite: *principium individuationis*. In being called to responsibility for the Other, I am singularized. Individuation is an event, the effect of what the Other does to me by the sheer fact of being-with me. In short: the Other cannot be with me without positing me as the one who has to be for him. "Proximity is only possible as responsibility."[6] This is the anticipated sense in which being-for is present in – inseparable from – being-with.

Since responsibility demands that I be for the Other whenever I am with him, responsibility means a readiness to give unconditionally. Concern with the Other's returns or favours is wholly absent. To allude to Kierkegaard, my act of giving qualifies as truly ethical insofar as it expects, nay desires, no returns. Responsibility is uncoupled from reciprocity.

Being a one-way affair, responsibility is compromised once it is seen as a product of dialogue. Exchange, symmetry, reciprocation: these are genuine products of human intentionality. Responsibility, by stark contrast, is not and cannot be negotiated. If responsibility obeyed the logic of something freely entered into, retreating from it would likewise pose an option. Such is the logic of a contract. In a contract, the transition from non-participation to partnership is one brought about by a decision, whose basis is the weighing of pros and cons. In responsibility understood as being-for there is no decision, no asking, What's in it for me?, no pondering, Shouldn't I rather stay outside of commitment? These are all non-options for the elemental reason that *morality* is not an option but a predicament, part and parcel of human existence. The Other commits me to being-for-him by his sheer coexisting with me.

Responsibility thus conceived is wildly implausible. But then again, morality is not a presence – a reality – in the world as humans come to exist in it by virtue of having been brought *argumentatively* into that world. Morality the phenomenon, responsibility the demand, have not awaited good or not so good reasons so as to be granted the characteristic of force and pull. Morality is something we can do or fail to do justice to. The demand silently yet unmistakenly operative in the Other's entering our room, turning to us, can be heeded or denied. The *how* of our exact response is up to us; the *that* – the givenness – of morality and demand is eminently not. Our way of responding to responsibility points to our freedom, brings freedom into being by presenting it with a task. If I were alone in the world, my freedom would have no ethical task, no agenda stretching beyond that demarcated by the preoccupations of self-interest.

But isn't this much too narrow an ethical doctrine? We started out complaining of the "puristic" conception of morality expressed in modern deontology à la Habermas and modernized contract theory à la Rawls. On the face of it, however, it seems that our steps away from today's leading ethical theories have landed us not in a richer and more differentiated moral universe but in an even narrower one. Excessive formalism, being fixed on criteria and the requirements of procedure, may still appear objectionable; but does the ascetic nature of morality and responsibility found in Levinas really fare any better? Moreover, if everything deserving the name ethical involves, even stems from, the Other, what's left for subjectivity? Doesn't the self-relationship also contain a truly ethical dimension?

These are no doubt crucial questions. Yet, as formulated here, they fail to do justice to Levinas' teaching. For Levinas, what matters to morality is responsibility. And responsibility – the burden and the task – is set in motion by the Other. Once set in motion by the Other and received by the I, everything to do with responsibility depends on the I. The *how* of moral (or not so moral) conduct is a matter resting squarely on the shoulders of the I. The concrete way of dealing with the Other is something for which the acting I has to answer. All alone. In cases of failing to do justice to the bestowal of responsibility that takes place in and as the proximity of the Other, the I would only deceive itself in trying to put the blame on others, or on society. This is the point where Levinas and Kierkegaard meet. For both, unselfish concern for others is the core of morality. In Kierkegaard, the highest expression of that concern is love, genuinely unselfish love for the Other regardless of her merits and attraction or lack of such; this is moral love. In Levinas, concern from the first has the form and content of responsibility, of being-for as overriding all negotiable modes of being-with, and so of reciprocity.

"It is not I who resist the system, as Kierkegaard thought; it is the Other."[7] We have not forgotten this remark in Levinas' *Totality and Infinity*. The objection seems in effect to side Kierkegaard with Heidegger, whose ontology "subordinates the relationship with the Other to the relation with Being in general".[8] Here and elsewhere Levinas construes an opposition between his own ethical thinking and that found in all others. He commits the fallacy he most tirelessly warns against, that of reducing everything otherwise to the same. Kierkegaard and Heidegger are wrongly grouped together. For, whereas in Kierkegaard the self achieves authenticity by way of the specific character of its enacted concern for the Other, Heidegger holds that authenticity turns on how the individual *Dasein* relates to the responsibility it bears for itself, not for others.

Much has been made of Heidegger's (largely unacknowledged) debt to Kierkegaard. But there is also a debt to the latter in Levinas. We have noted that they both side against Heidegger in depicting authenticity in terms of the response given to responsibility and concern for *others*. True, the self's concern with itself is a stronger motif in Kierkegaard than in Levinas. Yet when Kierkegaard criticizes the deceit, falsity, and conformism he observed in current forms of being-with, his aim was to make room for a truthful mode of being-for. His aim, therefore, is deeper than that of social critique. Kierkegaard objects to the primacy of the universal ("das Allgemeine" in Hegel). True, he does so in the name of the individual, not in the name of the Other. But again, this difference from Levinas is more due to the latter's predilection for philosophical boundary-building than to the matter under attack. Rightly understood, Kierkegaard's case against the primacy of the system is thoroughly ethical. So is Levinas' case against the "egoism" of ontology, detectable all the way from Plato to Heidegger.

What is wrong, blatantly wrong, with putting System and Categories first is that to do so misconstrues the nature of ethical responsibility and in effect helps to diminish it. It is the individual that is responsible; and he is so with respect to what is singular not universal. Here the contrast is not only with Hegel but with Kant too. Kant teaches that I must act out of respect for law. My bond with others is a subjection to the law in them. Others are bearers of the same moral law that I find in myself. Inviolability of the other person is derived from the fact that he is the locus of the same powers of autonomy and self-legislation that I myself am endowed with. Morality is about respecting what is shared; in the kingdom of ends, every person *anerkannt* will himself be an *Anerkenner*. The moral law defines a common humanity; it disallows private interests, person-bound sentiments, particularity of every sort. "Acting morally precisely consists in not taking oneself as an exception."[9]

What is lost in Kant is precisely the individual agent as irreplaceable. Nietzsche protested that to exist and to act with laws universal and necessary, laws valid for everyone, is to not have a law of one's own, a destiny one's own. It is to regulate one's life with a law in force in any other. This may successfully define humanity; it may capture the commonness of persons as formally conceived of. But the cost may still out-weigh the gain. For in enacting a law that is the same for everyone because present in the same formal way in every empirical agent, each agent makes herself interchangeable with any other. Each can replace another at her tasks. No one has tasks of her own.[10]

Universalism, it is true, represents an important improvement over par-ticularistic notions of the scope of the moral universe – be they notions restricting moral addressees in terms of race, sex, class, tribe, religion, or (witness Bosnia) ethnicity. For all the force of communitarianism's cri-tique of the excessive formalism already noted in present-day deontology, communitarianism is at a loss properly to secure the rights and interests of people who are simply individuals, and who for some (chosen or forced) reason enjoy no membership in some substantial collective (or in what for the time being may count as the politically "correct" collective). The instinct of universalism serves it right by dissociating rights and moral concern in general from the facticity of group membership. Conversely, communitarianism does not offer the individual moral secur-ity by declaring his rights to be an attribute of his communal belonging-ness. Proclaiming the moral–legal–political primacy of belongingness, so as to make moral status dependent on it, has the consequence of render-ing the individual – suddenly belonging to an ill-favoured group or poss-ibly none at all – vulnerable in a lethal sense. Rwanda showed no less, as did and does Bosnia.

There are two lessons here, both instructive with respect to the task placed before an ethics of proximity. First, we are reminded that univer-salism in scope of moral addressees is ill-fated or downright disastrous if the universalism is homogeneous instead of heterogeneous. *Within* the sameness of sharing equality in moral status (Kant: inviolability of all human persons), there must be room for the otherness of the human Other. The ethical reaching out to the Other by way of having been addressed by her is a reaching out to someone different from me though sharing a common humanity with me. Ethical response – responsibility – requires that such otherness be retained not wiped out.

The second lesson concerns the giver. It is the point where (as we have tried to show) the otherwise differently motivated aims of Kierkegaard and Levinas intersect. Kierkegaard warns against the life- and moral-ity-killing consequences of the fear of being an individual, hence of reluc-tance to do justice to the burden of responsibility. Attempts to merge with the "universal", to identify with society and what is everywhere expected of "one", to conform from the cradle to the grave – this invariably means to flee responsibility; such a person disavows his ethical being. The ethical relation is precisely what individualizes the individual. The otherness of givers is no less precious than the otherness of recipients. To be responsible for the Other is to be so uniquely.

Let us now turn briefly to the contributions to follow.

In "The Other's Face", Asbjørn Aarnes shows just how radical is Levinas' departure not only from current ethical theory but from Western philosophy since Plato. The relation with the Other is one neither of knowledge nor of being. This is so because, strictly speaking, the relation comes *to* the I instead of flowing from it.

Owing in particular to his book *Ich und Du*, Martin Buber is often discussed as a kind of founding father of an ethics of proximity. In "On Buber, Marcel, and Philosophy", Levinas once again brings his ethical thinking into sharp relief by contrasting it with two thinkers one would expect him largely to agree with. Levinas reproaches the I–Thou relationship presented by Buber for being reciprocal and symmetrical, thus committing violence against the "height" from which the Other issues the ethical appeal not to kill. Moreover, there is in Buber's portrait of the dyad a deplorable ring of self-sufficiency, a forgetfulness of the universe, the allowance of a preference for preference (Derrida) and thus a fencing in of moral concern so as to confine it to the near and dear one(s). What is lost from view in Buber's account is the distance which arises precisely in respect of the Other's proximity, the duality within proximity which (under the heading of apartness) will be especially focused on in Alastair Hannay's paper on Kierkegaard.[11]

In "Apropos of Buber: Some Notes", Buber is lauded by Levinas for having demonstrated the autonomy of the "dia-logual" I–Thou relation. In this brief but fascinating text, Levinas indicates his notion of justice as the principal source of a state's legitimacy. He goes on to formulate his idea of responsibility by way of a blunt analogy with the God of Judaism, subjected to *Bilderverbot* but present as a trace in the met-upon human Other. To quote: "The coming to mind of God is always linked, in my analyses, to the responsibility for the other person and all religious affectivity signifies in its concreteness a relation to others; the fear of God is concretely my fear for my neighbour."

In "Beyond Caritas: An Interview with Emmanuel Levinas", Levinas explains why the sentiments of caritas and love are inadequate to secure justice for all – the third as well as the Other. In doing so, he instructively compares his own view on the task of the modern state with that found in Kant and Hegel. In a manner characteristic of his later years, Levinas ends by dwelling on the close connection he increasingly perceived between ethics and religion.

As is well known, Levinas studied with Husserl and received enduring philosophical impulses from phenomenology. In his essay "End or Fulfilment of Phenomology?", Asbjørn Aarnes argues that, taken as a philosophy of experience, phenomenology runs up against its own limits when it encounters something experienced and yet beyond all representation, namely the Other. Levinas feels forced to depart from phenomenology because the face comes from and thus points toward what is non-phenomenal. The face – the upsurge of ethics, of responsibility – takes philosophy outside the ambit of *ordo cognoscendi*, thereby leaving ontology and epistemology (twins as far as Levinas is concerned) behind.

The Danish theologian Knud E. Løgstrup's text "On Trust" is taken from his monumental work *The Ethical Demand*. Trust, contends Løgstrup, is a given in human existence; it is the foundation of our encounter with the Other, and be it the stranger. The givenness of trust signifies that trust is not up to us. As human beings we cannot exist except by exposing ourselves to others, in every encounter laying something of our fate in the hands of the Other. In this vein Løgstrup speaks of the "silent demand" that is communicated by our vulnerability to the Other's way of responding, and so to the power he has over our fate. Human lives are inextricably linked with each other; Løgstrup refers to this as the givenness of interdependency. To be human means to expose vulnerability to affliction. The Other does so to me; I do so to the Other. We therefore meet in Løgstrup a more prominent concern with dependency and power as a two-way affair. As against the radical non-symmetry focused upon in Levinas' ethics, Løgstrup highlights how acknowledgement of the Other's vulnerability is mediated through insight into my own vulnerability. For all his concern with interdependency, however, Løgstrup no less than Levinas depicts responsibility as one-sided and unconditional.[12]

Trust is also a foundation short of which professional relationships would founder no less than would personal and intimate ones. The relation between a patient and her doctor is particularly dependent upon mutual trust. Today, however, the marketization taking place within an increasingly competitive and privatized health sector threatens to undermine the building of long-term professional relationships. Of course, a favourite charge against a *public* health service is precisely that it fosters anonymity and impersonality in nursing and so the very opposite of what the patient needs in order to feel treated as an individual. Yet it would be wrong to see the distinction between impersonal and personal health care as simply corresponding to the distinction between public and privatized health service. Commercialization of caring, putting as it does primacy on efficiency, time-saving in consultations, and generally increasing the number of patients treated (turnover), serves to impoverish the sheer *human* richness long associated with establishing an enduring – and so increasingly trust-based – relationship with a particular doctor. The current dangers of marketization aside, the doctor–patient relationship is one where finding the appropriate *balance* between closeness and distance will always be an issue for both parties. The paper by Robin Downie and Harald Jodalen is largely informed by the latter's experience as a practising doctor.

In her essay "Love and the Moral Point of View", Martha Nussbaum's aim is to help us appreciate the ways in which literature (especially novels) may sensitize us to the viewpoints of others and so to the interpersonal world of morality. Focusing on *David Copperfield* by Charles Dickens, Nussbaum gives us a strong impression of just how morally powerful novel-reading is "in and for life". Imagination and fantasy as fostered by reading the novels of authors such as Dickens, Dostoevsky, and Henry James shape our relations with the world in general and help expand our human and emotional ballast in perceiving the weal and woe of others. Nussbaum's argument for the morally sensitizing impact of novel-reading is also an argument for the indispensable role of emotions in moral agency.

In his essay "Is Man a Moral Being?", Arne Johan Vetlesen examines the divided opinions over whether we, simply as humans, find ourselves "always already" within the domain of morality. Are relations with others involving the burden of responsibility chosen ones, or must we rather concede that we are ineluctably moral beings, beings blameworthy for neglecting ethical responsibility even though we have never been in a position to decide whether or not to be the bearers of such responsibility in the first place? Taking its point of departure from Hobbes, the essay ends by criticizing Levinas' unreadiness to appreciate the extent to which being *able* to enact responsibility is a capacity developed thanks to others.

Alastair Hannay starts his "The Dialectic of Proximity and Apartness" by suggesting that the closeness required of the true ethical relationship presupposes genuine apartness. What is shared with the object of moral concern simply gets in the way of performing that concern. Hence philosophers stressing commonality as the only viable standpoint of ethics are on the wrong track. In contradistinction to Levinas, however, Kierkegaard is primarily preoccupied not with the otherness of the other but with the apartness of the self. The self as seen by Kierkegaard is not individuated – willy-nilly, as it were – by the sheer event of encountering the Other as face. Rather, the individuation of the self is a solitary task for each agent; he has to work on his own authenticity before he can enact responsibility for others in a non-replaceable, truly ethical manner.

Is there an ethics in Heidegger's *Being and Time?* This question has attracted rapidly growing attention during the past few years. In "Is and Ought" Joachim Renn explores the tension between responsibility and authenticity in Heidegger's fundamental ontology. Particular attention is paid to Heidegger's critique of the moral formalism found in Kant. Though initially siding with Hegel in his rejection of formalism, Heidegger goes on to indicate what may count as at least the outlines of an "existentialist" notion of freedom – freedom as modelled neither on Kantian reason-based autonomy nor on Hegel's account of a "substantielle Sittlichkeit" wherein all agents would be able to realize their freedom as situated yet universal. However, from the point of view of an ethics of proximity, the ethical potential of early Heidegger must appear meagre. When Heidegger speaks of responsibility, what he means is individual *Dasein*'s responsibility for itself, not for others. In the second part of his essay, Renn traces this negative conclusion to Heidegger's devaluation of intersubjectivity, be it in the face-to-face context or in the public sphere.

Zygmunt Bauman brings this anthology to a close by asking a most timely question: Can there be a Levinasian macro-ethics? As we have noted above, Levinas' moral world stretches between I and the Other. Only hesitantly did Levinas approach the entry of the third upon the scene, and with that the well-known problematic of justice, of being forced to decide who is to receive what, not least in cases where there simply isn't enough to go round. As long as there was only one Other – emphatically *the* Other – the *direction* of responding as responsible did not pose a problem. Once the third enters, by contrast, direction of response becomes a thorny matter of deciding who, in the midst of human neediness, is needier than others. Levinas approaches this complex problem by drawing a distinction between two "mutually independent" orders – one political, the other ethical. But this seems to restate the problem raised by the third, not to solve it. But can it ever be solved? Bauman reminds us just how grotesquely unjust is the world in which we live. The greater world of economy and politics, thus of power, thus of the silent structural violence upholding and reinforcing the abundance of the minority and the poverty of the ever-increasing majority – this greater world certainly seems vastly to transcend the moral impulse emanating from within the context of dyadic proximity. The Other most needy is precisely not the Other most nearby. To be moral – to enact responsibility – across the oceans and across the so-many boundaries set up by people between humans, today requires that one take up responsibility for those far off others too weak to address us. It means to respond even when there is no face to respond to. Who is given a face? Whose face (fate) is hidden behind anonymity? Granting someone a face, depriving others of theirs and so of their chance to express the wordless appeal "Thou shalt not kill!" – these are life-saving or life-robbing alternatives, ruled over by the manipulability of media coverage (four-year-old Irma becoming a face addressing the whole world thanks to CNN; at the same time, victims short of "being" a face because out of camera range are at a loss to elicit commitment). In the greater world of the five or six billion out there, where so many people's fate is determined by economic and political forces operating from afar and outside of their own control, moral commitment as sparked at home may seem simply to come to naught. And yet home is where morality begins and whence it always departs whenever it does depart, transcend, reach out to unknown others. At the end of the day, it remains true that proximity – closeness to the unique Other – is the context where moral sensitivity is born and gains its strength. Today more than ever, the task is to extend the scope of responsibility *beyond* the context of dyadic proximity in which it arises.

Notes and references

1. See Jürgen Habermas, *Moral Consciousness and Communicative Action*, Cambridge, MA: MIT Press, 1990; idem, *Justification and Application*, Cambridge, MA: MIT Press, 1993, esp. pp. 128ff. Relevant discussions of discourse ethics can be found in Stephen K. White, *The Cambridge Companion to Habermas*, Cambridge: Cambridge University Press, 1995.

2. Seyla Benhabib, *Situating the Self*, Cambridge: Polity Press, 1992, p. 184.

3. Jean-Paul Sartre, *Being and Nothingness*, New York: Washington Square Press, 1956, p. 329.

4. Ibid., p. 529. See also A. J. Vetlesen, "Relations with Others in Sartre and Levinas", *Constellations* 1–3, 1995, pp. 358–382.

5. Julia Annas, *The Morality of Happiness*, Oxford: Oxford University Press, 1993, pp. 440, 443. An excellent account of the moral point of view as pictured in virtue ethics is given by Martha Nussbaum, "Non-Relative Virtues: An Aristotelian Approach", in M. Nussbaum and Amartya Sen (eds), *The Quality of Life*, Oxford: Oxford University Press, 1993, pp. 242–269.

6. Fabio Ciaramelli, "Levinas' Ethical Discourse: Between Individuation and Universality", in Robert Bernasconi and Simon Critchley (eds), *Re-Reading Levinas*, London: Athlone Press, 1991, pp. 83–105. See also three other recently published books on Levinas: John Llewelyn, *Emmanuel Levinas. The Genealogy of Ethics*, London: Routledge, 1995; Adrian T. Peperzak (ed.), *Ethics as First Philosophy*, London: Routledge, 1995, esp. pp. 39–104; Brian Schroeder, *Altared Ground: Levinas, History, and Violence*, London: Routledge, 1996.

7. Emmanuel Levinas, *Totality and Infinity*, Dordrecht: Kluwer, 1991, p. 40.

8. Ibid., p. 46.

9. Alphonso Lingis, *Deathbound Subjectivity*, Indianapolis: Indiana University Press, 1989, p. 51.

10. I here draw heavily on Lingis, op. cit., p. 103.

11. See Robert Bernasconi, "'Failure of Communication' as a Surplus: Dialogue and Lack of Dialogue between Buber and Levinas", in R. Bernasconi and David Wood (eds), *The Provocation of Levinas*, London: Routledge, 1988, pp. 100–135, esp. p. 103f.

12. For a comparison between trust as a given, so-called "sovereign life-expression" in Løgstrup and truthfulness as a validity claim in Habermas, see A. J. Vetlesen, "Worlds Apart? Habermas and Levinas", in *Philosophy & Social Criticism* 23, 1997, pp. 1–20.

Chapter 2
The Other's Face

Asbjørn Aarnes

The Other's face is the focal point in Emmanuel Levinas' philosophy, fundamental ethics. This means that it offers an answer to my question as to what I – fundamentally – have to do in the world. It does not say what it means to be in the world; it gives no knowledge. One does not go to the Other as to the ant – to be "wise". Knowledge and wisdom would deprive him of his secret, that is his otherness, and return him to the Same. The Other's face shows me the significance, that is to say, the direction in which I must find my way:

> The face forces itself on me, without it being possible for me to remain deaf to its summons or to forget it, that is to say making it impossible for me to cease being responsible for its helplessness. Consciousness no longer has priority. . . To be I, means from now on to be unable to escape responsibility, as though the whole of creation rested on my shoulders. . . What is unique about me is the fact that no-one can be made responsible in my place.[1]

The Other's face is not "an idea of sensation". It does not manifest itself as something within the scope of perception. Characteristic of something that can be discovered by the senses is that it is revealed by degrees, as attention shifts from front to back, from side to side, so that the object makes its appearance in changing surroundings. The Face, as Levinas understands it, appears absolutely, that is "without surroundings", where all is revealed simultaneously and all is significance. "But in approaching another, where the Other is from the first under my responsibility, 'something' has overflowed my freely taken decisions, has slipped into me, *unbeknownst* to me, thus alienating my identity.[2]

Nor is the Face something thought, produced by my thinking; in Cartesian terms, there is no *cogitatum* linked to a *cogitatio*. The Other's face is something on the outside that I cannot form a relationship to, but that, unannounced, can form a relationship to me. It reaches its destination, in me, but not through the channels through which I normally communicate with the world and other human beings. It takes my active observation by surprise, strikes me before my defence is mobilized.

Nor is the Face the plastic picture that the portrait painter attempts to fasten to the canvas: it withdraws itself from the field of the visual. When Levinas occasionally connects it with a sense, he prefers hearing. The Other's face speaks; it is "a still small voice".[3] Levinas therefore prefers to call his philosophy *logos philosophy* – language philosophy:

> The neighbour who reveals himself in the Face, breaks through, so to speak, his own plastic form of being, as when someone opens the window in which his face has already been reflected. His manifestation consists in ridding himself of the form that has already made him visible. His appearance represents a *more*, in addition to the paralysis that inevitably follows the appearance. It is this we describe with the expression: The Face speaks. The manifestation of the face is the first Speaking. To speak is, above all, to come out from behind the appearing, from behind the form.[4]

The first Speaking says neither who the Other is nor who has sent him. The Other's face summons toward something higher, toward the Other who is higher than me in order and dignity. He is not "chosen" by me; it is he who chooses me to take responsibility for him. That I exist for the Other does not mean that I am called to serve under a foreign lord. This I, struggling in its being, first finds itself when responsibility has been imposed on it. Levinas can therefore say that his philosophy, in addition to being logos philosophy, is a philosophy of the I.

Therefore, to be struck by the Other's face means not that I am given freedom of self-assertion but, on the contrary, that I am chained to the responsibility; beyond the distinction free–unfree, there is "acceptance of good chains".[5]

The Other's face is a summons to break away from the *conatus* of being, from ontology, as Levinas says, and pass to ethics. And the ethical dimension cannot be understood in relation to such categories as intentionality or consciousness, either as successful or unsuccessful acts of consciousness. The change from ontology to ethics means that one is reminded that there is another aim for life than self-conservation and self-assertion. The significance establishes an unequivocal order: to be for the Other.

To leave ontology is to get away from the exercise of power, which is Being's struggle in time. The struggle of Being is constantly changing the shape of the world, by the rise and fall of existents. Through the ages, from antiquity, it has been the impossible passion of philosophy to grasp truth. Using force, I try to retain what is changing in the grasp of the Same. Time must be stopped, but to stop time is to assent to death, since "time is the pure unrest of life" (Hegel). To be for the Other is not to get out of time but to be for a time after my time, for the time of the Other.

For philosophers such as Martin Buber and Gabriel Marcel, with whom Levinas feels affinity, the relation to *you* is of a higher order than the relation to *it* in objectivity. Marcel calls the presence of *you* the *ontological mystery*, which has "more being" than the presence of the *object*. The transcendency of the I–You relation is to escape objectivity; in the meeting with *you* the *ego* mounts to a higher potency of being.

Levinas acquiesces to this critique of objectivity, but the question for him is not to get more or less of being. Hamlet's problem, he says – *to be or not to be* – was within ontology, for "not being" is negatively linked to being. For Levinas the question is to transcend ontology, summoned by the infinite that sounds "otherwise" than the finite.

In this conception of transcendency, Levinas seems nearer to Jean-Paul Sartre than to Buber and Marcel. When Sartre states that the Other's regard is a "hole in the world",[6] this surely means that, to him, to meet the Other's regard is to meet Nothingness, which annihilates my liberty. Levinas follows Sartre only so far as to deny that the Other's face belongs to the Being that, in Sartre's philosophy, has its counterpoint in Nothingness.

But it is as though the Other's face calls forth the nearness of an absence. Perhaps one could imagine a situation where brothers and sisters are gathered happily together when, suddenly, seeing the typical family features in the faces around them, they are reminded of someone who is absent: a mother, a father, a sister, or a brother. At such a moment, an absence is present.

It is the Other's face that makes me a human being, that establishes humanity. Humanism for Levinas is not a doctrine or an attitude based on the principle Human Being, against what offends this principle by making it either into something nobler or something less noble. What is human does not come from me; it is not something I have or do not have. It is established by the Other's face. And since the Other is a condition for human behaviour, ethics becomes the first philosophy or fundamental ethics. Responsibility for the Other forms the basis for both cognition and practice.

Other thinkers, such as Henri Bergson, have also separated ethics from cognition by asserting that our so-called good or bad reasons for behaving in this way or that are rationalizations, wisdom-after-the-event regarding an original action on behalf of *l'élan vital*. For Levinas, ethics and cognition differ not merely with regard to aims or argument. It is ethics that makes ontology possible, that is to say, knowledge of existence and existents. Responsibility lays a cloak of humanity around us, and around things and us. Wakefulness – *cogito* – does not come first; it is "brothership between human beings" that makes the watching eye that is sent out into the world acquire confidence in what it sees:

> The one is for the Other by virtue of a being that releases its hold, without making itself simultaneous with the Other, without being able to place itself by his side in a synthesis that reveals itself as theme. The One is for the Other as his brother's keeper, as the One responsible for the Other . . . the very nearness to the neighbour, through which alone is given a fund of fellowship between both, the one-ness of the human race, resulting from brothership between people.[7]

The philosophy of Levinas proposes a new social relationship in which responsibility is more important than cognition. In Western metaphysics from Plato to Heidegger, the intellectual model has prevailed: to be Man means to be able to know, and the subject of knowledge, the *ego cogito* in classical philosophy from Descartes to Husserl, played its part in "the nominative case", as Levinas puts it. Also Heidegger, whose aim was to bring Western metaphysics to an end, linked man to cognition (*Verstehen*). The *ego* did, in fact, disappear, but *Dasein*'s way of being is described as a cognitive structure, as a hiding and unfolding in the light of truth, the "essence" of *Dasein* being to reveal (*entdeckend*).

On this point too, Levinas deserts Heidegger, and perhaps Heidegger, for his part, built up a new metaphysics – the metaphysics of the ending of metaphysics. Perhaps fundamental ethics aims at no less than the closing of the era of knowledge, to which man was condemned as a result of having eaten from the Tree of Knowledge? To live in responsibility means to be at the mercy of the Other's supplication and commandment. But what are we going to tell each other, beyond cognition, beyond understanding?

The Other's face is a call to break away: towards infinity! Levinas's philosophy cannot therefore be called dialogue, or I–you philosophy. Confronted with infinity, he seems to hesitate between two interpretations: on the one hand a platonic interpretation in which infinity becomes the One that "frees itself from a thought that attempts to thematise it and from a language that seeks to hold it fast in the said"[8], and on the other hand a Jewish religious interpretation in which infinity becomes a person called Him, and the fact of being Him: *illéité* (from the Latin, *ille* = him/that one). He is placed over the relationship between the Other and me. He upholds the Other's otherness, and me as the one responsible for the Other, and, through him, I too am an other for my neighbour. In a difficult text Levinas shows how being Him – *illéité* – can mean God, without His becoming partner in a dialogue:

> In proximity the other obsesses me according to the absolute asymmetry of signi-fication, of the–one–for–the–other: I substitute myself for him, whereas no one can replace me, and the substitution of the one for the other does not signify the sub-stitution of the other for the one. The relationship with the third party is an incess-ant correction of the asymmetry of proximity in which the face is looked at. There is weighing, thought, objectification, and thus a decree in which my anarchic rela-tionship with *illeity* is betrayed, but in which it is conveyed before us. There is betrayal of my anarchic relation with *illeity*, but also a new relationship with it: it is only thanks to God that, as a subject incomparable with the other, I am approached as an other by the others, that is, "for myself". "Thanks to God" I am another for the others. God is not involved as an alleged interlocutor: the recipro-cal relationship binds me to the other man in the trace of transcendence, in *illeity*. The passing of God, of whom I can speak only by reference to this aid or this grace, is precisely the reverting of the incomparable subject into a member of society.[9]

The remark that God does not become "partner in a dialogue" tells us something important about Levinas' attitude to the religious. If God is indispensable to philosophical meditation, he must not become nomina-tive, not be located in the universe or be the object of worship. In that case he would become ontology's God – the God Nietzsche rightly declared dead. The Other's face does not reflect God, and in the world there is no sign of Him, no path from the world to Him. What is to be found is a trace of someone after Him – in the Other's face. One notes that in Levinas there is never talk of God's love of mankind, it is the lot of human beings to long, to long infinitely, without any guarantee of being heard. . .

Nor will we find anything in Levinas of the evangelical idea that I love my neighbour because God loves me. Does this mean that Levinas recog-nizes only *eros* – the longing that is directed upward toward God – and not *agape* – the love that rains down mercy over humanity? Is his God the God of Moses, who will not walk beside us, but only pass us by?

Stephan Strasser, who has written the standard monograph on Levinas, sums up his religious position thus:

> Efforts to deduce incontrovertible imperatives for the present out of the order of creation, do not sufficiently take into account the fact that the created world is not sign, but trace. Only by serving others who are found in the Creator's traces, can one approach nearer the Holy One. His unapproachable *illéité* means that we are referred to the human Other. To do service to our neighbour is to do service to God.[10]

We have attempted to describe a single element in Levinas' philosophy: the Other's face, "without horizons", that is to say without allowing the surroundings – ideas, themes – it appears in, and the background it is outlined against, to be drawn in. Nor has any attempt been made to show that, for Levinas, it was logically necessary to arrive at such a result.

Perhaps we approach here "the first speech" or the original intuition – the germ of his philosophy? Levinas' work is an epoque-making defence for a humanity that is moving out of modernity, a humanity that no longer believes that it owns itself, or rules over itself, and that in spite of this is not alienated because it is dedicated to the neighbour in responsibility for the Other's otherness.

"Let go!" could have stood as a motto over Levinas' fundamental ethics. Here we find loosened the epistemological cramp that wants to wring knowledge out of everything and reform everything into the Same. Before the Other's face the struggle for being – the sound of war, as Levinas also calls it – abates. Betrayal is not to forget Being – the famous *Seinsvergessenheit* of Heidegger – but to turn one's back on the Other's pleading. To forget one's neighbour, that is the betrayal.

Levinas is both Jew and "Greek", not Christian. But when we hear him say, "Those who hope to see God's countenance, will not see it before they have freed those who are in chains and fed those who hunger", who can fail to be reminded of that surprised question from "the righteous" – "Lord, when did we see you hungry and give you to eat, or thirsty and give you to drink?" – and the answer that marks the dividing line, in heaven and on earth: "Truly I say unto you: as you did it to one of the least of these my brethren, you did it to me".[11]

NOTES AND REFERENCES

1. Emmanuel Levinas, *Humanisme de l'autre homme*, Fata Morgana, Montpellier, 1972, pp. 49–50.
2. Ibid., p. 91, and *Collected Philosophical Papers*, trans. Alphonso Lingis, The Hague: Martinus Nijhoff, 1987, p. 145.
3. I Kings 19: 12.
4. Levinas, *Humanisme de l'autre homme*, op. cit., p. 48
5. Arnold Eidslott, *Vann og støv*, Gyldendal Oslo 1956, p. 10.
6. Jean-Paul Sartre, *L'Être et le néant*, Librairie Gallimard, Paris. 1943, p. 313.
7. *Humanisme de l'autre homme*, op. cit., p. 14.
8. Levinas, *Autrement qu'être ou au-delà de l'essence*, Le livre de poche, Kluwer Academic, 1990, p. 230.
9. Levinas, *Otherwise Than Being or Beyond Essence*, trans. Alphonso Lingis, Dordrecht/Boston/London: Kluwer, 1991, p. 158.
10. Stephan Strasser, *Jenseits von Sein und Zeit*, The Hague: Martinus Nijhoff, 1978, p. 213.
11. Matthew 25: 40.

Chapter 3
On Buber, Marcel, and Philosophy

Emmanuel Levinas

I and Thou, published in 1923, revealed the existence in Germany of a whole current of thought that, whether anticipatory or reminiscent, more or less converged with Buber's ideas. Texts conceived along the same lines preceded or followed the publication of his book by a short interval. They were signed by Ferdinand Ebner, Hans and Rudolf Ehrenberg, Eugen Rosenstock-Huessy, Eberhard Griesbach, and a few others. These authors, however, belonged to the same cultural sphere. The encounter between the work of Martin Buber and that of Gabriel Marcel is a more conclusive indication of a spiritual reality independent of the accidents of discourse. When Gabriel Marcel was writing his *Metaphysical Journal*, he did not know Martin Buber. He came from an intellectual tradition far removed, at that time, from the German academic atmosphere. By comparing, in their general traits, the speculative formulations of these two remarkable minds, so generously endowed in so many diverse domains, I would like to examine chiefly to what extent the thought expressed through their work, contrasting sharply with the style of the philosophy handed down to them, responds to the vocation of philosophy, how it renews it, and more specifically how the traditional privilege of ontology is affected by this new approach, in which the source and the model for the meaningful are sought in interhuman relations.

The relationship between Gabriel Marcel and Martin Buber was recently the object of a brilliant and profound study which appeared in Hebrew in a collection on "Jewish Thought vis-à-vis Universal Culture". The author, my friend Professor Mosche Schwartz of the University of Bar-Ilan in Israel, a specialist on Schelling and Rosenzweig who was to speak at the Beer-Sheva Colloquium on the subject of religious language in Buber, passed away a few weeks before the opening of this Colloquium.

Rereading his essay, I thought that for all matters concerning the historical comparison between Buber and Marcel I could borrow the essential from him. Thus a modest homage may be rendered to the memory of a friend who was a keen and sensitive thinker. Will I succeed, according to the rabbinic doctors' way of paraphrasing the Song of Songs 7: 10, in "making the sleeping lips speak"?

I

There is a remarkable commonality in the essential views of Gabriel Marcel and Martin Buber: the I–Thou relation described in its originality as distinguished from what Buber designates as I–It; the originality of sociality with respect to the subject–object structure, the latter not even being necessary to the grounding of the former; the Thou *par excellence*, invoked in God whom Buber calls the Eternal Thou and whom, according to Marcel, one would fail to apprehend were one to name Him in the third person; the invocation or addressing, in God, of an eternal Thou, which opens up a dimension that is the precondition for the meeting of a human Thou (even though the human may also allow of being treated as an object); and, thus, the founding of all truly interpersonal relations in an originative religion. That is the essential discovery that appears at first blush common to both the Jewish and the Christian philosopher. It consists in affirming that human spirituality – or religiosity – lies in the fact of the proximty of persons, neither lost in the mass nor abandoned to their solitude.[1] This bespeaks both the religious significance of inter-human relations and, conversely, the original possibility and accomplishment of the relation-to-God (that relation to the Invisible, the Non-Given) in the approach of one person to another, addressed as *Thou* – an approach that greets the other, an I–Thou relation, i.e. a relation fundamentally *other* than the perception of the other in his or her nature or essence, which would lead to truths or opinions expressed in the guise of judgements, as in the experience of any object whatsoever.

The object is not to the subject as the subject is to the object, whereas, in the Meeting between the *I* and the *Thou* in which the address is articulated, the relation is reciprocity itself: the I says "thou" to a Thou inasmuch as this *Thou* is an I capable of replying with a "thou". There is, then, on this view, something resembling an initial equality of status between the addressor and the addressee. But status here is only a manner of speaking. At best, such a term might be appropriately applied to the subject and object, terms positing themselves or being posited for themselves. The *I* and *Thou* do not bear within them the ratio of their relation; the I–Thou relation contrasts sharply with the subject–object one precisely because, in Buber, it is somehow traced out prior to the terms, as a "between" (*Zwischen*). And Marcel, early on, in his *Metaphysical Journal*[2] discovered the necessity of an energetic analysis of this "between": "the eminent value of *autarkia*, or personal self-sufficiency", is depreciated in the affirmation that "only a relationship of being to being can be called spiritual". And in his study on Buber in the collective work of 1963,[3] Marcel seems to confirm his agreement on this point, writing: "In all these situations, the meeting does not take place in any sense in one or the other participant, nor in a neutral unity embracing both, but in the truest sense between them in a dimension accessible to them alone".

The two philosophers agree in questioning the spiritual primacy of intellectual objectivism, which is affirmed in science, taken as the model of all intelligibility, but also in Western philosophy, from which that science emerged. Buber and Marcel challenge the claim of the intellectual act of knowledge to the dignity of the spiritual act *par excellence*. It is a challenge they share, in a sense, with the philosophy of existence. Buber and Marcel join the latter in the search for an ecstatic fullness of existence as a whole and for a presence that, in the objectivity of things-to-be-known, becomes limited and distorted. This is what allows these philosophers to elevate concrete terms with an anthropological ring, which hitherto had occurred only in psychology, to the rank of categories (or existentials, as they are called since Heidegger). But, for the philosophers of coexistence, the "ekstasis" around which concrete human plenitude gathers is not the thematizing intentionality of experience but the addressing of the other, a person-to-person relation, culminating in the pronoun "thou". It is not truth that is the ultimate meaning of that relation, but *sociality*, which is irreducible to knowledge and truth. Let us note before proceeding that, although Buber and Marcel, in their descriptions of the Meeting or the Relation, as Buber calls it, break away from an ontology of the object and of substance, both characterize the I–Thou relation in terms of *being*. "Between" is a *mode of being*: co-presence, co-esse. If we are to go by the letter of the texts, being and presence remain the ultimate support of meaning.

It would be important, however, to determine whether both philosophers turn to ontological language for the same reason – whether, in Buber, the break with ontology does not intimate a more radical rupture, whether the persistence of ontology in his work is not more anomalous than in Marcel's, who, although remarkably free from any school, or scholasticism, and so deliberately hostile to the objectivist interpretation of being, remains deeply rooted, despite all the disruption introduced by the idea of the Thou, in ontology. Thus Marcel appears to continue the high Western tradition for which the supreme characterization of the Divine amounts to identifying it with being; and for which all relation with being is, in the final analysis, reducible to an experience (that is, to knowledge) and remains a modality of that being. The philosophy that affirms the originality of the I–Thou relation, on the contrary, proposes that *sociality* is irreducible to the *experience of sociality* – that, as extreme rectitude, it does not inflect back upon itself as does the *esse* of being, which always *gives* itself, that is, is destined to the "understanding of being", lending credence, ever anew, to idealism. But this is a dis-interested élan, the sense of which signifies in an absolutely straightforward thought. Reflection can find only an ambiguous trace of it.

II

Already in his stance on the medieval dispute about universals, Buber favours nominalism. He rejects the tendency that, in his opinion, would recognize the absolute only in the universal, and consequently imply the privilege of knowledge. The latter, according to Buber, even in Spinozan monism, is but an escape from lived experience – contemplation, the visual, optic life – that is, precisely recourse to ideal notions. The knowledge of the object, impossible without idealization, is but the congealed form of an existential state. It would put an end to the personal fullness attained in the Meeting, in the Relation in the covenant between individuals, a covenant that rests solely on the pure coexistence of the I with the absolute Thou, on the *with* – pure transcendence!

To wonder how such an alliance between the singularity of the *I* and the absolute *Thou* is possible is to suppose that which, according to Buber's message, is superseded: the concern for a unitary principle underlying the essential duality of the Relation. Buber's fundamental thesis is: In the beginning was the Relation. The concrete mode in which that relation is accomplished is language, which thus reaches the confines of divinity. Here "dialogue" is not a metaphor. In his analyses, Buber insists on the movement inherent in the word, which cannot be accommodated within the speaker, and already seizes upon or is received by the listener, whom it transforms into an answerer (even if he or she remains silent). The word is the *between par excellence*. Dialogue functions not as a *synthesis* of the Relation, but as its very unfolding.

Beyond the immediate essence of the Meeting as it is accomplished in the *between* of the word, nothing can be grasped that is not already a retreat from language, nothing that does not move away from presence, from the living Relation. Relation through language is conceived as a transcendence irreducible to immanence. And the "ontology" (for it remains ontology nonetheless) that is thus formed derives all its significance from that irreducible transcendence.

Marcel, in his studies[4] on Buber, accepts the latter's views, but says he does not go as far in his agreement on "the elucidation of the structural aspect of the fundamental human situation".[5] And yet, already in these reservations that appear directed to points of detail, a different philosophical attitude emerges. "To be sure", he writes, "Buber's fundamental intuition remains unconditionally valid in my view, but there remains the question of knowing how it can be transposed onto the level of language without degenerating in the process. That transposition raises great difficulties".[6] Marcel has a Bergsonian mistrust of language. In his view, language is inadequate to the truth of the inner life, whereas the *I–Thou* is lived as immediacy of co-presence itself and, consequently, above the level of words, above dialogue. This structure is approached by Marcel through the notions of "human incarnation" and "ontological mystery".

Incarnation, according to Marcel, is "the central given of metaphysics". It is "the situation of a being that appears to itself as attached to a body". By contrast with the *cogito*, it is "a given not transparent to itself".[7] A non-transparent given: the incarnate I is not, in its consciousness of self, for itself only; it exists in such a way as to have something impenetrable within itself. Not a foreign body! Its being-toward-itself is immediately a *being exposed to others* and, in this sense, it is itself obscurity. "It is the shadow that is at the center".[8] The impenetrable "something" in it is not the addition of an extended substance to a thinking substance, but a way of being of the spirit itself by which it is, before all thematization of the universe, *for* the universe and thus united with it. It is a way of being toward oneself precisely as being toward the other-than-oneself – which identifies it. It is an ontological modality, a modality of the verb *to be* that is mediation itself. That is one of Marcel's most beautiful speculative constructions: "Of this body I can say neither that it is I, nor that it is not I, nor that it is *for* me (object)".[9] And yet the *I* and the body cannot be distinguished: "I cannot validly say, 'I and my body'".[10] There is no Cartesian separation between me and my body, nor a synthesis, but immediately an unobjectifiable, lived participation. The body is essentially a mediator, but irreducible to any formal or dialectical mediation. It is the absolute or originary mediation of being: "In that sense, it is myself, for I can distinguish myself from it only on the condition that I convert it into an object, that is, that I cease treating it as the absolute mediator".[11] Hence, "we are tied to being".[12] And, conversely, every existent refers back to our body: "When I affirm that a thing exists, it is always the case that I consider that thing as linked to my body, as capable of being put in contact with it, however indirectly".[13] And along the same lines: "One might well ask whether the union of the soul and the body is of a different essence than the union between the soul and other existing things: in other words is there not subtending, as it were, all affirmation of existence, a certain experience of self as attached to the universe?"[14] Hence Marcel can say that "a blindfold knowledge [*connaissance aveuglée*] of being in general is implied in all particular knowledge".[15]

With incarnation, a universal structure of being is declared; its coherence is not, to be sure, secured by a few ideal ties, but neither is it secured by dialogue. "All spiritual life is essentially a dialogue"[16] – but the dialogue is not the ultimate instance of communication. Being is tied together into unity through human incarnation. The one *with* the other of being is thus reduced to the incarnation of the *I*, placed on an "existential orbit", as in a magnetic field. The interhuman encounter is but a modality of that ontological coherence mediated by the incarnation in which the I is *for* the other. Here we are on the hither side of the Buberian Relation, but at the heart of co-presence: participation founding all relation. Participation is not a dialogue. It is an intersubjective nexus deeper than the language that is torn away, according to Marcel, from that originative communication. As a principle of alienation, language petrifies living communication: it is precisely in speaking that we pass most easily from "Thou" to "He" and to "It" – objectifying others.[17]

Whereas for Buber to say "Thou" is an absolute relation having no

foundational principle behind it, Marcel opposes language understood as
the *element* of the Meeting; he opposes the very term *Relation*, preferring
"meeting" or "tension" (*Spannung*). [18] He denounces the conceptual character attaching, in his view, to terms in a "relation" and to their objectivity, suggested by that word.[19] Going to a deeper level than incarnation, he
is anxious to replace *relation* with the more fundamental structure of the
ontological mystery. "It seems to me", he writes, "that it is inaccurate to
say: 'In the beginning was the Relation.' In the beginning there is rather
a certain presentiment of unity that continuously dissolves, giving way to
a Whole that will be formed by reciprocally linked notions". Marcel's
intent is certainly not to set up, in opposition to Buber's Relation (or to
imagine behind it), some reality conceived on the model of objects or ide-
alities or any sort of closed system. The concern is rather to establish a
concrete life that overflows and leads man to the heart of his being, where
the originative bond, or love, is bound – to the heart of his being, which
is not entirely his. "We are not entirely ours". That is one of the consequences of Marcel's analysis of the ontological mystery: the subject is not
entirely his or her own. The divine being that we are not, the absolute
Thou whom we meet as transcendent, is also the being that sustains and
loves us. Marcel reproaches Buber for designating the situation of the
I–Thou meeting as *Gegenwärtigheit*. It is certainly not the reference to
presence as a modality of being, the implicit recourse to ontology, that
seems reprehensible to him, but rather the idea of the *gegen*, the *against*,
calling to mind the *gegen* of *Gegenständlichkeit*[20] and suggesting the possibility of a pure exteriority, whereas what is invoked as transcendent,
according to Marcel, already grounds that invocation and the invoker.
The mystery of being is the way our being which "goes toward God"
already belongs to God, and it is the way the being of God holds the *I* of
man. The *I* of man is no longer the middle, or the beginning, or the end
point of the Whole.

This mystery is recognized, for example, in the question "What is it to
be?" An initial reflection discovers that the questioner is already in that
which he or she puts in question; the problem proves to be meta-prob-
lematic. Nothing is pure problem, nothing entirely put forward: in thinking about being, I participate, in this thinking, in what I am thinking
about. The questioning is in the final analysis not in me but in being itself;
and the I thus discovers itself, in a second-degree reflection or meditation,
as not belonging totally to itself, but as if plunged in the "ontological

mystery" that envelops its functioning as subject.

The meeting with the absolute Thou is thus enveloped within the mystery of being: "The *heart* of my existence is that which is at the center of what I might designate as important to my life; it is the nucleus from which I draw my life; moreover it is not, most of the time, an object of clear consciousness for me. The heart, the nucleus of my existence, is also the community between thee and I, in which the mutual membership is all the more real and essential, the closer it takes place to this heart".[21]

Contrary to Buber's view, the meeting of the neighbour, of the human Thou, presupposes a "sharing of the same history" or the same destiny, and not the unconditionality of the approach. According to Marcel, we do not "meet" everyone we happen to run into.[22] The I–Thou does not occur just anywhere. For example, it is fear for our existence in a train that stops in an unusual manner in the middle of the countryside that brings us together – we travellers, we who were nevertheless side by side with one another – by tearing us away from our banal, egocentric perspectives. It is not, as in Buber, the mere appearance of the other that constitutes meeting.

According to Gabriel Marcel, the ontological mystery receives, in meditation, a luminosity of its own – precisely that of faith – which is seen not as an incomprehensible and unreflective act but as the height of intelligibility. Through the discovery of the I–Thou, Marcel remains faithful to the spirituality of knowledge. The spirit directed toward God as Thou is also the event of the *ens manifestum sui* [being that is manifest to itself], the fact of being's self-revelation. Saying God as Thou does not underscore transcendence, but is a modality of the revelation and truth of the Absolute. As the common source of thought and being, the mystery of love signifies the immanence of Myself to God and of God to myself. It is, as Schwartz summarizes it, what Schelling would call transcendence made immanence. Buber eliminates the gnoseological foundation of the Meeting. The unconditioned event of the Meeting overflows thought and being. It is a pure dialogue, a pure *covenant* that no pneumatic common presence envelops. I am destined for the other not because of our *prior* proximity or our substantial union, but because the Thou is absolutely other.

III

The achievement of Marcel and Buber – henceforth the classic example of the philosophy called (overlooking the difference between Buber and Marcel) the philosophy of dialogue – is not only the discovery of an intellectual novelty alongside objectification, a "curious" relation, called relation with a Thou. For the history of ideas, that accession to God as to an Eternal Thou or absolute Other would seem, at any rate, to mark the end of a certain metaphysics of the object, in which God is deduced as the unconditioned, setting out from that object, by a movement of founding or conditioning. The "philosophy of dialogue" also shows a questioning of the exclusive *intelligibility* of the *foundation* and the questioning of objectification and even thematization as sole sources of the meaningful. But how does dialogue respond to the very vocation of philosophy?

What was that vocation? It was traditionally understood as an appeal to live in such a way as not to undergo social, cultural, political, and religious decisions and imperatives passively, not to be taken in by ideologies – which is probably the negative definition of thought itself and of reason in their age-old opposition to opinion; and, in the final analysis, it is being able to say *I*, to think in saying *I* – the ability to say in all sincerity: *cogito*. What sustained this ability in our Western world was objective knowledge, fulfilled in communicable patency, attaining unshakeable, substantial being, affirming itself on the firmness of the earth – knowledge attaining that same substantiality and firmness, in the presence, the identity of being in its being as such, miraculously equal to the knowledge that sought it, marvellously *made to measure* for that knowledge. Knowledge and being – correlation, the most perfect match! The rigorous development of this knowledge led to the fullest consciousness of self. To think being is to think on one's own scale, to coincide with oneself. And the way the ability to say *I* was understood in that adequate knowledge which equalled itself in equalling being, without anything being able to remain outside that adequate knowledge to weigh it down, was called freedom. But, on that royal road as well, philosophers found they had been duped.

Let us not dwell on the fact that the intellectual mastery of being eventually proved to be the technological mastery of being as world, and that, though freed by scientific reason, man became the plaything of technological necessities dictating their law to reason. It was also the presence of being to reason – the reason of pure speculation – that became problematic.

The history of thought reflects a growing uncertainty about (a) the precise significance of the rational, once wrested free from opinion and ideology; (b) the presence of being itself as opposed to its false semblance in the forms embracing it, in which *appearing* remains suspect of appearances; and (c) the foundation and significance of science, which, despite its success, does not know from what place in being and under what conditions its so self-confident voice sounds forth. The history of philosophy is an ever-renewed struggle against the imprudence of the spontaneous exercise of reason, incapable of ensuring its security and protecting itself from paralogisms, and thus from the resurgence, in ever-unexpected forms, of naivety at the heart of reflection. Kantian philosophy itself [*le criticisme*], which has lent reason its form and figure, was still misled by a traditional logic accepted as fixed, and needed a phenomenology, whether Hegelian – overcoming the separations of logical understanding by a form of reason in movement – or, more humbly but more radically, Husserlian, seeking full lucidity on the hither side of logic in a *living present*, in its proto-impressions and their syntheses and "passive explications". In Husserl's view, that full lucidity has already been diminished by the first constituted structures of objectivity, which block the horizons of critical scrutiny.

Whence a privilege of presence, which is precisely what is called into question by one whole current of contemporary French philosophy, a current that may be characterized as a "merciless critical inquiry" – a critique born of a reflection on all the conditions and all the "mediations" of supposedly immediate experience: political, social, epistemological, psychoanalytic, linguistic, poetic. It is no longer the worlds-behind-the-world that are challenged. There would seem to be a transcendental illusion in the immediately given, in the world spread out before us with nothing hidden. It is a critique one can be tempted to reproach for not applying its critique to its own possibility; but it is impossible to use that reproach to avoid taking it seriously. It is not a question of adopting it as one might a fashion emanating from a large Western metropolis. But not to see in it the testimony of a crisis that befalls us on the royal road of philosophy which identifies meaning and intelligibility with the intellectual act of knowing would be even more frivolous.

The philosophies of dialogue of Buber and Marcel, despite all that separates them, indirectly bear witness to that crisis ehat doubtless already began between the two world wars, but was not just a malaise of circumstance. I have asked: Does their contestation of the philosophical privilege of the *relation* to the *other* understood as a *being* thematized and assimilable to knowledge through the power of ideal generalities, and their doctrine of the *relation to the other* as ensuring the alterity of the other, and thus his or her transcendence as that of a *Thou* addressed in God, and in the other person met in the wake of that address – does that thought respond to philosophy's vocation?

Both philosophers clearly still have recourse to ontological language to describe the meeting with the Thou – and we will return to that point. But the question remains: Does the doctrine, in its novelty, ensure the ability to say *I* without founding it on the freedom of a consciousness equalling being?

IV

Let us return, in order to answer the question, to the relation of transcendence, conceived by Buber as ultimate and irreducible in the I–Thou, and enveloped by no deeper unity. The comparison between Buber and Marcel allowed us to point that out. Language – dialogue – would appear to be the proper element of that transcendence. Can it measure up to that immediacy? Even if Marcel thinks he must trace the I–Thou back to a prior connection, deeper and not dialogic (to the structure of the incarnation and the ontological mystery), is not his criticism of language as the element of the Relation independent of his fundamental position? Is not language [*le langage*] also a particular language [*une langue*], words and a system of words in which no signification is immediate, in which all depends upon a conjunction of signs? To Marcel's criticism of language, nourished by memories of Bergson, we must add all that contemporary thought, and especially present-day French thought, has taught us about the persistence or infiltration of linguistic symbolism into the most immediate lived experience, and the metaphor's mystification, and verbal idealization. Can language as *Said* respect the immediacy of the I–Thou Relation?

But above all, as *Said*, language speaks of something and expresses the relation of the speaker to the object of which he or she speaks, saying how it is with it. To the extent that it is understood that one speaks in order to say something and not for the sake of speaking, dialogue itself appears as a modality of the I–It. Is not the relationship with the other, then, a frequentation alongside truth and objectivity, rather than the I–Thou? Which is, for example, the conception of intersubjectivity in Husserl's Fifth Cartesian Meditation.

But what of language as *Saying*? Is it absorbed into the *Said* without distinction? Can it not be examined in its purity? It says this or that, but at the same time it says *Thou*. The word *Thou* is a *Said*, but it is a *Said* that is not, like this or that, simply something it is possible to say: it is the *Said* of the *Saying* as such. The *Saying* says *Thou* – often without saying it – by its nature of direct discourse which it is or to which, in the final analysis, it belongs. That address in which, even without leaving the lips, the word *Thou* is said and *appeals* to the other – does it still have the structure of an experience and the wariness of an aim? In this vocative, it is not sufficient to recognize, as a grammarian, an incomparable *case* among the other *cases* of the declension. In it there resounds a call, an event that does without mediation, even that of a precursory knowledge or ontological project. It is all the irruption, without ceremony or preface, of informal address [*tutoiement*] which is also the risk of disinterest,[23] all the grace, all the gratuitousness – but also all the ethics of sociability – of covenant, of association with the unknown that is, I think, pure allegiance and responsibility. Does not the immediacy of the I–Thou of which Buber speaks reside – rather than negatively in a thought totally disengaged from any recourse to the conceptual systems of the world and history – in the very urgency of my responsibility that precedes all knowledge?

Here we are indeed taking a few steps outside Buber – not "to understand him better than he understood himself" but to try to apprehend and recognize him as a pioneer. Is it not the irreducibility of the association with the other to any prior knowledge that he is teaching us, in declaring the independence of the I–Thou, inconvertible into I–It? That the Thou *par excellence* signifies the Thou of God and the Thou in God – this also means that *saying Thou* is not an *aim* but precisely an allegiance to the Invisible, to the Invisible thought vigorously not only as the non-sensible but as the unknowable and unthematizable *per se*, of which one can say nothing. The saying of Thou to the Invisible only opens up a dimension of meaning in which, contrary to all the other dimensions of thought, there occurs no recognition of *being* [*essence*] depicted in the Said – neither representation nor knowledge nor ontology, but a dimension in which the other person, addressed from the start as Thou, is placed.[24]

It is a dimension of meaning in which persons encounter one another, an ethical dimension that thus specifies or determines the religious character, the excellence or elevation of the revelation of the Eternal Thou. The relation with the other is possible only in the wake – be it unknown, unavowed, denied – of originative religion; and, conversely, describing a circle in no sense vicious, it is from the relation with the human Thou that Buber glimpses the relation with the Eternal Thou itself – the latter being, in the final analysis, the foundation of the former. And that is the case even if the Relation, taken by surprise in the relation with others, is extended to realms having nothing ethical about them – the world, spiritual entities! The I–Thou Relation, reciprocity of the dialogue, which sustains all human intercourse, is described in Buber as a pure, and in a sense formal, confrontation, a face-to-face, but it appears in his texts as immediately qualified: responsibility of one for the other, as if the face-to-face were, from the beginning and constantly thereafter, ethical concreteness. The "responses" constituting the dialogue signify – without this being a simple pun – "responsibility". And even Marcel insists on the link between these words in Buber and sees the response as a condition of responsibility.[25] Intersubjectivity thus appears in Buber's work as a reciprocal responsibility, in keeping with the ancient Talmudic expression: "All in Israel are responsible for one another".[26] Buber's entire oeuvre is a renewal of ethics, which begins neither in a mystical valuation of a few values having the status of Platonic ideas, nor on the basis of a prior thematization, knowledge, and theory of being, culminating in a self-knowledge of which ethics would constitute a consequence or appendix, nor in the universal law of Reason. Ethics begins before the exteriority of the *other*, before other people, and, as I like to put it, before the face of the other, which engages my responsibility by its human expression, which cannot – without being changed, immobilized – be held objectively at a distance. This is an ethics of heteronomy that is not a servitude, but the service of God through responsibility for the neighbour, in which I am irreplaceable. We are probably on the hither side of freedom and unfreedom. The radical distinction between the I–It of knowledge and the I–Thou of dialogue, and the *total* independence of the latter from the former – a thesis Buber and Marcel share, despite their differences – signify that new ethics and that new order of the meaningful.

But this new ethics is also a new way of understanding the possibility of an I, and consequently responds to the vocation of philosophy. In this case, it is a question not of the freedom that a knowledge of the totality of being would ensure, but of the ethical responsibility that also signifies that no one can take my place when I am the one responsible: I cannot shrink before the other man, I am *I* by way of that uniqueness, I am *I* as if I had been chosen.

This is an ethical interpretation of transcendence, but one that is surely not always ensured against a relapse into a view in which the I–Thou, the ethical, is again interpreted as a certain mode – a privileged mode – of presence, that is, as a modality of being. I have stressed, in the present study, Buber's recourse to ontological terms to describe the relationship with the Thou, and his stated search for an ontology, setting out from the I–Thou, as if being (or the being of beings) were the alpha and omega of meaning. There is reason to ask oneself whether the I–Thou relation, in its transcendence, encounters being primordially, whether it does not name it in an act of reflection that is only secondary, whether that act of reflection is always legitimate, whether the Thou as God in his invisibility does not have a significance of sociality that eclipses the clarity of the givens and their being. Does not the ethical relation signify precisely the non-significance of being, even if theologians, reflecting, persist in finding its meaning in the trace of sociality, and interpret sociality as an experience? And to use once more, in articulating it, the word that expresses that non-significance, the Relation – is it not dis-inter-estment itself, the uprooting from Being – straightforwardness of élan without a return toward self? Disinterestment that does not signify indifference, but allegiance to the other.

It is not a simple matter of vocabulary. The interpretation of the I–Thou relation as presence, coexistence, or the superlative that the meaning of the word *being* would assume in the *co-esse*, the proposition "all real [*wirklich*] life is meeting", the inverse of which should also be true – do they attest, in the final analysis, to the impossibility of thinking outside or beyond being? Do they call us back to the necessity of thinking matters through to the end, and of finding being there again? Does reflection claim to apprehend a modality of being in disinterestment itself? In that case, the philosophy of dialogue would be but a specification of ontology and the "thought of being". If that is so, then all theology, all ethics, all theophany, and all religion would turn out to be "thought of being" in the Heideggerian sense, or transcendental idealism.

Such is, in fact, the destiny of the philosophy that has been transmitted to us; the last pages of Husserl's *Krisis* show this to us in its modern metamorphosis and noble grandeur. Here is psychology, thought as science, thought through to the end, which reveals itself progressively (except for a special methodological procedure accomplishing the "phenomenological reduction") to be transcendental philosophy. All being is reduced to the noemata of constituting intentions from which the experience of that being is made, and which phenomenological reflection analyses apodictically; and through this process all being is confirmed and clarified in its Being – all beings, even other people. Others, it is true, in a privileged way: as presupposed in the "consciousness-of-world" as long as, along the path leading step by step to the ultimate epochè of transcendental consciousness, the "reduced" subject still retains its human condition, before positing itself as absolute subject. Husserl writes: "it is unthinkable, and not merely [contrary to] fact, that I could be man in a world without being *a* man".[27] And a little further: "everyone, in his commerce with others within his world-consciousness, at the same time has consciousness of others in the form of particular others".[28] He goes on to add: "within the vitally flowing intentionality in which the life of an ego-subject consists, every other ego is already intentionally implied in advance in the mode of empathy [*Einfühlung*]".[29] *In the mode of empathy*, which Husserl understands as experience, "it [each soul] has empathy experiences, experiencing consciousness of others".[30] It is thus by a certain structure of experience that the egological consciousness is linked to other consciousnesses. Husserl, faithful to the history of our philosophy, converts the welcoming of others into an experience of others, that is, he grants himself the right to reduce the unmotivated nature [*gratuité*] of the relation-to-others to knowledge that will be surveyed by reflection. The relation-to-others presupposed by the *human* perception of the world is therefore not necessary to the transcendental subject as absolute, for whom that entire relation must yet be constituted.

> [W]hen I practice the reducing epoché on myself and *my* world-consciousness, the other human beings, like the world itself, fall before the epochè; that is, they are merely intentional phenomena for me. Thus the radical and perfect reduction leads to the *absolutely unique ego* of the pure psychologist, who thus at first absolutely isolates himself and as such no longer has validity for himself [*Selbstgeltung*] as a human being or as really existing in the world, but is instead the pure subject of his intentionality, which through the radical reduction is universal and pure, with all its intentional implications".[31]

Hence, in the final analysis, even the privileged relation the ego held with others in the consciousness-of-world and psychological discourse on that consciousness – which, as scientific discourse, is held *with* and *for* the others – harks back to a monologue going *from oneself to oneself* as does thought, according to Plato – a silent discourse of the soul with itself. "What I say here scientifically, I say from myself to myself; but at the same time, paradoxically, I say it to all the others as being transcendentally implied in me and in one another".[32] This implication is based on the *Einfühlung*, which, as experience, is convertible into knowledge.

Is not Husserl's intent in thinking things *through to the end* to find, by reflecting on our relation to the other, *Einfühlung* in the form of experience? And can we seriously question whether or not it is right to think things through to the end, whether or not one should think reflectively? The very raising of such questions elicits condemnation by the thinking portion of humanity. Unless such questions are asking only whether thoughts that do not return to the self – pure élans – are unthinkable. Unless they are questioning whether the necessity of thinking through to the end is suspended *only* as a result of the non-thought and non-meaning of blind passions, frivolous distractions, or a lapse into the preoccupations of daily life. Unless they are asking whether the relation to the other person, the solicitation of our fellow human beings, the exigencies of *sociality*, all that returning toward the others, to those close to us, to all that sociality we hear around us, waiting for us when we leave the laboratory or study, close the book, put down the pen (all that going back in which, as Husserl admits, the ties to the life-world, the *Lebenswelt*, are retied, but in which the founder of phenomenology saw nothing more than a still provisional level of the epochè) – whether all that turning back is no more than an interruption of pure concession to the weakness of our non-angelic natures. Is not the philosophy of dialogue precisely – by reference to that which, outside all ontology, *otherwise*, but just as rigorously, has the value of *source of meaning* – the affirmation that it is impossible to encompass within a theory the Meeting with the others as if it were an experience whose meaning reflection could recover? And the affirmation that it is impossible to contain the meaning of the human face in any concept? Reasonable meanings that Reason does not know![33] Has not the philosophy of dialogue made us attentive to the ambiguity or the enigma of thoughts that think the world and the other person, knowledge and sociality, being and God together? Is not alternation henceforth the lot of the modern mind?

An ancient Talmudic apologue relates the protest of the angels when the divine Torah was going to leave Heaven to be given to men. The Eternal comforts them: the laws contained in the Torah are made for the earth; they do not apply to angels, who are neither born nor die, neither work nor eat, neither own nor sell. The angels submit. Did they fall silent solely because their pride was flattered? Did they, on the contrary, catch a brief glimpse of the superiority of earthly beings capable of *giving* and of being-for-one-another and thus beginning the "divine comedy", above and beyond the understanding of the being to which pure spirits are consigned?

NOTES AND REFERENCES

1. See the collective work on the Buber which appeared in German (1963) and then in English, under the title *The Philosophy of Martin Buber*, ed. Paul A. Schilpp and Maurice Friedman (La Salle, Illionois: Open Court Publishing Co.; London: Cambridge University Press, 1967); read the article by Gabriel Marcel, p. 42.
2. Gabriel Marcel, *Metaphisical Journal*, trans. B. Wall (London: Rockliff, 1952), pp. 210-11. [*Translator's note*: Translation slightly altered.]
3. *The Philosophy of Martin Buber*, p. 41.
4. Besides the study published in *The Philosophy of Martin Buber*, there is another essay of Marcel's on Buber entitled "Anthropologie philosophique de Martin Buber", in the collection published in 1968 by Editions de l'Institut de Sociologie de l'Université Libre de Bruxelles: *Martin Buber. L'homme et le philosophe*, pp. 17–41. I will cite it by this last title.
5. *The Philosophy of Martin Buber*, p. 41.
6. Ibid., p. 45.
7. *Being and Having*, trans. K. Farrer (New York: Harper & Row, 1965), p. 11. [*Translator's note*: I have modified Farrer's translations slightly.]
8. Ibid., p. 14.
9. Ibid., p. 12.
10. Ibid., p. 14.
11. Ibid.
12. Ibid., p. 28.
13. Ibid., p. 10.
14. Ibid., p. 11.
15. Ibid., p. 28.
16. *Metaphysical Journal*, p. 137.
17. *The Philosophy of Martin Buber*, p. 44.
18. *Martin Buber. L'homme et le philosophe*, p. 19.
19. *The Philosophy of Martin Buber*, p. 45.
20. Ibid., pp. 45–46.
21. Ibid., p. 47.

22. Ibid., p. 46.
23. [*Translator's note*: In French, "*risque dés-inter-essé*". Levinas nearly always hyphenates *dés-inter-essé* to bring out the Latin etymological meaning: "not-within-being". The overall sense of the expression would then seem to be: the risk of leaving "being" in the discursive address, which constitutes a leap toward the other.]
24. Is not Brentano's famous thesis, that every psychic phenomenon is either a representation or founded on a representation (a thesis that never ceased to preoccupy Husserl), refuted or at least contradicted by the I–Thou psychism, which requires no I–It for its foundation? See, on the contestation of the "autonomy" of the I–Thou, the very important book by Yochanan Bloch: *Die Aporie des Du. Probleme der Dialogik Martin Bubers* (Heidelberg: Lambert Schneider, 1977).
25. *Martin Buber. L'homme et le philosophe*, pp. 31–32.
26. Babylonian Talmud, Tractate Shevuot, p. 39a. An expression in which Israel is to be understood as shorthand for humanity.
27. Edmund Husserl, *The Crisis of European Sciences and Transcendental Phenomenology*, trans. David Carr (Evanston: Northwestern University Press, 1970), p. 253.
28. Ibid., p. 254.
29. Ibid., p. 255.
30. Ibid.
31. Ibid., p. 256.
32. Ibid., p. 258.
33. [*Translator's note*: This phrase echoes Pascal's "The heart has its reasons, that reason does not know".]

Chapter 4
Apropos of Buber: Some Notes

Emmanuel Levinas

I

The statement that others do not appear to me as objects does not just mean that I do not take the other person as a thing under my power, a "something". It also asserts that the very relation originally established between myself and others, between myself and someone, cannot properly be said to reside in an act of knowledge that, as such, is seizure and comprehension, the besiegement of objects. The object, supposedly external, is in fact already encompassed by me; hence the ambiguous status of immanence and transcendence. The relation to others is precisely the end of that ambiguity and of the old tradition of idealist philosophy, in which the advent of language is only a supplemental factor, a means by which to make known on the outside what strictly speaking takes place within ourselves, or to serve inner thought as an instrument of analysis, or as a repository in which its acquired results can accumulate. In the relation to others, that inferiority is immediately broken open and language – the saying that says, if only implicitly, *thou* – is not just the (always optional) account of a meeting. It is the event of that meeting itself, the very bursting forth of thought dialogically coming out of itself, and quite otherwise than a noesis that projects itself through the same toward the object it gives itself.

Martin Buber discovers that bursting forth or that turning of intentionality into language. He therefore begins his philosopher's approach with the primal word, the fundamental word, the *Grundwort*, instead of reflecting on the *cogito*. The *Grundwort* I–Thou is ultimately the opening condition of all language, even the language that states the relation of pure knowledge expressed by the *Grundwort Ich–Es* (I–That); for the I–That, precisely because it is language, also addresses an interlocutor, and is already dialogue, or residue of a dialogue.

That valuation of the dialogual relation and its phenomenological irre-ducibility, its fitness to constitute a meaningful order that is autonomous and as legitimate as the traditional and privileged subject–object correla-tion in the operation of knowledge – that will remain the unforgettable contribution of Martin Buber's philosophical labours. The multiplicity implied by social proximity is no longer, in relation to unity (or the syn-thesis or totality of being sought by learning or science), a degradation of the rational or a privation. It is a fully meaningful order of the ethical relation, a relation with the unassimilable and thus, properly speaking, in-com-prehensible (alien to the grasp, to possession) alterity of others. The discovery of that order in its full originality and the elaboration of its consequences, and, if one may designate them thus, its "categories", remain inseparable from the name Buber, whatever may have been the concordant voices in the midst of which his own made itself heard – voices as commanding as that of Gabriel Marcel in his *Metaphysical Journal*. But even ignorance of the fact that in walking and working the ground of dialogue one treads on land already cleared by another does not dispense the researcher from allegiance to Buber. Nothing could limit the homage due him. Any reflection on the alterity of the other in his or her irreducibility to the objectivity of objects and the being of beings must recognize the new perspective Buber opened – and find encouragement in it.

Therefore in my remarks on Buber, though I indicate a few points of divergence, it is not to question the fundamental and admirable analyses of *I and Thou*, and even less to embark upon the perilous or ridiculous enterprise of "improving" the teachings of an authentic creator. But the speculative landscape opened up by Buber is rich enough, and still new enough, to make possible certain perspectives of meaning that cannot always be seen, at the start at least, from the trails masterfully blazed by the pioneer.

My remarks, which distinguish differences between Buber's positions and those I take up in my own essays, are formulated as working notes on various themes. They do not supply the underlying insights that found them, and often take the form of questions rather than objections. It may not be impossible to find answers to them – or even to find a place for the ideas that inform them – in Buber's texts. But that would involve a study not undertaken here today.

II

One further preliminary remark is in order. It might astonish some that – faced with so many unleashed forces, so many violent and voracious acts that fill our history, our societies, and our souls – I should turn to the *I–Thou* or the responsibility-of-one-person-for-the-other to find the categories of the Human. That astonishment may be shared by many noble minds. This was certainly the case with our dear departed friend, Professor Alphonse de Waelhens, – when, after having devoted so many fine works to phenomenology, he spoke of the distance separating philosophical anthropology and the face of true human misery, and when, in order to look that misery in the eyes, he began frequenting (after so many libraries) psychiatric hospitals. But perhaps seeking the secret of the human in the ethical structures of proximity is not the equivalent of trying to close one's eyes to that misery. It is not by confidence in progress, based on a consoling dialectic or the empirically gathered signs portending a new Golden Age, that this research on ethics as first philosophy is justified. It is undoubtedly the implacable necessities of being that explain the inhuman history of mankind, rather than an ethics of alterity. But it is because the human has sprung up within being that those implacable necessities and those violent acts and that universal inter-estment are in question and are denounced as cruelty, horrors, and crimes – and that humanity both perseveres in being and at the same time declares its opposition to the *conatus essendi* through the saints and the righteous, and is to be understood not only on the basis of its being-in-the-world but also from books. The humanity of the human – is this not, in the contranatural appearance of the ethical relation to the other man, the very crisis of being *qua* being?

III

To Buber, the *Thou* that the *I* solicits is already, in that appeal, heard as an *I* who says *thou* to me. The appeal to the *Thou* by the *I* would thus be, for the *I*, the institution of a reciprocity, an equality or equity from the start. Whence the understanding of the *I* as *I*, and the possibility of an adequate thematization of the *I*. The idea of the *I* or of a Myself in general is immediately derived from that relation: a total reflection on myself would be possible and thus the elevation of the Myself to the level of the concept, to Subjectivity above the lived centrality of the I; an elevation that, in traditional rationalism, passes for "better" or more "spiritual" than centrality, and is said to signify a "liberation" with respect to partial subjectivism with its intellectual and moral illusions.

In my own analyses, the approach to others is not originally in my speaking out to the other, but in my responsibility for him or her. That is the original ethical relation. That responsibility is elicited, brought about by the face of the other person, described as a breaking of the plastic forms of the phenomenality of appearance: straightforwardness of the exposure to death, and an order issued to me not to abandon the other (the Word of God). Methodological importance is given to the face and its originality in the perceived, according to a significance independent of that given it by the context of the world. The ineradicable centrality of the I – of the I not leaving its first person – signifies the unlimited nature of that responsibility for the neighbour: I am never absolved with respect to others. Responsibility for the other person is a responsibility neither conditioned nor measured by any free acts of which it would be the consequence; it is gratuitous responsibility resembling that of a hostage, and going as far as taking the other's place, without requiring reciprocity. It is the foundation of the ideas of fraternity and expiation for the other man. Here, then, contrary to Buber's I–Thou, there is no initial equality. (Is the use of the familiar I–Thou form justified?)[1] Ethical inequality: subordination to the other, original diacony:[2] the "first person accusative" and not "nominative". Hence the profound truth of Dostoevsky's *Brothers Karamazov*, often quoted: "We are all guilty of everything and everyone, towards everyone, and I more so than all the others". That superlative degree of guilt does not, of course, refer to any personal history, or to the character traits of the individual making that statement.

IV

It is a non-transferable responsibility, as if my neighbour called me urgently and called none other than myself, as if I were the only one concerned. Proximity itself resides in the exclusivity of my role. It is ethically impossible to transfer my responsibility for my neighbour to a third party. My ethical responsibility is my uniqueness, my election, and my "primogeniture". The identity and uniqueness of the *me* does not seem to be a problem in Buber. They are not derived from the correlation of the dialogue itself, in which the *me* is concrete. Does not its "individuation" remain implicitly substantialist in Buber?

V

As regards relation with the other in reciprocity, in Buber, justice begins within the *I–Thou*. From my perspective, on the other hand, the passage from ethical inequality – from what I have termed the dissymmetry of intersubjective space – to "equality between persons" comes from the political order of citizens in a state. The birth of the state from the ethical order is intelligible to the extent that I have also to answer for the third parry "next to" my neighbour. But who is *next to* whom? The immediacy of my relation to my neighbour is modified by the necessity of comparing persons with one another and judging them, by recourse to universal principles, locus of justice and objectivity. Citizenship does not put an end to the centrality of the I. It invests it with a new meaning: an irrevocable meaning. The state can begin functioning according to the laws of being. It is the responsibility for the other that determines the legitimacy of the state, that is, its justice.

VI

Does not the thought to which dialogue organically and primordially belongs, in Buber, remain within the *element* of consciousness? It has seemed to me essential to stress the irreducibility of responsibility toward others to the intentionality of consciousness, to a thought that knows, to a thought closed to the transcendence of the *Other*, and ensuring, as knowledge, equality between idea and *ideatum* – whether it be in the strict noetic–noematic parallel, or the adequation of its truth, or the fullness of the intuition "fulfilling" the goal of the *Meinen* [to mean], satisfying it as one satisfies a need. The ethical relation to the other person, the proximity, the responsibility for others is not a simple modulation of intentionality; it is the concrete modality in which there is produced a non-indifference of one to the other or of the same to the *Other*, that is, a relation from the Same to what is *out of all proportion* with the Same, and is, in a sense, not of the "same kind". The proximity ensured by the responsibility for the other is not the makeshift link between "terms" that cannot coincide, cannot be fused into one because of their difference, but rather the new and proper excellence of sociality.

There is, here, in my manner of proceeding, something like a deduction of "concrete situations" from abstract significations whose horizons or "*mise-en-scène*" are reconstituted – a manner inspired by phenomenology, and often used since *Totality and Infinity* (for example, the "at home" as an inflection of the Me, sought after in the concreteness of the dwelling, and the interiority of the dwelling leading back to the feminine face). There is an emphasis, moreover, on the limit that the concreteness of the "ethical content" imposes upon the necessity of purely formal structures: "subordination" can exclude servitude when it is the Infinite that commands; the *greater* is in the *lesser* in the Cartesian idea of God; possibilities are beyond the limits of the possible in paternity, and so on. Doesn't Husserl's very important distinction (*Ideas*, chap. 1, para. 3) between the formal, which is empty, and the general, which is always still *sachhaltig* [possessed of thing-like content], contain the possibility (despite the subordination of genus to form) of a certain distortion of form by content?

VII

God, to Buber, is the Great Thou or the Eternal Thou. The relations between persons intersect in Him, end in Him. I have shown that I am less certain that what is called the Divine Person resides in the Thou of dialogue and that devotion and prayer are dialogue. I have been led to have recourse to the third person, to what I have called *illeity*, to speak of the Infinite and the divine transcendence, which is other than the alterity of others – illeity of God who sends me to serve my neighbour, to responsibility for him. God is personal insofar as He brings about interpersonal relations between myself and my neighbours. He signifies from the face of the other person, with a significance articulated not as the relation of signifier to signified, but as order signified to me.[3] The coming to mind of God is always linked, in my analyses, to the responsibility for the other person and all religious affectivity signifies in its concreteness a relation to others; the fear of God is concretely my fear for my neighbour. It does not revert, Heidegger's schema of affectivity norwithstanding, to a fear for oneself.

VIII

Cannot Buber's dualism of the fundamental words I–Thou and I–That, a dualism of the social relation and objectification, be overcome? I have already alluded to the entry of the third party into the relation to my neighbour, motivating thematization, objectification, and knowledge. But is not the *for the other* itself of sociality concrete in *giving*, and does it not presuppose *things*, without which, empty-handed, the responsibility for others would be but the ethereal sociality of angels?[4]

IX

Does Buber's language, so faithful to the novelty of the relation with others in contrast with the knowledge going toward being, break entirely with the priority of ontology? Is not I–Thou spoken as its own way of reaching being? I have attempted to think through the relation to others and the Infinite as dis-inter-estment in both senses of the term: as gratuitousness of the relation, but also as the eclipse of the traditional problem of being in the relation with God and others. The problem of the meaning of being becomes, in this manner of thinking, the questioning of the *conatus essendi* that, in the "understanding of being", remained the essential trait of being: the being of *Dasein* meant having to be. In the responsibility for the other person, my being calls for justification: being-there, is that not already occupying another's place? The *Da* of *Dasein* is already an ethical problem.

NOTES AND REFERENCES

1. [*Translator's note*: "I–Thou" is my translation of Levinas's "*Je–Tu*", which in turn is his translation of Buber's "*Ich–Du*". The French (and German) pronouns are those used familiarly, between friends or equals. Levinas questions their appropriateness to designate the relationship between self and other because (differing from Buber on this point) he considers the other to be higher and greater than the self, and the relation to be asymmetrical and non-reversible. In fact, the relation with the other (person) takes place in the "trace" of the relation of self to God. This latter is to be understood in terms of "illeity", i.e. as an "I–It" relationship, though it should not be confused with the one Buber and Marcel reject in favor of the "I–Thou" to describe the human encounter. See Levinas, *En découvrant l'existence avec Husserl et Heidegger* (Paris: Vrin, 2nd ed. enl., 1988), p. 202.]

2. [*Translator's note*: Levinas uses this term in its etymological sense of the function of a servant. See *En découvrant*, pp. 194–197.]

3. [*Translator's note*: Levinas is playing on two senses of the French verb *signifier*, which means (usually) "to mean", but also "to command".]

4. See on this question pp. 51–55 of my *Noms propres* (Montpellier: Fata Morgana, 1976). I refer the reader also, for a discussion of the problem raised by these Notes on Buber, to Stephane Strasser's beautiful study, "Buber und Levinas, Philosophische Besinnung auf einen Gegensatz", in *Revue internationale de la Philosophie*, 1978, pp. 512–525.

Chapter 5

Beyond Caritas
An Interview with Emmanuel Levinas

Arne Johan Vetlesen and Harald Jodalen

On a brilliant summer day in June 1993, we were warmly welcomed by Emmanuel Levinas and his wife in their home in Paris. In an atmosphere of great hospitality, a two-hour conversation took place, from which the interview printed here is an excerpt.

Q: The great ethicists – Plato, Aristotle, Hume, Kant – were all committed to specific assumptions about human nature. By contrast, and notwithstanding the anthropocentrism that is at the core of your ethical thought, you are for the most part silent about anthropological assumptions. Why? Is it because you, coming from Husserl, view ethics as part of phenomenology?

A: A hard question. In phenomenology, the overall focus is on the meticulous laying out of the main structures of human existence. On the other hand, when one turns to Aristotle, attention is from the very beginning devoted to the issue of moral education; that is, to how a person may acquire the virtues by habituation, by following the example of the virtuous person, by taking part in the practice of a community. In this sense moral education, as you indicate, always rests on certain assumptions about "man", about the sort of condition in which philosophy, or ethics, finds the human agent as he "is" prior to the workings of moral education, be it of Aristotelian or of some other kind. In phenomenology, by contrast, education and pedagogy are matters of secondary importance. What is important in phenomenology is the analysis itself, without seeking to draw conclusions – substantial conclusions – for education and morals.

Q: Is there anything in Aristotle's moral philosophy that has influenced your own thinking?

A: Aristotle, you know, is simply the best there is – the first and the best. But again, from a phenomenological viewpoint, there is no real "analysis" in Aristotle; more to the point, there is no examination of intentionality.

Q: Perhaps we should simply say that your questions are different from those raised by Aristotle? I mean, would you say that Aristotle's question, What does the good life consist in?, is a predominant question in your own ethical thought?

A: No.

Q: Since your starting-point in ethics obviously isn't Aristotelian, what is it? Let me put it this way: Is the dyad – the I–thou relationship – sufficient as the point of departure? Or is it necessary to include the "third" from the very start, thus replacing the dyadic relationship with a triadic one?

A: Speaking about the ethical relationship, we must first of all speak about openness. Of what kind is this openness? To begin with, it is not love; it is much wider in scope than love. Love is exclusive, selective. However, love is ambiguous. We must distinguish between the one person who is one's "love" and love of mankind. Only by loving can one fully realize what it is to be a human being. Without love, or rather without loving, a person's full humanity cannot unfold. But love is not sufficient as a basis for ethics. Love's selectivity is only overwon in friendship, which is truly universal. Indeed, in the European spirit – if I may use such an expression – friendship enjoys a higher standing than love. Remember that for Kant love is nothing more than a sensuous tendency ("eine sinnliche Tendenz").

Q: But this still leaves the question concerning the role of the third unanswered. Now, in your major work *Totality and Infinity*, it is only when the issue of justice is raised that the third enters the picture. What is, in your view, the core of justice?

A: The core of justice is that the other never be considered a mere means. Like I have said before, justice is the way I respond to the fact that I am not alone in the world with the other. I will explain what is involved here by returning to your earlier question. We may say that caritas is part of the basis of our relation with others; but caritas too is insufficient from the ethical point of view. Now, as soon as the third appears on the scene, the question becomes: who is the other and who is the third? Caritas is inadequate to respond to this question; accordingly, this marks the point where justice must make its entry, and justice means the state. So the issue of justice arises once there is a triad as opposed to a dyad; and matters of justice cannot be settled by caritas. What is required for justice is a court of law, a tribunal, and in this lies the beginning of the state. The universality of caritas is possible only, if at all, within the state.

Q: It strikes me that your position comes very close to Hegel's, and surprisingly so. Hegel too, especially in his early works, starts out with love (as experienced in the family, in a setting of intimacy) and moves over solidarity (as facilitated in civil society) to end up positing justice ('Recht") as the principle realized in the state and in the state only; justice in the full-blown universal sense.
A: Well, the spiritual ("das Geistige") is realized only in the state. And only in the state does the third truly have a say, as it were. It is crucial that there be a third party, and not only for reasons elucidated by Hegel. For only when there is a third party is one forced to judge, to make a decision. In this sense, what is exclusively human (i.e., having to judge, to decide with a view to justice) can unfold only by way of participation in the state. In fact, only in politics can we talk about humanity's realizing itself.

Q: Now you sound just like Aristotle. But isn't Aristotle a bad guide in these matters? I mean, for all the emphasis he puts on friendship, even the complete friendship so highly praised by Aristotle is a relationship between equals, between "people similar in virtue". And politics too is a matter among equals, whereby justice in the modern, universalist meaning is denied to those of lower standing – i.e., to women, to slaves, to strangers; and hence, I wish to add, to *the other* as conceived in your ethical thought.
A: Certainly. One must be very cautious here. For – Aristotle aside – there is a corruption of politics, or more precisely, a decay in political life. And probably exactly at this point there will be a re-emergence of love; caritas will again prevail. But, to repeat, caritas is and will always remain as between two only; caritas will always be a matter of selection.

Q: I would like to return to Kant in order to bring your position into sharp relief. In Kant, the other that I recognize is himself a recognizer – that is to say, I recognize someone capable of recognizing me. Hence there is what I would call structural reciprocity. Isn't this conception fundamentally different from yours?

A: Well, I do in fact think that Kant too has recognized the point you expect me to make. Kant saw, no less than did Hegel, albeit in a different way, that true recognition of one subject by another is something that is possible only in a state, in a just state, that is. Indeed, this is precisely what constitutes the problem, or the task, of the just state.

Q: Okay, but this still leaves out of the picture the radicality in your conception of the ethical relationship that I was getting at. I believe that what is radical in your position is your insistence that my responsibility for the other is prior to the other's responsibility for me. In other words, you uncouple responsibility from reciprocity: I am responsible for the other; I alone am so, and I am so totally; I am without substitute, and I am without choice. Thus I am responsible regardless of whether or not the other will return my favours, will reciprocate my responsibility.

A: Yes, of course, and this is unlike Kant. Practically, in real life, it is very difficult. But, speaking about Kant and Hegel, what separates us from them is that we have experienced the decline of the state, being citizens of the 20th century. Therefore we have to reflect anew about the state, about the conditions of recognition, of justice to the third party. In fact, it is necessary that our reflection transcends the state, goes beyond it. Or, alternatively, in the wake of the disasters we have witnessed, one chooses to become sceptical; one says, the human – humanity – has limits.

Q: It seems apt that we turn now to your views on ethics and religion.

A: In my opinion, the decline of the state is perhaps something that points to the religious. Our thinking about this today must proceed in an altogether novel fashion. What I refer to as "the religious" is still not accomplished. The limit of the secular state marks the point where the religious enters and comes into its own. This does not mean that the state is going to hell. But certainly there emerges now a novel form of religion – a new way in which to acknowledge God. However, I do not wish to talk about what is unfulfilled.

Q: In an interview in 1986 you stated: "What I have said about ethics, about the universality of the commandment in the face, of the commandment which is valid even if it doesn't bring salvation, even if there is no reward, is valid independently of any religion".[1]

A: Yes, that is right. But concerning religion – every religion is a vivid expectation of renewal; Messiah continues to be expected. The Messianic moment is still not fulfilled. I am talking about an experience, one which is to be taken very seriously, especially in our time.

Q: What you are saying reinforces my impression that religion plays an ever more important role in your thinking. Am I right?

A: Yes, certainly. But the fact is that I have always been in close contact with the Holy Scriptures.

Q: Do you consider hope for humankind to reside in religion?

A: Indeed. But you know, as for philosophy – I do not regard Husserl's philosophy as decalogue. I used to say, only partly as a joke, that philosophy is a sickness; a lifelong one, to be sure.

Translated from the German by Arne Johan Vetlesen

NOTES AND REFERENCES

1. See "The Paradox of Morality: An Interview with Emmanuel Levinas", in Robert Bernasconi and David Wood, *The Provocation of Levinas*, London: Routledge, 1988, p. 177.

Chapter 6

End or Fulfilment of Phenomenology?
On the Philosophy of Levinas

Asbjørn Aarnes

I

Phenomenology was – and is – a philosophy of experience, and is perhaps best known for the widening of the conception of experience to which it has contributed. The highest authority for knowledge is the so-called *self-given* (*das Selbstgegebene*). It has been maintained that this philosophy represents a turn towards subjectivity.[1] This may be correct in the case of some of those who followed and who moved in the direction of existence philosophy or existentialism. As understood by its founder, Edmund Husserl, however, phenomenology was thought of rather in the perspective of objectivism, a new objectivity.

Under the influence of positivism, a number of phenomena lost their status of reality and were relegated to psychology, the department for all that has status "only" as feeling. Husserl and his pupils made a systematic attempt during the first ten years of the 20th century to overcome this *psychologism* by rehabilitating objects within former and newly established regions of study.

Interest in art and literature, for example, had under positivism fallen into two separate fields, one of "strict" study, another of "personal" intercourse with works of art within the framework of culture and education. Phenomenology underlines the connection between the two attitudes: both, each in its own way, may be related to something real. The impression received when one reads a poem, for example, or looks at a painting – the representation, known as *noema* – possesses something that can be described. It is not part of the activity of consciousness, *noesis*, but something of which one is conscious.

It has been said that Emmanuel Levinas has given phenomenology a new and deeper dimension.[2] That it has played an important role in his thinking can be documented throughout his works, where Husserl and, especially, Heidegger are the names most often quoted.

When Levinas leaves phenomenology, he does so not with a clear break but by gradually widening the perspective. In fact, he even asks himself whether it is not by leaving phenomenology that he can best remain faithful to fundamental impulses in this philosophy. Its motto was, after all, to stay faithful to experience and respect the nature and quality of experience. *Nothing within the reach of experience shall be alien to the philosopher!*

But Husserl's philosophy was a philosophy of representation: if nothing within the reach of experience was to be alien to him, it must reach him through its representation – the *idea*. This is not to say that what was experienced was his representation. "The Aspects" (*die Abschattungen*) from the material world that via *noema* reached *noesis* brought him new knowledge, but this took place under "self-control", through the act of representation, with vigilance and awareness, through the *idea* – the representation.

When Husserl revealed himself as an idealist in 1913 – with *Ideen I* – this came as a surprise to certain students who had believed that they were working to found a new realism.[3] But the leading word *idea* was there right from the start, and surely it is legitimate to say that a philosophy that makes representation the point where the philosopher meets the world, and where the world meets the philosopher, will end in *idealism?*

When Levinas goes beyond phenomenology, it is phenomenology considered as a philosophy of representation that he deserts. He knows that the *idea* is a window on the world and an opening toward the depths in the self, and if one stops up at ontology – i.e. at the description of existents and existing – one cannot have any better access than *the idea*. But Levinas found that he could not stay faithful to the motto "nothing within the reach of experience shall be alien...", without renouncing control, vigilance, awareness – that is to say, representation. Thus it was in phenomenology itself that the impulse to transcend phenomenology – as a philosophy both of representation and of experience – was to be found. Something comes to him without a warning knock at the door. Something breaks in and finds him beyond all representation: *the face of the Other*, or, more exactly, *the trace of him in the face of the Other*. Phenomenology means attention to that which reveals itself, but in the face of the Other he in fact does not reveal himself. He bears witness only through the trace, bears witness that he is in fact not present, but that he, in an immemorable past, has passed by.

It is at this point that Levinas parts with phenomenology – and with Bergson and Marcel, both of whom were "philosophes de la présence" – and, paradoxically enough, approaches Jean-Paul Sartre, though here a reservation must be made: Levinas finds Infinity where Sartre finds Nothing. He understands Sartre when the latter says that the Other is simply "a hole in the world". Both Bergson and Marcel would have said "presence" rather than hole, plenitude given to consciousness. The idea of the "hole" is not incompatible with Levinas' thinking, but for him "the hole" opens out toward Infinity. Sartre was impatient, "the hole" disturbed him, hindered his work in the world, threatened his freedom. For Levinas' philosophy, which is not a philosophy of consciousness and not a philosophy of representation, the face of the Other is not a threat but a testimony of my responsibility for the Other. What is given to consciousness is never immediate, therefore – says Levinas – the title of Bergson's treatise of 1889, *Essai sur les données immédiates de la conscience*, is a *contradictio in adjecto*.[4]

II

Ego cogito made its appearance under Descartes and was further developed under Kant, as an active, thinking I. It was in the nominative, as subject, and its predicate was thinking. Traditional humanism thought in the same way: it is what a human being does that makes him a human being. The dignity of man, humanism's highest conception, is bound up with an *ego agens*, an *ego* that *thinks* and that *wills*.

In its understanding of *comprehension* as being openness to what is given, phenomenology prepares a break with this epistemological schema. It is what Levinas points to as "the passive synthesis" in phenomenology. The break, however, was not complete. A central idea in phenomenology is in fact *intentionality*, which means that the notion of an acting *ego* is maintained. True enough, it suffers a metamorphosis under the various "reductions" – forms of the *époché* – but it rests in the nominative, as the *transcendental ego*, who according to Husserl *constitutes* the whole cosmos: all beings, *alter ego*, and society. Husserl's phenomenology is therefore humanism in the traditional sense. Perhaps one might even say that it was in order to save humanism that Husserl ended up in idealism? The realist interpretation of the motto "To the things themselves" would be that man is exposed to the threat of object-ivity, the threat of Being.

According to Levinas, this is what has happened in the case of many of phenomenology's successors. *Ego* as a counterpoint to everything, extra-mundane, takes its energy from everything that is *not* itself. The story of Descartes' *res cogitans*, which in the Age of Enlightenment was rejected as an unnecessary metaphysical "appendix" in favour of *res extensa* and physics, seems to have repeated itself. Criticism of the philos-ophy of the subject was developed precisely by philosophers who had been under the influence of phenomenology: Derrida, Foucault, Lyotard, Deleuze, and – to a certain extent – Paul Ricoeur. Criticism found new vitality in the philosophies of Suspicion, even in a form of materialism (not Ricoeur), and established itself as *anti-reason* (*Widervernunft*, Karl Jaspers),[5] dismissing the subject and giving priority to objectivity, Structures, or the System.

One of the most remarkable aspects of philosophy today according to Levinas, is that these efforts to "deconstruct" subjectivity correspond to the philosophy that was developed by Husserl's first pupil, Martin Heidegger. Heidegger does not speak on behalf of objectivity, Structures, or the System. His criticism is to be found at a deeper level. It is in order to make up for 2000 years of "Forgetfulness of Being" that he calls on man, as "Being's herdsman", to let being be (*das Sein sein lassen*). It is as though all the powers that be – progressive and regressive – have con-spired against the *ego cogitans*!

Levinas stands neither on the side of Being nor on the side of the subject, and he is outside post-modernism's "deconstruction of logo-centrism". He speaks for a new understanding of humanity, in which what makes man a human being is not what he does, but what happens to him. The *ego* has moved into the case of the sufferer, the accusative, *ego patiens*, where the *ego* has become the summoned, the prosecuted, the accused.

It is, however, not the Other who summons, prosecutes, and accuses. If it had been the Other, then Levinas' philosophy would have been a "phil-osophy of dialogue", like Buber's and Marcel's. It would have taken the form of an "internal affair" between "the two of us", myself and the Other. The Other would have ceased to be other and would have entered together with me into the Same.

In the face of the Other, Levinas finds trace of a third person – He who has crossed our path. One asks who this is: is it God or Man – the man in all human beings who is to be recognized not by *cogito* but by his vulnerability, his sensitivity, the being who speaks and is spoken to through the face? He is different from Thou, who together with me represents We. He is a stranger. I know Him only through responsibility.

This is what makes fundamental ethics different from the philosophies of dialogue and "social ontology" (Michael Theunissen).[6] The concept of intentionality has disappeared on the way to the Other, but one can ask whether the very *logos* in phenomenology is not itself "dismantled", as in post-modern philosophy. Not so. But with the disappearance of intentionality the epistemological schema is turned upside down, and with it all its constituent parts. Most decisive is perhaps the extension – or the exploding – of the category *sign*.

III

After Ferdinand de Saussure we know that communicating through signs presupposes a sender and a receiver, as well as, among other things, a code for deciphering the signs. When we find signs, we can conclude that someone has wished to give someone a message. The world of sign rests on the idea of intentionality. It is an intelligible world; it can be explained. It is a social world that invites us to understand.

When Levinas introduces the idea of *trace*, he brings confusion into the world of the sign. Trace as he understands it is the result of an unintentional act, a "by-product", for example of the act of giving a sign. When we stand face to face with the trace, we can say: here someone has passed by, but no one has wished to say anything, to convey a message. We are outside the world of communication and community. The trace testifies to something which has never been in consciousness, never been actually present, and which consequently cannot be remembered.

The trace becomes a leading idea for Levinas.[7] It is the trace that decides the new ethic, the fundamental ethic that goes before ontology, aesthetics, and theology. His thoughts about the Work (*l'Oeuvre*) have an ethical perspective: to create a work of art, for example, is to go beyond the order of the Same; it is to operate for a time that is not my time, the time when the Work will be met by others and will be exposed to the happening of Otherness.

Levinas takes comfort in the thought that everything that today is mine and ours will continue to exist without me, without us, in a time in which we no longer exist. He does not regret that *tempus fugit*. What is human is for him connected with the defeat of egotism: life *for* the Other heralds the birth of humanity. And to live for the Other can also mean to die for the Other. Life is not, therefore, a "being-to-death" (Heidegger) but a being-beyond-death, for a time that is the time of the Other.

To approach the Work is to approach the Other, an endless wandering. Thus, when we approach the work of others, we must respect its Otherness. The work of the Other is analogous with the face of the Other!

Along these lines, Levinas' philosophy has relevance for the problems of methodology in the humanities. If we try to interpret a work of art with reference to the conditions under which it has come into existence, to the author's life, social position, etc., we are attempting the impossible: to proceed as though the work has not been created. For it was precisely in *this* biography and in *this* society that the author had his starting point, and his work became his answer to that which was originally given. To interpret the work in the light of the originally given is to deprive it of its Otherness and bring it back to the Same, which is to wish it undone.

If the work were a sign, this procedure would be legitimate. It would then be a case of "deciphering" the work, that is to say, of finding out what the sender wished to communicate – or, to use the language of art and literature, of finding the *intention*. But for Levinas no intention is accessible. What is accessible is the meaning of the work, its significance as trace. It is in its character of trace that the work is "ineffable". Interpreted by Levinas, this is to say that the work continues to speak without intentional guidance, and it affects us directly, without our seeing it in relation to an intention. The reader/viewer is left to interpret infinitely and, because she knows that she can never hope to complete an interpretation of the work, she succumbs to the temptation to call its language *ambiguous*, even though it may appear to speak more clearly than all other forms of speech.

In a "theological" context confusion is caused when messages no longer function as signs.[8] So long as they functioned as signs, God mediated between guilt and innocence. We interpreted the signs, learned to recognize guilt so that we could pray for forgiveness. But when God's speech – this expression is in itself meaningless for many people – has become trace, access to the code is gone. And, when the code is gone, our own actions also become traces. Or, in other words, the death of God means the disappearance of meaning.

That our actions are accepted as traces means that they appear to be without intention, as if they occur accidentally. If we consider what is the greatest threat to mankind today, the threat to the world and to life on earth, it is not easy to point out who is guilty, or what has been the intention behind it all. Everything has been done with the best of intentions: to release man from the yoke of the elements and to establish the dignity of man. Unintentionally, by accident, the "work" found another channel and thus turned against precisely that which it was intended to safeguard.

Things have gone wrong, but is it possible to say "I have done something wrong" and pray for forgiveness? One must not believe, says Levinas, that man today feels himself free from guilt, that he has nothing for which to ask forgiveness. On the contrary, the dilemma is that actions without intention seem to be outside the order of pardon. For what he has done by accident, man is only half-way guilty, but he will never be able to rid himself of this half-guilt.

Thus guilt and innocence are intermingled. What makes the situation most difficult is that neither the one nor the other can be clearly defined. This is Franz Kafka's dilemma in *The Trial*, and this is why Kafka's book speaks so strongly to people today. Josef K. lives suspended between guilt and innocence. He has not forgotten the distinction between guilt and innocence, but he has no one to advise him or mediate for him. If he maintains innocence, he is reminded – anonymously – of guilt. When he considers the possibility of guilt, and seeks help to defend himself, he is overwhelmed by distractions: women, the lawyers, the artist . . .

Under the Law it seems that a vacuum occurs when acts free themselves from intention and become acts without actors. An answer is to be found under the sign of Grace, which does not suspend but fulfils the Law. The answer comes from Jesus himself when, on the way to Golgotha, he prays: "Father forgive them, for they know not what they do". The Gospel tells us that we do not need to feel that we are responsible for our acts in order to ask for forgiveness. Nothing in our hearts is hidden from Him, even if it has never appeared to our consciousness as an actual presence. That the same conviction is also alive in the Old Testament we find when we read David's Psalm (19:12), where he prays to the Lord: "Cleanse Thou me from secret faults".

The best answer to the question of what God means for Levinas is perhaps that given by Stephan Strasser:

> In personal contact, in the ardent care for one's neighbour, in unselfish effort for the Other, the Holy reveals himself. He reveals himself in this way without becoming the object of intentionality, without becoming the object of comprehension, or being made a theme for a statement. He is "un-imaginable", not because he is too great, too distant or powerful for imagination, but because he speaks to us from a past that was never actual presence for us or ever could be actual presence. *His infinity is neither beginning nor end, but an-archy* . . . it cannot be thought in connection with a common goal. Translated to a time-philosophy, this means that *His transcendence is "diachrony"*. And the transcendent God nevertheless reveals himself. *He reveals himself in basic ethical situations – in no other way does he reveal himself.* Levinas, as philosopher of religion, draws this conclusion: In our era it is no longer possible to talk of God in the language of ontology or of theology, but only in the language of ethics.[9]

IV

In the age of modernity the ego expanded, emancipating itself from all restrictions on its way to realize the autonomous, self-sufficient subject.

Criticism that arose in the 18th century (Rousseau), and was further developed in phenomenology and Bergsonism, has tried to show the price that had to be paid for autonomy: the degradation of Nature to a resource for exploitation, the reduction of human beings to "managers of knowledge" – or"slaves to knowledge", as though the objective were to master the world, not to live in it.

Let us return to Heidegger. His definition of man as *Dasein* is considered the most radical attempt in recent philosophy to think man back into his environment. Man as *Dasein* has no "inner life" but, like his surroundings, lies open, as one can say that a town lies "open" for the conqueror. In this openness lies man's privilege. In other words, man *ek-sistiert* – stands out from existing into Existence.

How radical in fact is this definition? Pascal speaks of man as a *thinking reed*, who by means of thinking is able to include everything that exists in an actual presence of consciousness, and who by virtue of this actualization masters the world. Is this so very different from Heidegger's *Dasein*, who because of his openness to Being is superior to all other beings? To raise these questions is to attempt to bring Heidegger back into the Western metaphysics that he wished to bring to an end.

But it is also possible to stress the distance from this tradition. Man is called to be Being's *herdsman* and the origin of the "little" action to *let* be, in *Sein sein lassen*. Wouldn't *Dasein* then have to live at the mercy of Being? Even less will remain of the subject's sphere of action when Heidegger speaks of man as *be-Dingt*, i.e. as under the command of things.

Is it strange that those who speak in support of the modern project find this somewhat regressive? Is not autonomy squandered here in favour of a "primitive mentality", an animism of Being? Is not the work of enlightenment hereby obscured?

Where does Levinas stand in this debate concerning *progress* and *regression?* He will not sacrifice the idea of *humanism*. Unlike Heidegger, who sees in Being the "favour-giving" and "redemption-promising" before which *Dasein* must bow in thoughtful gratitude, Levinas feels a threat coming from Being, a threat to vulnerable man. He talks of the "rumbling" of *conatus*, the striving to remain in Being. Being's rise and fall can be heard like the clamour from a battlefield, now distant, now right up against the ear. What is it that makes this rumbling noise? It cannot be called an entity, as it is at the same time too small and too great. It is *le pur exister sans existant*, the pure Existing without existent that Levinas calls *il-y-a*:[10] it exists, it is going on, it happens, it occurs, endlessly, as impersonally as when we say "it's raining", "it's snowing". It is like lying in bed and trying to sleep, not knowing how to lose consciousness and fall asleep. There is nothing definite that keeps one awake, no clock that ticks, no water that drips, no "hum of traffic from the town" (Paul Verlaine). It is simply nothing – only this *hustle and bustle* (described by the Norwegian poet Emil Boyson in his poem "Before the ship sails") that envelops the consciousness that is kept awake. It is not Bergson's "immediately given". Neither is it the sound of Being in *es gibt* in the later Heidegger. It is neither something *given* nor *giving*. It is something that *takes*, that is out to get me.

Levinas sees humanity in a social perspective. Perhaps we may say that the Face has for him the same precedence as Nature had for the great romantics. For them Nature was a trace or sign left by the Creator. Although Levinas was born, as he has said, "in the country with the great and beautiful forests", he would not be likely to say, with the Norwegian poet Rolf Jacobsen, "It is well that timber is still to be found in the world".[11] No eye looks at us from "under the stones' crust" (Nerval).[12] No face reveals itself on timber or on stone. Nothing is more absurd than to ask the stars for advice before one acts, as Levinas writes in *Humanisme de l'autre homme*. As for the sailors who sailed at night along the coasts of Thessaly and heard a loud voice calling out "Pan is dead!", so, also for Levinas, is Nature's god dead, "dead as only gods can die – from lack of incense and reverence, forgotten and struck to the heart by ingratitude".[13] Levinas' world is an "enlightened" and not a mythical world, a world in which man alone is entitled to have a face.

Levinas knows no "naturally religious soul" (*anima naturaliter religiosa*). Man is naturally egocentric, "stuck" in the struggle of being, i.e. striving to remain in Being, in contest with other beings. If it were not for the Other, the *ego* would have been able to live in satisfaction with itself, even happy. The Other disturbs the order in the home, causes a disquiet that never quietens, because it is Longing for Infinity.

But man has at no stage of his existence been only nature, and no state of society is absolute. To wander, to part from one another, to find one another, to rest and start anew, that is the rhythm in everything, breathing out and breathing in. Would it perhaps be possible to divide the history of mankind into periods of rest and of departure?

Modernity has been a period of migration, under its motto "What will bring us *forward?*" The modern nomad has never been in doubt about the direction.

Now, after so many unfulfilled hopes, it would seem that the time has come to call a halt – to have a day of rest. Each step forward leaves us with an unpaid bill. We no longer have confidence in knowledge: it was after all from knowledge that the mistakes arose. Now we need each other, not under the command "Workers of the world unite!"; not as contracting parties to a treaty promising mutual support; but with the Other's face as a supreme measure for meaning.

This sounds like a philosophy for flower children, who demand *love* and not *war*, who are infatuated with "happenings". But Levinas' language demands the greatest patience: it puts one to the test.

Philosophy for him is certainly more destiny than profession. But he does not consider himself an oracle, and he is not in a hurry. He listens to the voices in the dialogue from Platon to Heidegger, faithful to the culture of learning.

But responsibility and love have a higher status than knowledge, and readers of Levinas are not completely mistaken if they feel that he has a special sympathy for the young, who find it so easy to *seek together* without consideration for what they are seeking. In contrast to the

Hegelian "evening philosophy" that is preached when Minerva's owl "flies out toward the night", this is a morning philosophy, after a long day's journey into night, a longing for the happening – the ethical happening before the face of the Other.

V

The end of phenomenology – or phenomenology's final accomplishment? Certain features of Levinas' philosophy tell us clearly that we are no longer confined within phenomenology's horizon of science. We are beyond science, beyond knowledge, yes, even beyond the "intellectual sympathy" that Bergson called the intuitive approach to Being.[14] Strange as it may sound when speaking of such an important work of the mind, we find ourselves with Levinas outside *ordo cognoscendi*, the order of the knowable.

It is not merely that a research programme or the preference of a particular school has changed when we think of Husserl's – and we can also say Bergson's – confidence that new generations will continue our progressive approach to truth. With Levinas we have left an epoch; or, put differently, modernity's optimism for the future is left behind.

If we read Heidegger's philosophy as phenomenology, the question of affinity to Levinas becomes more difficult. Their positions are intertwined in such a way that a profound study of each is needed in order to draw the distinctions.

A real difference, as both have explicitly underlined, lies in their view of man, in their attitude to humanism.[15] Heidegger rejects a humanism that is built on the *ego cogito* tradition because it sacrifices *Sein* for the subject. If anything is sacrificed in Heidegger, it is the *ego cogito*, in favour of Being. But does this really mean the end of the subject's hegemony? Perhaps the *Gelassenheit* (the "letting-be") is a "ruse of reason" to remain in possession of power? The sound of Being that comes to the herdsman's ear from Poets and Pre-Socratists announces the return of the gods, who now "alone can save us".

The sound of Being can also be heard in Levinas – his *il-y-a* – but here it has a warning note for man attempting to uphold the *cogito* state of awareness. Man lacks Being's strength, he is related only distantly to Being. He is Being in a moment of weakness. Humanity, Levinas asks, is that not *Being that weeps?*[16]

After modernity . . . This does not adequately characterize the "un-actuality" in Levinas' philosophy. We must go back – or forward? – to the Orient, to the time before *dis-orientation*[17] set in and the warnings manifested themselves in traces: back to childhood, before ontology began to ask: "What was that?".

Heidegger's aim was to bring Western metaphysics to a close; the metaphysics that implied the Forgetfulness of Being. Levinas sees the Forgetfulness of Being as part of man's vocation: mankind is called upon to forget Being in favour of the Other. By this ethical *volte face*, Levinas succeeds perhaps where Heidegger failed – in bringing metaphysics as ontology to an end.

The task of philosophy becomes practice, training in readiness for the rescue of the Other. Not an exercise in awareness, as in the *ego cogito* tradition, but a practice in "diaconia".

All ties to phenomenology are not broken, however. As Levinas has several times pointed out, there is a paradox in this philosophy that swears by the evidence, by that which is "self-given" in experience as the ultimate source of all experience, while at the same time it confirms that everything seen and experienced has its basis in something unseen and not experienced that makes the evidence possible: *the horizons*. This is to say that in phenomenology's "work of enlightenment" a hint is given of the significance of that which cannot be revealed in the light of consciousness. In this sense phenomenology is a philosophy not of consciousness but of meaning.

Levinas calls his philosophy logos philosophy. Meaning is not established by the intentionality of a subject, but *springs out of* the face of the Other. The expression "springs out of" is used to stress its "passive synthesis": meaning is not primarily something that "appears" or that I produce or "understand". It *comes to me directly* from the face of the Other.

Many of Husserl's pupils have described his research enthusiasm and his identification with phenomenology. Levinas himself says that "it was always Phenomenology one met when one visited Husserl".[18] But in everything that is written about Husserl one finds time and again the description of his exceptional patience, as though life were just a matter of *wait and see*. Do we hear an echo of this in Levinas, whose ethics seems to confirm that the Good always comes as *a favour and a gift*?

NOTES AND REFERENCES

1. See Dagfinn Føllesdal in *Spor etter mennesket – Minneskrift til A. H. Winsnes*, Aschehoug, Oslo, 1989, pp. 291–304.
2. See Stephan Strasser, *Jenseits von Sein und Zeit. Eine Einführung in Emmanuel Levinas' Philosophie*, The Hague: Martinus Nijhoff, 1978, p. 384, and in the German translation of *Humanisme de l'autre homme*, Fata Morgana, Montpellier 1972, *Humanismus des anderen Menschen*, Felix Meiner, Hamburg, 1989, p. 131.
3. See Roman Ingarden, "Innføring i Edmund Husserls fenomenologi" – ten Oslo lectures, 1967, *Idé og Tanke* no. 23/24, 1970.
4. See Levinas, *Entre nous. Essais sur le penser-à-l'autre*, Bernard Grasset, Paris, 1991, p. 23.
5. See *Tanke og Mistanke*, ed. Asbjørn Aarnes and Helge Salemonsen, Aventura, Oslo, 1987.
6. Gabriel Marcel and Martin Buber take philosophical standpoints that have been called I–Thou philosophy or philosophy of dialogue; "social ontology" is an expression that is found in the sub-title of Theunissen's *Der Andere, Studien zur Sozialontologie der Gegenwart*, Berlin 1965, 1978², in which social relations are analysed from an ontological definition of what it means to be in relation to another human being.
7. See Levinas, *Humanisme de l'autre homme*, op. cit. pp. 57 ff.
8. Levinas, *Entre nous*, op. cit., pp. 25–52, in the chapter "Le moi et la Totalité".
9. Strasser, op. cit. p. 302.
10. See, e.g., Levinas, *Le Temps et l'autre*, P.U.F., Paris, 1989, pp. 26–27.
11. The poem is entitled "Tømmer" (Timber) and is found in the collection *Hemmelig liv*, Gyldendal, Oslo, 1954.
12. Nerval's poem has the title "Vers dorés", and is found in the collection *Chimères*, included in the collection of short stories *Les Filles du Feu*, 1854. The poem has as its motto a quotation attributed to Pythagoras, "What? Everything has feeling!", and expresses a pantheistic view of nature, see *Oeuvres de Gérard de Nerval*, édition de la Pléiade, Paris 1952, pp. 34–35.
13. A quotation from Gérard de Nerval; see Asbjørn Aarnes, *Diktningen hos Gérard de Nerval. Estetikk og poesi*, Tanum, Oslo, 1957, p. 45.
14. See e.g. Bergson, "Introduction à la métaphysique" in *La Pensée et le mouvant*, 1934; Henri Bergson *Oeuvres*, P.U.F., 1963, pp. 1392–1432.
15. See Heidegger, *Über den 'Humanismus'. Brief an Jean Baufret*, A. Francke Verlag, Bern, 1947, and Levinas, *Humanisme de l'autre homme*, op. cit.
16. *Humanisme de l'autre homme*, op. cit., p. 15.
17. Ibid., p. 55.
18. See Levinas, "La ruine de la représentation" in *Edmund Husserl 1859–1938*, The Hague: Martinus Nijhoff, 1959, p. 73.

Chapter 7

On Trust

Knud E. Løgstrup

Trust as a Fundamental Part of Human Existence

It is a characteristic of human life that we naturally trust one another. This is true not only in the case of persons who are well acquainted with one another but also in the case of complete strangers. Only because of some special circumstance do we ever distrust a stranger in advance. Perhaps some informer has destroyed the natural trust which people spontaneously have toward one another, so that their relationship becomes oppressive and strained. Perhaps because of strife in the land, where the land is ruled by men who have no respect for law and justice, people lose confidence in one another. In normal circumstances, however, we accept the stranger's word and do not mistrust him until we have some particular reason to do so. We never suspect a person of falsehood until after we have caught him in a lie. If we enter into conversation on the train with a person whom we have never met before and about whom we know absolutely nothing, we assume that what she says is true and do not become suspicious of her unless she begins to indulge in wild exaggerations. Nor do we normally assume a person to be a thief; not until he conducts himself in a suspicious manner do we begin to suspect him. Initially we believe one another's word; initially we trust one another. This may indeed seem strange, but it is a part of what it means to be human. Human life could hardly exist if it were otherwise. We would simply not be able to live; our life would be impaired and wither away if we were in advance to distrust one another, if we were to suspect the other of thievery and falsehood from the very outset.

To trust, however, is to deliver oneself over into the hands of another.[1] This is why we react vehemently when our trust is "violated", as we say, even though it may have been only in some inconsequential matter. Violated trust is trust that is turned against the person who does the trusting. The embarrassment and danger to which we are subjected by the violation is bad enough. But even worse is the fact that our trust was scorned by the other person. For the other person to have been able to violate it, our trust must simply have left her cold. However much she may seem to have accepted it outwardly, she did not actually accept it but merely exploited it. And it is a question whether it is not the indifference thus manifested toward us in her violation of our trust, even more than the unpleasant consequences of the violation itself, that evokes our bitter reaction.

That trust and the self-surrender that goes with it are a fundamental part of human life is seen not only when trust is violated. We see it fully as much in those conflicts which are caused by a collision between two persons' respective spirits and worlds.

The peculiar point here is that, although the collision is due to the fact that a purely personal expectation is not fulfilled by the other person, it takes the form of moral accusations – even though moral evaluations of the other person's behaviour are quite beside the point and the accusations themselves are therefore obviously unreasonable. Why is this? We need to know the answer. We need to explain why conflicts which in themselves have nothing to do with morality or immorality, with right or wrong, but which are entirely due to a difference between our respective spirits and worlds – why these conflicts nevertheless turn into questions of sheer morality and self-justification and cause reproaches and accusations which are plainly unreasonable.

First, an expectation which requires that the other person personally fulfil it usually makes itself apparent in one way or another, perhaps through general attitude or conduct, or perhaps directly through some particular word or action. Whatever its form, whether articulated or silent, the expectation manifests itself in the presupposition that the other person is to fulfil the expectation. This is to say that by manifesting the expectation one has already surrendered oneself to the other person – even before it is certain that there will be any fulfilment. In other words, the manifestation is necessary for bringing about the fulfilment – perhaps simply in order to make the other person aware of what we expect from her.

Now, if the fulfilment does not take place, the manifestation is in vain and perhaps meaningless. But what is worse is the fact that in the manifestation one has exposed oneself. One's expectation, exposed through its manifestation, has not been covered by the other person's fulfilment of it. And it is this exposure which causes the encounter to erupt in moral reproaches and accusations.

Second, when one dares to extend oneself in the hope of being accepted, and then is not accepted, this gives the conflict such an emotional character that, even though no one has done anything wrong, one must turn it into the kind of conflict that results from the other person's having committed a wrong. One finds it necessary to invent a suffered wrong by which to motivate one's strong and deep emotional reaction. In short, it is the emotional element in the situation that causes one to grasp at the moral reproaches and accusations which, precisely because of their moral character, are emotionally loaded.

The simple conflict within a conflict, namely, that one has dared to extend oneself in the hope of being accepted but was not accepted, makes everything either black or white and makes one's accusation correspondingly irrevocable. For it is precisely to the degree that things are black or white in our moral evaluations that our moral accusations become irrevocable.[2]

But there is a third reason why the conflict vents itself in moral accusations. It must at all costs never become apparent to the other person, and preferably not even to ourselves, that it is a matter of disappointed expectation, because though we have been exposed we are at pains not to admit it. We would much rather admit blemishes and weaknesses, mistakes and stupidities than admit to our having been exposed. The collision in the encounter must therefore be covered up. It must be externalized even though we may have to go far afield for the reproaches and may have to invent the most unreasonable accusations in an effort to cover up the real conflict. The accusations, having nothing to do with morality, betray the fact that it is a matter of a conflict which at all costs must be covered up, even at the cost of our having to invent the most absurd accusations.[3]

If communication between persons in conflict with each other is cut off, sparks of moral reproach and accusation begin to fly, because there is self-surrender in all forms of communication. Rejected self-surrender expresses itself in moral accusations because the situation is emotional and plain, and because the exposure must at all costs be kept covered up.

In E. M. Forster's novel *Howard's End*, we have the account of a rift between Leonard Bast and the Schlegel sisters. Their respective milieus were as different from one another as they could possibly be. Leonard was a penniless office clerk whose married life was very drab and whose entire existence would be bleak indeed were it not for his consuming interest in culture. However, he was not equal to this interest; his hunger for books and music was and remained artificial. The Schlegel sisters, on the other hand, had never known anything but economic security. They were fairly wealthy. Since they had grown up in an atmosphere of cultural appreciation and had become the centre of a large social group where these things were discussed, their life was rich in terms of experience and delightful variety.

On an altogether casual occasion Leonard Bast came into contact with the Schlegel sisters. He received an invitation to afternoon tea with them. It turned out to be a fiasco. Leonard was disappointed in his expectations for the afternoon. He had hoped to discuss books and to keep his visit with them in a romantic vein and at all costs to keep it from getting mixed up with his routine, uninteresting life at the office.

The Schlegel sisters, however, had an entirely different purpose in inviting him, a very practical purpose, namely, to get him out of the firm in which he was employed inasmuch as they had secret information that the firm was about to go bankrupt. And they had another, an indirect, purpose too: to help him in his interest in culture, because though his love of books was artificial they detected that underneath there lay a desire for authenticity.

The ensuing conflict was inevitable. It could not be warded off. For the Schlegel sisters' idea in issuing the invitation was entirely different from Leonard's idea in accepting it. The two parties were blind to one another's worlds. Leonard's anticipation of an afternoon spent in undisturbed enjoyment of books blinded him to the Schlegel sisters' desire to help him. Disappointed and embittered, he was carried away with outrageous and stupid accusations that they had low motives in inviting him, namely, that they wanted to use him for spying upon his firm. As for the Schlegel sisters themselves, not until afterwards did they have any inkling of the two worlds in Leonard's life and of how important it was for him to keep them isolated from each other.

Leonard Bast and the Schlegel sisters disagreed about many things, but it was not an objective disagreement which caused the collision between them. Nor was the collision caused by one of them committing wrong and the other being wronged. Rather it was because Leonard was disappointed in his expectation that the Schlegel sisters would satisfy his cultural craving by engaging him in conversation about books. Their failure to do this immediately turned into a moral issue.

Those who are implicated in it never, or at least very seldom, are aware that the conflict has nothing to do with right or wrong. Only observers on the outside who have an incisive insight into the worlds of both parties – dramatists and novelists, theatregoers and readers – are able to see this.

The fundamental character of trust is revealed in yet another way. In love and sympathy there is no impulse to investigate the other person's character. We do not deliberately try to picture to ourselves who he or she is. In the event that we already have such a picture, it shows only those features which immediately stand out. We are aware only of those peculiarities which force themselves upon our attention. Of ourselves we make no conscious effort to picture the other person, for the simple reason that there has been nothing about him to arouse our suspicion.

If, on the other hand, we are not in sympathy with the other person, or if there is a certain tension between us and her because of something about her regarding which we are uncertain or against which we react with irritation, dissatisfaction, or antipathy, then we begin to form a picture of her character. We then begin to see in her a variety of dispositions because we are on our guard in relation to her.

When we are in direct association with her, however, this picture usually breaks down; her personal presence erases it. It is not erased because of any particular words, deeds, or conduct; this would of course only mean that the facts contradict the picture we have had of her, forcing us either to correct it or to set it aside entirely. No, it means something altogether different. It means that the actual presence of the other person leaves no room for a mere picture. Her presence and my picture of her are irreconcilable. They exclude each other, and it is the picture that must give way. Only where the proof of her unreliability has in the most positive sense become an ingrown distrust, or where the irritation and antipathy have shut me off from her completely, does the picture continue to stand.

Why does the picture break down? This is a difficult question to answer, because what happens in this connection is something fundamental, something anterior to morality and convention. An adequate explanation is impossible. Only through paraphrase and metaphor, only by approaching the phenomenon from different angles are we able to suggest the answer.

To associate with or encounter personally another person always means to be "in the power of" his words and conduct. Psychology refers to this as the power of suggestion. There are many degrees of suggestion. It may be very weak, only strong enough to understand what the other person says and does, or it may be so strong that we are, as we say, grasped or taken captive by it.

But there is also something more fundamental than this. Not to let the other person come into his own through words, deeds, and conduct, but to hinder him instead by our suspicion and by the picture we have formed of him as a result of our antipathy toward him is a denial of life, his life and our own. It is in the very nature of human existence that it does not want to be reduced to reactions – even wise reactions – which are determined solely by what has already transpired. It is in the very nature of human existence that it wants to be just as new as the other person's new words, new deeds, and new conduct. We assume, as it were, that because they are contemporary they are new, and so we also insist upon taking a similarly new attitude to them. We might call this a trust in life itself, in the ongoing renewal of life. Later we discover that the words, deeds, and conduct were after all not new, and we vow that we will never again let ourselves be tricked or fooled or be naive or in any other way let our trust get the better of us.[4]

In its fundamental sense, trust is essential to every conversation. In conversation as such we deliver ourselves over into the hand of another. This is evident in the fact that in the very act of addressing a person we make a certain demand of him. This demand is not merely for a response to what we say. And the self-surrender is not essentially a matter of what is said: its content or importance or intimate character. What happens is that simply in addressing him, irrespective of the importance of the content of what we say, a certain note is struck through which we, as it were, step out of ourselves in order to exist in the speech relationship with him. For this reason the point of the demand – though unarticulated – is that, as the note struck by the speaker's address is accepted, the speaker is himself accepted. For a person inadvertently or even intentionally not to hear the note in what we say, therefore, means that it is we ourselves who are being ignored, provided it is we ourselves who made the over-ture. That all speech takes place in such fundamental trust is evident in the fact that the most casual comment takes on a false note if one believes that it is not accepted in the sense that it is intended.

A particular point of the analysis we have made thus far – one might call it an analysis of a phenomenological character – is in fact supported by such sciences as psychology and psychiatry. Their investigations have clearly shown how a child's life may be permanently determined by the manner in which adults behave toward her. For example, one might mention parents' ambitious pride in relation to their children. In the ambiguity of everyday living this is regarded as very commendable, but humanly speaking it is a detriment to the children because it can result in an upbringing which deprives them, perhaps forever, of something of paramount importance, namely, joy in living, the courage to be. This is due not least of all to the fact that the child, in contradistinction to the adult, is never content to trust only partially. To trust with reservation is possible only for one who has learned to hold back something of herself. But this the child has not learned consciously and deliberately to do. For her, reservation takes place as a matter of psychic automatism. This is why the disappointed trust, restlessness, and insecurity which go with it create in the child far-reaching and fateful consequences.

Although it is in the child's relation to the adult that the one is surren-dered to the other in the most far-reaching and fateful sense – which is why science has here been able to establish it – it is nonetheless in one degree or another true also of all the relationships in which we deal with one another. A person never has something to do with another person without also having some degree of control over him. It may be a very small matter, involving only a passing mood, a dampening or quickening of spirit, a deep-ening or removal of some dislike. But it may also be a matter of tremendous scope, such as can determine the very course of his life.

Unconsciously, we nonetheless have the strange notion that one person has nothing to do with another person's world. We have the curious idea that a person constitutes her own world, and that the rest of us have no part in it but touch upon it only now and then. If the encounter between persons therefore means, as it normally does, nothing more than that their respective worlds touch upon each other and then continue unaffected on their separate courses, the encounter can hardly be very important. According to this reasoning, it is only when a person accidentally breaks into another person's world with good or bad intentions that anything important is at stake.

This is really a curious idea, an idea no less curious because we take it for granted. The fact is, however, that it is completely wrong because we do indeed constitute one another's world and destiny. That we usually ignore this fact can easily be explained.

It is a common observation that the most elementary phenomena of our existence are the ones we are least aware of. It should be added that the phenomenon we are discussing here is highly disquieting. For the sake of our own peace of mind it is perhaps fortunate that we are not more aware of the extent to which by what we were or said or did in our relationship with them we have actually determined other people's joy or pain in living, their sincerity or duplicity.

In describing the nature of trust, we have in the foregoing used several different expressions. We have spoken of a person surrendering himself, of his going out of himself, of his placing something of his own life into the hands of the other person. These expressions are metaphorical and subject to misunderstanding. In order to avoid one serious misunderstanding, one that is easily suggested by the metaphors themselves, it should be said that trust does not mean to turn oneself inside out. Trust has nothing to do with the abandonment of all spiritual modesty. To surrender oneself by turning oneself inside out in the presence of another does not require trust. In fact this sort of thing is rarely even related to trust; it usually demands nothing of the other person except that he play the role of an observer.

It is quite another thing, however, to surrender oneself in that trust of the other person whereby a requirement is always imposed upon him insofar as one comes to him with an expectation. In expecting something of the other person we undertake an action which amounts to a delivering of ourselves over into his hand. This self-surrender, whatever form it may take, need not necessarily mean that we confide in the other person. It can of course mean that too, but it can also mean all kinds of other things; for example it may mean that we rely upon him to speak the truth, or that in speaking to him we adopt a particular tone of voice. Correspondingly it means that the self-exposure, through the trust which was not accepted, consists in one's having risked the chance of being rejected. It has nothing to do, however, with exposure in an exhibitionist sense.

The Demand That Grows out of Trust

Through the trust which a person either shows or asks of another person she surrenders something of her life to that person. Therefore, our existence demands of us that we protect the life of the person who has placed her trust in us. How much or how little is at stake for a person who has thus placed her trust in another person obviously varies greatly. It depends upon many different factors: upon her psychic constitution and momentary condition, and upon the situation, which is determined not least of all by who and what the other person is. But in any event this trust means that in every encounter between human beings there is an unarticulated demand, irrespective of the circumstances in which the encounter takes place and irrespective of the nature of the encounter.

Regardless of how varied the communication between persons may be, it always involves the risk of one person approaching the other in the hope of a response. This is the essence of communication and the fundamental basis of ethical life. Therefore, a consciousness of the resultant demand is not dependent upon a revelation, in the theological sense of the word, nor is the demand based on a more or less conscious agreement between the persons with respect to what would be mutually beneficial.

If trust and the self-surrender that goes with it were determined by our own arbitrary decision, so that without any loss to ourselves we could ignore the trust and the surrender, then life together with other people would present no demands other than those which one person might arbitrarily decide to place upon another person, whether they be conventional, sentimental, or paranoiac demands. Such is not the case, however. Trust is not of our own making; it is given. Life is so constituted that it cannot be lived except as one person surrenders something of himself to the other person. either by trusting him or by asking him for his trust.[5]

By our very attitude to one another we help to shape one another's world. By our attitude to the other person we help to determine the scope and hue of his world; we make it large or small, bright or drab, rich or dull, threatening or secure. We help to shape his world not by theories and views but by our very attitude toward him. Herein lies the unarticulated and one might say anonymous demand that we take care of the life which trust has placed in our hands.[6]

The Twofold Function of Conventional Forms

Usually we trust one another with great reservation. We hold ourselves in reserve and do not allow ourselves completely to trust one another. Not even in an emergency situation when we desperately need help do we trust without some reservation. Hence what is normally expected of us in everyday living is concern not for a person's life but for the things which belong to conventional courtesy. Social convention has the effect of reducing both the trust that we show and the demand that we take care of the other person's life.

The conventional forms have a twofold function. For one thing, regardless of how these forms originated, they facilitate our relationship with one another, making it smooth and effortless, not least because they protect us against psychic exposure. Without the protection of the conventional norms, association with other people would be intolerable.

When we thus refer to "spiritual modesty" does this mean that there are certain things which simply are not to be mentioned? Must we, by keeping silent about them, act as if they did not exist? Are there feelings which can exist only as long as we refrain from expressing them but which die the moment we allow them to come to the surface in speech? Does that which is most vital in life wither in the light of day?

No, what we mean is rather that there are certain things which cannot exist in a formless state. That which is most vital in a person's life cannot tolerate banality. Formless expression destroys it. Spiritual immodesty is not a harmless affair.

Spiritual modesty keeps the most vital human relationships from being spoiled by banality. It gives form to a person's life. That which is most vital demands a controlled, structured, indirect expression.

The will to form is not limited to the elect, to creative artists. It is something fundamentally human, something native to any person even though she may have very little to do with what we usually call art. And because we cannot ourselves create the necessary forms we adopt the conventional forms.

Life has been given to us. We have not ourselves created it. This is why we cannot give it a direct expression. If we attempt to do so all the same, we falsify it in pathetically or sentimentally unstructured effusion.

In the second place, however, we employ the very same conventional forms for reducing trust and its demand. Instead of allowing convention to give needed form to our life, we use it as a means for keeping aloof from one another and for insulating ourselves. The one who trusts has in advance, by way of convention, guarded himself; he has rendered his trust conventionally reserved, and the one who is trusted is thus relieved of hearing the demand contained in that trust, the demand that he take care of the trusting person's life.

The important thing is that, if a person's trust is not accepted, it turns into distrust. This distrust is not necessarily the result of animosity; it is just as likely the result of indifference, reservation, and rejection. Not wanting to run the risk of being distrusted, one neutralizes one's own trust in advance. The alternative given in and with human existence, namely, that whatever is not in the nature of care for the trusting person's life ruins it, is thus broken by a third possibility, which is the neutral possibility of social convention. Unable to bear the given alternative of care or ruin, we tacitly agree to avail ourselves of convention as a form of existence whereby we avoid the alternative.

The child, however, will not go along with this. She is able to trust only without reservation. When she shows trust she gives herself completely. The child, being yet outside of convention, still stands in the power of the given alternative. If she fails to encounter love, her future possibilities are destroyed – as psychology and psychiatry have amply shown.

The Unspoken Demand

The demand which is present in any human relationship is, however, unspoken and is not to be equated with a person's expressed wish or request. It is not expressed in his spoken or implied expectations. Any correspondence between the spoken and the unspoken demand is purely accidental; usually they are not at all alike. The other person's interpretation of the implications of the trust offered or desired is one thing, and the demand which is implicit in that trust as, one might say, a "fact of creation" which I must interpret is quite another thing. And these two interpretations may well conflict with each other. The situation may be such that I am challenged to oppose the very thing which the other person expects and wishes me to do for him, because this alone will serve his best interest. In other words, the challenge rests on the assumption that I know better than he does what is best for him.

If this were not true, communication between two persons would in fact be impossible. If it were merely a matter of fulfilling the other person's expectations and granting her wishes, our association would mean nothing less than – irresponsibly – making oneself the tool of the other person. Our mutual relations would no longer present any challenge but would consist merely in reciprocal flattery. However, what we are speaking of is a demand for love, not for indulgence. The risk of conflict is therefore an ever-present possibility.

This is not mere theory. What is regarded in ordinary parlance as a "very good" or "very kind" thing to say is usually only a case of accommodating oneself to the other person, abstaining from any contradiction which we know would irritate him, refraining from any criticism which would offend him, avoiding the confrontation which would not be well received. It is a matter of shying away from contradiction in an effort to lead the conversation on to something regarding which one knows that the other person can agree with. It is refraining from criticism and instead looking for something for which one can praise him. It is an avoidance at all costs of confrontation in order to be able to settle down cosily in mutual agreement about something irrelevant. What men commonly commend as good or kind usually represents in reality the kind of accommodation that results in an insecure relationship. What men commonly call love is usually an affectation which shuns like the plague truth between people. And this situation is not altered by the fact that sacrifice is sometimes both demanded and given. Where there is no will to truth, even sacrifice turns to flattery. In short, if there were no difference between the challenge implicit in every relationship and the other person's expressed request, our life together would consist in abandoning ourselves to the crowd. And the crowd can very well consist of only one person. Indeed, this is the case if it is a person I am willing merely to follow – however much that following may involve me in great sacrifice and may even be interpreted as goodness or kindness.

In other words, the demand implicit in every encounter between persons is not vocal but remains silent. The individual to whom the demand is directed must herself in each concrete relationship decide what the content of the demand is. This is not to say that a person can arbitrarily and capriciously determine the content of the demand. In that event there would be no demand. But the fact is that there is a demand. And since the demand is implied by the very fact that a person belongs to the world in which the other person has her life, and therefore holds something of that person's life in her hands, it is therefore a demand to take care of that person's life. But nothing is thereby said about how this caring is to be done. The other person cannot herself say anything about this, even though she is the one directly concerned, since, as we said before, it might very well involve something diametrically opposed to her own expectations and wishes. It is of the essence of the demand that with such insight, imagination, and understanding as she possesses a person must figure out for herself what the demand requires.

The Sovereignty of the Individual

In the light of what has been said one might ask: Does not the demand then encourage arrogant encroachment upon the other person? How can one know what is best for him, especially if that which presumably is best for him is clearly disappointing to him or even resisted by him? The answer is that this is something which one learns from one's own outlook on life. But of what concern is my outlook to the other person, who perhaps does not even share it? Why must he have an outlook imputed to him or even forced upon him which is entirely strange to him and which he can neither use nor appreciate?

A prominent idea in the idealistic ethics of the 19th century, largely through the influence of Kant, was respect for the other person's independence. Idealistic ethics is severely criticized today by both philosophers and theologians, and not without some justification, because this matter of mutual respect for one another's independence threatened to become the major consideration. Morality came to consist in self-realization, and respect for the other person in his self-realization. Respect for the other person's independence was used to legitimate one's own self-realization, and this inevitably resulted in a kind of adulation of personhood. At the base of this idea was the notion that every person is a world unto himself and that others are not a part of that world. Consequently there was no awareness of the conflict in which the idea of respect for the other person's independence arises and belongs. This conflict may be expressed in the form of a question: What does my outlook have to do with the other person if it leads me to think I know better than he what is best for him?

Outlook on life is a very abstract concept. It can mean many different things. It can even be a matter of something very fundamental. To disappoint a person's desire for flattery could hardly, except by the disappointed person himself, be regarded as an attempt to impose a foreign outlook upon him. We may even assume that there is a certain basic conception of human existence which is inevitable and common to all.

However, the outlook on life can take on more and more definite features; it can take on a firm structure and thereby become more and more narrow. It can become hardened into an ideology which a person comes to regard as something absolute. The more this happens, the more the relation of the individual to other people becomes an occasion for arrogance and possibly for encroachment upon them. In other words, the ideologically hardened outlook becomes, so far as the individual is concerned, her life's meaning, but in the sense that the order of values is inverted so that her life exists for the sake of her outlook on life instead of the reverse. It is a case not so much of her own life giving content to her outlook as of her outlook determining the content of her life, a life which without the outlook is empty. The outlook simply becomes a cause for which she exists. Whatever concerns her own life must logically concern the life of all others as well. The ultimate truth which she possesses must be the ultimate truth also for them – obviously, because otherwise it would of course not be ultimate truth! In the name of this ultimate truth she therefore also knows – with incontrovertible certainty – what is best for the other person. Consequently she need not concern herself with the idea of respect for other people's independence. It follows that the further this process advances, the easier it becomes with a good conscience to violate the other person. You see, it is the ultimate truth, the perfect outlook for which one is responsible!

It is possible to lose all sense of the problem here under discussion through a pandering to the lower instincts, through a mutual admiration of one another, or through indifference toward one another – always under the guise of respect for the other person in his own world. But it may also be lost when the outlook on life becomes so hardened and so religiously ultimate that we come to believe that we know what is best for the other person, when we come to believe that it is only through our outlook that not only our own life but also the lives of other people have meaning and content.

We are, in other words, dealing with two different perversions of communication between people. The one is the kind of association which, owing to laziness, fear of people, or a propensity for cosy relationships, consists in simply trying to please one another while always dodging the issue. With the possible exception of a common cause against a third person, there is nothing which promotes a comfortable relationship quite so much as mutual praise. At any rate, mutual admiration can hardly fail to create such a relationship. The understanding here revealed is not the kind which in the interest of honesty is willing to be uncharitably received. It is rather the kind regarding which one knows in advance that he will be warmly welcomed; the other comes to covet such understanding, almost as a tribute which is his due.

What makes this kind of association so attractive is that it calls for no appreciable inconvenience. It demands very little of us. So long as the other person is accorded all the understanding she desires, and even a little more, she causes no further inconvenience. When each one receives her due in the form of the desired praise and understanding, we can enjoy the peace or indifference toward one another. In reality, however, no communication takes place, despite the fact that to all appearances the persons involved are very much taken up with their association.

We commonly think that it is only among persons who are comparative strangers to one another that men say always what the other person wants to hear; we tend to think that honesty increases only as the degree of acquaintance increases. However, the opposite may equally well be true, namely, that the closer persons are united in friendship, the more dishonest they become in their relation to one another; they find it easier to be honest toward persons they do not know quite so well.

An opposite form of perverted communication consists in our wanting to change other people. We have definite opinions about how they ought to be. These opinions are lacking in understanding because, the more definitive the opinions are, the more necessary it becomes that we not be distracted by too much understanding of those who are to be changed. Understanding must be temporarily suspended. The mania for perfection turns everything which is said and done into something provisional and preparatory. Understanding must be postponed until perfection has been attained.

Taking these two perversions of communication into consideration we are, in other words, caught in the conflict between a regard for others which is in fact indulgence, compliance, and flattery on the one hand, and a disregard for others which in the interest of our own outlook turns into arrogance and violation on the other hand. Although this conflict can be resolved only in specific instances by the exercise of one's own individual judgement, we can nonetheless advance some fundamental considerations to guide us in such judgement.

In our discussion up to this point we have spoken metaphorically of having something of the other person's life "in our hands" or "delivered over to us". Precisely what in the other person's life is in our hands, what of the other person has been delivered over to us, may vary greatly. It may vary all the way from his most passing mood to his entire destiny.

However, there is one thing which a person does not directly surrender, and that is his individuality which determines his reactions to what we say and do. The fact that we are one another's world does not mean that we hold another person's will in our hands. We cannot intrude upon his individuality and will, upon his personhood, in the same way that we can affect his emotions and in some instances even his destiny.

We often have the other person's more or less passing mood in our hands in the most direct way. However, we are not able in the same direct way to determine how she either conquers or succumbs to the despondency, for example, which we have caused in her. Correspondingly, an individual often in a most direct way holds another person's destiny in his power. For example, he may determine the success or failure of his spouse's marriage. Inconsiderateness of one kind or another on his part may turn the marriage into lifelong suffering for his spouse. However, this does not mean that the inconsiderate partner has power in the same direct way to determine how his spouse reacts to his inconsiderateness, how she defends or does not defend herself against it. The partner who by his inconsiderateness determines his spouse's fate does not in the same way hold his spouse's individuality and will in his power. In other words, he cannot control whether the spouse resigns or does not resign herself to her fate.

Nevertheless, the boundary between one's ability to determine another person's fate and one's inability to determine how that other person will react to his fate is fluid. The individuality and the will of both adults and children – particularly children – may be affected through assaults upon their emotions and their fate.

This much can therefore be said: whatever a person may say or do out of concern for what he believes will best serve the other person's welfare, it is not his prerogative to control the other person's reactions to what he says or does. One is not to try to determine what use the other person makes of what is said or done. To this we have no right, be our intentions ever so good. The will to determine what is best for the other person – and to speak or remain silent, or to act in harmony with our insight into what we believe to be best for him – must be coupled with a willingness to let him remain sovereign in his own world. The demand to guard that part of the other person's life which has been delivered over to us, irrespective of the words and actions which the demand may indicate, is always at the same time a demand that the other person be given ample time and opportunity to make his own world as expansive as possible. The demand is always also a demand that we use the surrender out of which the demand has come in such a way as to free the other person from his confinement and to give his vision the widest possible horizon.

On the other hand, the person who out of a fierce perfectionism tries to refashion people will stop at nothing, not even at the violation of their personalities and wills. In her effort to dominate their reactions, even to the point of crowding out their individualities, she capitalizes upon the fact that the boundary line is fluid. The other person is to be completely changed from the ground up, including his will.

However, no one has the right to make himself the master of another person's individuality or will. Neither good intentions, insight into what is best for him, nor even the possibility of saving him from great calamities which would otherwise strike him can justify intrusion upon his individuality and will.[7]

To "have something in one's hand" is a metaphor. Usually it is used in speaking of the comparatively rare situation in which everything hangs in the balance. The situation is one of suspense; the scales may tip in either direction, leading to one outcome or the other. Added to this is the fact that the entire weight of the situation rests upon the individual. He determines the outcome of the situation. Therefore, everything which happens or does not happen is traced back to him; it is the consequence of what he does or fails to do.

To speak as we do here of "holding another person's life in one's hand" endows this metaphor with a certain emotional power. The emotional significance of the metaphor grows out of the contrast in the relationship to which it refers, namely, that we have the power to determine the direction of something in another person's life, perhaps merely her mood or in an extreme case her entire destiny. Now it is altogether reasonable that we should have power to control things and animals. It is reasonable that legal authorities should have definite delegated and legally defined power over people in order to keep them from violating others. But it is altogether unreasonable that one person should possess direct power over another person, because such power has not been delegated to him, has not been defined by existing law, and does not serve to protect other people's rights. Wielding such power over another person is unreasonable because every person is an independent and responsible individual; yet we are to a large extent inescapably dependent upon one another so that, whether the thing at stake is our mood or our destiny, we are mutually and in a most immediate sense in one another's power.

Out of this fundamental dependence and direct power arises the demand that we take care of that in the other person's life which is dependent upon us and which we have in our power. However, this same demand forbids that we ever attempt, even for his own sake, to rob him of his independence. Responsibility for the other person never consists in our assuming the responsibility which is his.

NOTES AND REFERENCES

1. Gogarten makes this point in some of his helpful remarks concerning the basis of law. Friedrich Gogarten, *Die Verkündigung Jesu Christi*, (Heidelberg: Schneider, 1948), p. 108.

2. Regardless of how vehemently our opponent may refute our moral accusation and inveigle into replying and getting involved in discussion, and though the discussion may have a moderating effect upon us and even cause us to revoke our moral accusation – that accusation is nonetheless final and irrevocable in its original intention.

3. We have reference here to resentment. The person who has been offended advances unreasonable reproaches and accusations. He will not admit that they are unreasonable, though he knows very well that they are. By nourishing his resentment he is unable to reason clearly. He allows himself to be dominated by the purely emotional inertia of his resentment. It is characteristic of resentment that it wants to hide its own emotional origin in the exposure, and to divert our own and others' attention from it by unreasonable accusations. It is an opaqueness which knows that it is opaque without wanting to become transparent. Consequently it must in self-pity, one might say, cling to its own unreasonable accusations and reproaches. Resentment is the cheapest form of taking pleasure in pain, because the pain is imagined, and one knows that it is imagined.

4. This is not to say that it is in the nature of human existence for a person to try to prevent his being in any way determined by what has already happened. To

be determined by the past can mean two things. It can mean that out of what one has heard, said, done, experienced, and thought there arises an outlook on life which gives perspective to one's judgement. It can also mean that these give rise only to security measures and, especially, countermeasures whose purpose is to prevent one from undertaking anything regarding the outcome of which we are uncertain. This makes the word old even before it is spoken, the action old even before it is taken.

5. Trust and distrust are not two parallel ways of life. Trust is basic; distrust is the absence of trust. This is why we do not normally advance arguments and justifications for trust as we do for distrust. To use a modern philosophical expression, distrust is the "deficient form" of trust.

6. Someone will probably argue that the fact that a person gives himself to another person by trusting him is one thing, whereas the demand that we take care of the life thus committed to us through trust is quite another thing, in other words, that there must be a difference between a fact and a demand, between an opinion about what is and an opinion about what ought to be. This argument raises a number of questions too extensive for treatment here; they must be dealt with elsewhere.

Our concern here is only to point out the intimate connection between the fact and the demand, to point out that to a great extent the demand grows out of the fact. In other words, the fact forces upon us the alternative: either we take care of the other person's life or we ruin it. Given man's creatureliness, there is no third alternative. To accept the fact without listening to the demand is to be indifferent to the question whether life is to be promoted or ruined.

7. Lady Bertha in Henrik Pontoppidan's *De Dødes Rige* is not in the least doubt about what would be best for her daughter Jytte – a life together with Torben Diehmer. But Jytte Abildgaard is completely unnerved by an unconquerable distrust of life. She does not dare to face it. One day her love for Torben Diehmer conquers, but she has no sooner said yes to him than the unconquerable distrust asserts itself and causes her the next morning to retract her yes to him. At this point Lady Bertha's wrath is aroused. She is angered by the lighthearted trifling with life and death and she is struck by the wild notion that it might be her duty to bring force to bear upon Jytte. But this notion has no sooner come to her than she dismisses it, because there is nothing which gives a person the right to dominate another's will, not even if to do so would save that person from the greatest catastrophe. Says Pontoppidan: "It was only a momentary flash of anger in Bertha. She knew too well that she would never dare to wrest her child's fate out of the hands of life's hidden powers in order to shape it according to her own will. She found herself here at the boundary of her courage and acknowledged her impotence. Though she was certain about the path Jytte would have to follow to attain peace and fortune, she dared not take the responsibility upon herself" (Vol. 1 [Copenhagen: Gyldendal, 1918], p. 111).

Chapter 8
Love and the Moral Point of View

Martha C. Nussbaum

I

The summer my daughter fell in love with James Steerforth in Dickens' *David Copperfield*, she was 14 and I was 40. We were traveling around England, and, in response to her Dickensian longing, we had ended up in Yarmouth, to inspect, so to speak, the scene of the crime. I had indulgence, but little sympathy, for this literary infatuation. For I felt that I had known long ago, and would have known even if I hadn't made it my business to write on ethical topics, that he was simply not worthy of a good person's love. And I suspected her, as well, of immature reading. For surely, as I remembered it, it was Dickens' intention to make the reader judge Steerforth from the moral point of view, not to encourage her, or him, to fall in love with Steerforth. Full of maternal superiority, and bored with the garish coarseness of Yarmouth – in 1987 a place of oil refineries and cheap summer holiday facilities -- I undertook to reread the novel in order to establish my point.

My composure survived the first encounters, where I firmly took the side of Mr Mell, censured Steerforth for selfishness and egotism in his relation to the other boys, even concurred with Agnes in warning innocent David against his bad angel. And then one afternoon, sitting on the Yarmouth beach in the early July sun, my back turned to the ugly casinos, the cheap hotels, the pink and blue cottages, my eyes shifting from the pages of the novel to the generous sweep of the dark blue sea that beckoned onward before me, I felt a wind in my face and an excitement in my heart, a sensuous delight in the fresh presence of each thing that seemed to be connected, somehow, with the vividness of the chapters, with the power, above all, of Steerforth's presence. I felt my heart quite suddenly take itself off, rushing happily from the firmness of judgment into the eager volatility of desire. And, as I read on, the very words made my "heart beat high" and my "blood rush to my face", until, with tears and with love, maternal authority utterly vanquished, I saw him there before me, "lying with his head upon his arm, as I had often seen him lie at school".[1]

The question I want to ask in this essay is, quite simply, what has happened here? First, how is the point of view of love related to the moral point of view, and what, precisely, are the tensions between them? And also: how does novel-reading, the reading of this novel in particular, explore these tensions, constituting its readers as hybrid transmoral agents who slip dangerously back and forth from one world, one point of view, to the other?

II

The subject of romantic and erotic love is not often treated in works on moral philosophy, especially in the Anglo-American tradition. In part this has been a matter of reticence – for that philosophical tradition has lived within a conventional morality that disapproves, on the whole, of the public expression and even the public discussion of deep feelings. In part, too, it has been a matter of *style*: for the plain unadorned nonrhetorical style that the Anglo-American moral tradition both chooses and justifies as the most appropriate for moral reflection is not a style in which the topic of romantic/erotic love can be very easily or very fully discussed. (We see this, for example, in the thinness of Hume's account, which hardly compares to his analyses of pride or sympathy in persuasive and intuitive power.) The topic seems to demand for its convincing treatment a more literary style, a style that uses metaphor and narrative, that represents and also awakens powerful feelings. And all of this Anglo-American moral philosophy has usually avoided.

But these views about public expression and about style do not simply express, on the part of these philosophers, an unreflective adherence to cultural conventions. Philosophers are creatures of habit, to be sure. And one sees the effect of this tradition's habits of writing in the work of some contemporary moral philosophers who defend the moral centrality of intimate personal relationships, romantic love prominently included, but who write, nonetheless, as if philosophy would be better off not going too deeply into the texture of these relationships, not investigating too closely or too concretely the contribution they have to make to the good human life. But, as I say, habit is not all that is motivating philosophers in this tradition. There are deeper motivations too, arising from beliefs about morality and the moral point of view, beliefs that make it questionable whether romantic love could ever correctly be included inside morality, or be anything but subversive of the moral point of view.[2]

Some of these deeper reasons are, roughly speaking, Kantian. Romantic love is not something that is governed by the will. It is, instead, something with respect to which we are, at least in part, *passive*. It seems that we can't choose to fall in love with someone; it simply *happens* to us. And we can't altogether govern the way in which, or the goodness with which, it will happen. As Pindar long ago observed, some are lifted up by "the gentle hands of necessity", but "others with other hands" (*Nemean* VIII). So if one believes that the domain of morality is the domain of the will-governed and the actively chosen, one will be likely to feel, as Kant does, that romantic/erotic love must lie outside the domain of morality.

This is the motivation for Kant's remarkable distinction, in the *Doctrine of Virtue*, between *pathological love*, his name for the romantic, non-will-governed variety, and *practical love*, an attitude of concern that one can will oneself to have toward another human being, and which is, for that reason, a part of morality.[3] If one believes, in addition, that the realm of morality is of special and perhaps of supreme importance in human life – a belief that it seems fair to attribute to Kant – one will be likely, having once made that distinction, to ascribe high *human* worth to practical love, and far less worth to the pathological variety. In fact, since the relationship between the two loves for Kant is not simply neutral, since pathological love, indulged, actually draws us away from the correct moral attitude, sapping and subverting it, and since the moral attitude, actively cultivated, on the other hand activates our wills, making them less likely to succumb to the lures of pathological love, the Kantian will be likely to ascribe to pathological love a low human value indeed, probably a disvalue.

All this would not exactly suggest that moral philosophy should not be concerned with the topic of pathological love: for one who makes the negative judgment might become preoccupied, as, for example, Spinoza is preoccupied, with showing exactly what sort of threat love is to morality, and how this threat might be headed off.[4] But the negative judgment on love does imply that a treatise written from the point of view of morality will not display the value of love as lovers see it, or investigate the experience of love with empathy, from within.

But it is not this objection to love that I want to consider in the body of this essay. The Kantian objection, based on the distinction between activity and passivity, has certainly been influential in explaining the absence of love from our moral philosophy. But the objection is, in the context of our interest in understanding the properties of *love*, too large-scale and, so to speak, unrefined an objection. It throws out too many things to show what might be morally problematic about love in particular. For it holds, if it holds, not only against (romantic) love, but also against all the other sentiments, inclinations, passions, and even perceptual states with respect to which we are, in a manner, passive. The specifically Kantian tradition on the sentiments and passions finds moral problems in pity as well as love, in friendly feeling as well as erotic passion, in anger, fear, even sympathy – all these are morally problematic insofar as they are not will-governed. It is beyond my purpose here to criticize that general line of argument against the sentiments.[5]

What is more revealing, if it is romantic love we wish to understand, is the absence of this love from moralities based upon compassion and other sentiments. For it is plain that philosophers who argue that morality ought to be based upon sentiment and who insist that the ideal moral viewpoint is one that is rich in feeling, including a lot of what Kant would call *pathological* feeling, still find romantic love morally problematic in a special way. They still hold that it is to be left out of the moral point of view (not counted as a part of what animates someone who sees from that point of view), for reasons that have nothing to do with a general rejection of passivity. So if we want to understand what is uniquely troublesome about love in our moral tradition, we would do best to examine those arguments. It is also plain to me that if our interest is in the absence of love from modern writing in the Anglo-American tradition, it is this sentiment-based line of argument that explains our current situation – and our related ambivalence about the relationship between moral philosophy and the novel – to a far greater degree than does the Kantian tradition. Finally, if we need one further inducement to examine these arguments against love, I suggest that we have one in their power and cogency. I believe that they perspicuously describe a tension that really exists betweeen love and morality, and, in this way, they advance our understanding of the question: What role might romantic love play, or not play, in the good life for a human being?[6]

I shall turn first of all to a succinct philosophical statement of the argument in which I am interested, in Adam Smith's *The Theory of Moral Sentiments*.[7] Smith himself suggests that we develop our sense of the objection and its force by considering our experience as readers of works of literature or as spectators at plays; so we shall investigate the parallel. But the experience of readership has, it seems, as a moral experience, a more complicated character than Smith allows. In pursuit of this complexity, we shall return to *David Copperfield*, which I take to be one of the most profoundly interesting treatments in the English novel of the tension between the point of view of romantic love and the point of view of moral sentiments. We shall ask about the relationship between Agnes' arm, which points morally upward, and the opposing gesture of Steerforth, who lies with his head reclining easily on his arm. And this will lead us to wonder what the relation of the narrator might be to both morality and romance, and how his narrative moves, and moves both him and us, between these two opposing viewpoints.

III

In *The Theory of Moral Sentiments*, Adam Smith argues that the ideal moral point of view, the point of view of the "judicious spectator", is a viewpoint rich in feeling. Not only compassion and sympathy, but also fear, grief, anger, hope, and certain types of love are felt by this spectator, as a result of his active, concrete imagining of the circumstances and aims and feelings of others.[8] The spectator's feelings are not just willed attitudes of concern, they are really passions; and Smith clearly believes that it is both possible and essential to cultivate the passions, making people not less but more responsive and, so to speak, passive, in certain ways at certain times. Correct feeling is, for Smith, both morally *useful*, in showing us what we ought to do, and also morally *valuable* in its own right, as a kind of proper recognition of the ethical character of the situation before us. For Smith, who refers back to the Greek Stoics here,[9] the passions have a cognitive dimension – they are at least partially made up out of beliefs – so that it is natural for him to think of them both as guides and as pieces of recognizing.

The link between passion and the deliberately undertaken is forged by the imagination. By cultivating our ability to see vividly another person's distress, to picture ourselves in another person's place – and this, he makes clear, is something that we can set ourselves deliberately to do – we make ourselves more likely to respond with the morally illuminating and appropriate sort of response. It is clear that Smith attaches considerable importance to literature as a source of this kind of moral development; and literature is also, for him, an artificial construction of ideal spectatorship, which leads us into the morally good viewpoint naturally, and offers us in that way a model we can refer to in real life. For frequently, in order to show his reader what he means by a certain claim about the ideal spectator's responses, or in order to support his assertion that the spectator in a certain case will respond this way and not this, he refers to our experience as readers of stories and watchers of plays, asking us to notice what sentiments we experience in that role.[10] He proceeds as if readership and spectatorship are more familiar to us, more securely and concretely grasped, than the moral problems of life, concerning which he wishes to persuade us. He also assumes that we will agree that literary readership is structurally isomorphic to the spectator's moral role, so that a dubious issue in the real-life moral sphere can legitimately be pinned down by appeal to literary experience. The experience of readership is a moral activity in its own right, a cultivation of imagination for moral activity in life, and a test for correctness of real-life judgment and response.

What is, however, very remarkable, in the midst of this tremendous emphasis on the cultivation of the passions, is that two types of passion that play a prominent role in our lives and (or so we might have suspected) our literary experiences are considered by Smith to be totally absent from the judicious spectator and therefore totally to be omitted when we describe the limits of moral propriety. Whereas most passions are moderated and channeled, but still assiduously cultivated within the moral point of view, these two sorts are omitted from it altogether. The two are the bodily desires, including sexual desire, and the so-called "passions which take their origin from a particular turn or habit of the imagination". The salient example in the latter category is romantic love. If we combine the two passages, we have a sweeping rejection from morality and the moral viewpoint both of love and also of the erotic desire that is, Smith himself emphasizes, a prominent component of it. We also have, as I think we shall see, a claim in its own way as uncompromising as Kant's concerning the subversive relation between love and morality – though this claim is defended with arguments that have nothing to do with the rejection of passivity.

How does the argument work? Let us take the bodily passions first. Smith asks us, first, to imagine his judicious spectator looking on at someone else's hunger for food. The spectator, as elsewhere, is imagined as someone who is a concerned friend of the parties, emotionally involved with their good and ill, able to imagine vividly what it is like to be them. At the same time, he lives a life distinct from theirs and connects himself to theirs primarily through imagining rather than interacting. As I have said, Smith's frequent way of getting us to see what such a spectator is like and what he will feel is to ask us to think of him as like us when we read a novel or see a play, caring about the characters and vividly responding to their predicament. And seeing what this spectator will feel gives us a test to determine the proper sort and degree of feeling for us to have in our own real lives, in situations where we are not spectators but actively involved as moral agents. (For example, we will learn not to have excessive anger in a personal case of our own by reminding ourselves that the friendly spectator would feel anger for our situation only up to a certain limit.)

Smith now argues as follows. When we read a story about hungry people (in, he says, "the journal of a siege, or of a sea voyage") we can sympathize with, both respond to and assume in our empathetic imagining, their grief, fear, and "consternation" at being in such a predicament. What we can't take on as readers is the hunger itself, since that is based on a physical condition that we are not in. Therefore hunger is not, by itself, a moral response, or a part of the moral point of view.[11] We could better convey the centrality of this point of view in Smith's account of human agency by saying that hunger is not a constituent part of a fully and adequately human response to the world. This doesn't mean that we should never feel hunger, or should feel guilty about our hunger; it just means that we should not identify ourselves with it, think of it as a good human thing or any part of our true humanity.

The same, Smith now continues, is true of "the passion by which Nature unites the two sexes"[12] It is a very strong passion – in fact, "naturally the most furious of the passions". But, unlike other strong passions such as anger and grief, it proves altogether improper and extramoral when we apply the spectator test. The claim seems to be that we do not become sexually aroused when we look, as spectators, at people who are themselves sexually excited by one another. The closest we get to their excitement in our own state is, says Smith, a spirit of "gallantry" and "sensibility" toward them. As in the food case, Smith would presumably wish to say that reading about erotic arousal does not cause us to become, ourselves, aroused – although the absence here of any explicit remark to that effect (in contrast to the hunger case, where literature is prominent) may indicate that he is familiar enough with pornography to sense a difficulty in his argument at this point. In any case, the conclusion, as before, is that sexual desire is outside of the moral viewpoint on the world, and to be judged improper when we look at the world from that viewpont. "All strong expressions of it are upon every occasion indecent, even between persons in whom its most complete indulgence is acknowledged by all laws, both human and divine, to be perfectly innocent".[13]

Smith now adds a further point. The ancient philosophers, he says, hold that the reason these bodily passions are problematic is that we share them with "the brutes". Not so he replies: for we share with "the brutes" many passions:

> such as resentment, natural affection, even gratitude, which do not, upon that account, appear to be so brutal. The true cause of the peculiar disgust which we conceive for the appetites of the body when we see them in other men, is that we cannot enter into them. To the person himself who feels them, as soon as they are gratified, the object that excited them ceases to be agreeable: even its presence often becomes offensive to him; he looks round to no purpose for the charm which transported him the moment before, and he can now as little enter into his own passion as another person. When we have dined, we order the covers to be removed; and we should treat in the same manner the objects of the most ardent and passionate desires, if they were the objects of no other passions but those which take their origin from the body.[14]

In other words, there is a point of view that we are deeply committed to, which expresses something very fundamental about our humanity. And it is because the bodily passions do not appear in us, when we assume that viewpoint, that we must reject them from morality, not because they arise from some brutish element in us.

There are some problems with Smith's account of the spectator in this passage: a tendency to blur the distinction between empathy and sympathy; a tendency to confuse propriety in feeling with propriety in the public expression of feeling.[15] But we see the general shape of the argument well enough. What a concerned friend or a reader cannot respond to out of friendly concern (and I think that the point can be made without Smith's assumption that all sympathetic response involves having the *very same* feeling), what the reader can't, as a reader, be moved by, is somehow morally suspect. We turn now to the next group of banned passions; for it is here that romantic love itself gets rejected.

Among the passions derived from the imagination, Smith writes, are some that "take their origin from a peculiar turn or habit it has acquired". And these are always morally problematic:

> The imaginations of mankind, not having acquired that particular turn, cannot enter into them; and such passions, though they may be allowed to be almost unavoidable in some part of life, are always, in some measure, ridiculous. This is the case with that strong attachment which naturally grows up between two persons of different sexes, who have long fixed their thoughts upon one another. Our imagination not having run in the same channel with that of the lover, we cannot enter into the eagerness of his emotions. If our friend has been injured, we readily sympathize with his resentment, and grow angry with the very person with whom he is angry. If he has received a benefit, we readily enter into his gratitude, and have a very high sense of the merit of his benefactor. But if he is in love, though we may think his passion just as reasonable as any of the kind, yet we never think ourselves bound to conceive a passion of the same kind, and for the same person for whom he has conceived it. The passion appears to every body, but the man who feels it, entirely disproportioned to the value of the object; and love, though it is pardoned in a certain age because we know it is natural, is always laughed at, because we cannot enter into it. All serious and strong expressions of it appear ridiculous to a third person; and though a lover may be good company to his mistress, he is so to nobody else. He himself is sensible of this; and as long as he continues in his sober senses, endeavours to treat his own passion with raillery and ridicule. It is the only style in which we care to hear of it; because it is the only style in which we ourselves are disposed to talk of it. We grow weary of the grave, pedantic, and long-sentenced love of Cowley and Petrarca, who never have done with exaggerating the violence of their attachments; but the gaiety of Ovid, and the gallantry of Horace, are always agreeable.[16]

We can, he continues, enter into the lovers' hopes of happiness, or their fear of disappointment – but not into the love itself, making its seriousness real and vivid for ourselves.

Smith's point seems to be that romantic and erotic love is based upon a strong response to morally irrelevant particularities, in such a way that it can't be explained; it retains always an element of the surd, the mysterious, the impenetrably arbitrary. We can't imagine *why* it has happened between these two people in this way at this time – and so we can't see the love from the lovers' own viewpoint. This is all the more so, presumably, because this romantic love contains within it the bodily arousal that Smith's argument has already rejected, and which Smith here calls "perhaps, the foundation of love".[17]

Smith now returns to the issue of literary spectatorship. For it would appear to be a natural objection to his argument that romantic and erotic love are a staple of literature, and among the things that, in literature, most move and engage the reader's imagination. This Smith now denies. The lovers' wish for happiness and their fear of reversal – *these* are certainly staples of literary experience; and these are the foundation of our interest, he claims, both in pastoral poetry and in "modern tragedies and romances". But the *love itself* is not the object of the reader's interest, except in the comic manner already mentioned:

> The author who should introduce two lovers, in a scene of perfect security, expressing their mutual fondness for one another, would excite laughter, and not sympathy. If a scene of this kind is ever admitted into a tragedy, it is always, in some measure, improper, and is endured, not from any sympathy with the passion that is expressed in it, but from concern for the dangers and difficulties with which the audience foresee that its gratification is likely to be attended.[18]

Smith adds that romantic love, since it is frequently mixed with "humanity, generosity, kindness, friendship, esteem", is not, despite its extravagance and its mysteriousness, found actually revolting or odious – only, perhaps, a little ridiculous. In order to understand Smith's argument here, we must first attempt to say more plainly what romantic love is, as he sees it. Unlike his Stoic predecessors, unlike, as well, Descartes and Spinoza, Smith does not offer definitions of the passions; so this is a little hard to do. But I think that we can infer from his examples and descriptions in this passage that he takes romantic love to contain, as necessary ingredients, at least the following elements:

1. Mutual feelings of sexual attraction and arousal.

2. Beliefs (on both sides, presumably) about the supreme importance of the object, beliefs that go beyond any reasoned justification that the lover could articulate to others – even though they may contain, as well, some articulable element of esteem.[19]

We can add that the romantic love Smith describes appears to connect these two elements closely: sexual arousal is felt towards the person *seen as* supremely valuable and important.

3. A complex intimate way of life that involves the exchange of affectionate communications, both verbal and erotic; a way of life in which lovers are totally wrapped up in one another, attending for long periods of time to nobody else, and in which, characteristically, they take themselves off into privacy, not inviting or wanting any scrutiny or even company, seeking a "perfect security". For the lovers, this life has the charms of mystery, secrecy, and intimacy; from the outside it is simply mysterious.

Once again, we can add that the third element is closely connected with the other two: sexual desire is felt toward the person seen as part of an intimate way of life, apart from others; intimacy enhances the sense of importance; and at the same time sexual desire and the belief in importance are strong motivations to undertake the way of life in the first place.

I should add that, by insisting on this last, very complex, element, Smith seems to me to go beyond his philosophical predecessors on this topic, who all seem to define love as some sort of combination of feeling and belief,[20] without sufficiently taking account of the fact that love cannot exist in a single instant, but requires a pattern of exchange and mutuality, of mutual attention evolving over time. In this way he brings to the analysis of romantic and erotic love the insight first introduced in the sphere of friendly love by Aristotle:[21] love is fundamentally a relation, not something *in* a single person at all – a relation that involves the give and take, over time, of feeling, thought, benefits, conversations. Smith adds that this relation, where romantic love is concerned, evolves its own mysterious habits and delights in the charm of its secret routines, so inscrutable to the nonparticipant.

Smith's objection to this relation seems to be based, precisely, on its mysteriousness and exclusivity. We might expand his point about the spectator as follows. Lovers wrapped up in loving conversation (and it is, I think, significant that his paradigm scene of love is a scene of conversation) are not, insofar as they are lovers, also spectators. Being in love is

altogether different, as a kind of attention, from being a judicious spectator; for lovers do not look around at the entirety of their world, but are
exclusively wrapped up in one another. They do not enter into anyone
else's predicament; their imaginations do not see out. By the same token,
if we imagine the judicious spectator looking at her world, she will not be
able to find in it, no matter how fine her imagination, the passion that
they feel for one another. It is a mystery to her; she can't see into it.
Lovers, then, neither see nor are seen with the judicious eye of sympathetic moral concern.

We now must confront an ambiguity in Smith's account. For there are
two ways in which the moral function of the spectator might be understood. (These two possibilities arise in interpreting most ideal-judge views,
beginning with Aristotle's.[22]) On one reading, the judicious spectator is
merely heuristic: moral appropriateness and propriety in passion exist
independently and can in principle be specified independently of his
response, and imagining his response is a useful device for us in finding
out the appropriate response. On this reading, there is something inappropriate about love, something that demands apology, apart from the
spectator's inability to enter into it, and the spectator shows us the way
to the correct conclusion. On the second, and stronger reading, however,
the spectator's responses are themselves constitutive of what is and is not
morally appropriate. The fact that she cannot enter into love is not a sign
that points beyond itself to some independently existing inappropriateness
in the relation. It is the very fact that she cannot enter in that *makes* the
passion inappropriate. It is what is deficient, or excessive, about it.

The second reading can, I believe, be strongly supported from a
number of passages in the text. To confine ourselves to the sections we
are discussing, we might recall Smith's vigorous insistence that the *reason
for* the inappropriateness of bodily passion is not some separate brutish-
ness in hunger and sexual desire; rather, the "true cause" of our negative
view is "that we cannot enter into them". This may just be a psychological remark; but it looks like something more. Not just the cause, but the
justification for our negative view, seems to be found in the fact of the
spectator's incomprehension.[23]

What, in that case, is the deeper significance of the spectator's failure to
enter into these passions? What is the moral significance of the spectatorial stance?[24] I think that Smith's underlying point is this. Morality essentially involves thinking of oneself as one person among others, bound by

ties of friendship and sympathy to those others. These ties, in turn, involve, essentially, two further things. First, they require us to look around us, taking thought, so to speak, for all that we can see. And they involve, too, general social conversation, the giving and receiving of justifications and reasons. Therefore, they require that we permit ourselves and our actions to *be seen*. These practices both express our concern for our fellow beings and bind them to us in a network of mutual concern. The presence of these features in the spectator explains why assuming, in thought, the spectator's position can be a way of assuming the moral point of view. We have built into the account of the spectator the most essential features of our moral humanity.

And that, we may now also add, thinking of Smith's reliance on literature, is why going to plays and reading novels and stories is a valuable part of moral development: not because it points beyond itself to a separately existing moral realm, but because it is among the ways in which we constitute ourselves as moral, and thus as fully human, beings. For we find, as we read novels, that we quite naturally assume the viewpoint of an affectionate and responsive social creature, who looks at all the scene before her with fond and sympathetic attention, caring for all the people, and caring, too, for the bonds of discourse that hold them all together. Interpreting a novel or play involves one, indeed, in a kind of sympathetic reason-giving that is highly characteristic of morality; for we ask ourselves, as we try to enter into the plot, why the characters do what they do, and we are put off if our inquiries lead to nothing but mystery and arbitrariness.

But mystery is what love is all about. And the fact that we cannot, where love is concerned, enter into the essential forms of moral give and take is the very thing that makes love, as a relation, inappropriate to our highest humanity, and subversive of the moral community.

IV

Smith's idea about the moral stance and his connection of that stance to the experience of the reader of fiction has had a long history (whether through direct influence or through a more general cultural dissemination) in the reflections of English novelists themselves about the moral role of their craft.[25] I have argued elsewhere that Henry James takes a very similar view about the reader's activity and its moral worth. And

James has related worries about the role, in the moral vision that sustains his novels, of personal love and of related emotions such as jealousy and the desire for revenge. Love, as James sees it, requires both hiddenness and a willful self-blinding, both a turning from the good of others and a request that others turn away their eyes. For these reasons it threatens a valuable norm of moral attention. And I have suggested that it is for this reason that strong personal love, in James, occurs only, so to speak, in the margins of the novel – in the silence beyond the ending of *The Golden Bowl*, after Maggie has buried her eyes in her husband's embrace, tragically surrendering her equal vision of the claims of all; in the boat where Chad and Marie de Vionnet are sailing, before that boat has been recognized by the spectator Strether and become a part of his, and the reader's, vision; in the trip of Charlotte and the Prince to Gloucester, where they step out of the novel's vision into a silence prefigured by their determination to "go" for that one day, only "by" each other. As readers, we are not encouraged to fall in love with any of James's characters, nor are we at all encouraged to take up a stance toward them that would make this a possible response. We are not seduced, not led, ourselves, into their silences. In this way we are borne up morally, held as "participators by a fond attention"[26] in the adventures of all the characters, even when we are reminded that there are silences into which the morality of fine-tuned social perception has no entry.

But Smith's nonerotic idea of readership and James's similar but more complex idea, which complicates the austerity with erotic silences, are not all that novel-reading has morally to offer us. For if Smith's claim that we don't get seduced by fictional characters seems, up to a point, correct as an account of certain novels, for example the novels of James, we know well, also, that there are other experiences of novel-reading that are, although still profoundly moral, also disturbingly erotic. And perhaps by investigating the relationship between moral community and erotic privacy in the novels that do have a seductive dimension we can better understand the tension between love and the moral viewpoint. And we might even discover, as Smith did not discover, a path between them, a way in which morality itself, most richly and generously construed, leads beyond itself into love.

I shall, then, for the balance of this essay turn to Dickens' *David Copperfield*, and to the question with which I began: Why is it that, morally attuned as the reader of this novel is made to be, the reader nonetheless falls in love, as David also falls in love, with James Steerforth? Why, and how, does this novel, which begins with an open question about who the hero of David Copperfield's life actually is, and which ends (apparently) with the upward-pointing gesture of morality, lead us, at times, outside of morality into the "shadowy world" of moonlight and love, of magic, and an arm curved along the pillow?

V

I shall begin by enumerating, simply, certain facts.[27] That David Copperfield was born with a caul – which signifies that he would never drown at sea (p. 49). That the hour of his birth, midnight on a Friday, signified that he would be unlucky in life but be "privileged to see ghosts and spirits". That it is his persistent fantasy that he himself was born as a traveler out of that "shadowy world" (p. 60). That, in consequence of Betsey Trotwood's conjecture that he would be born a girl, he has, as well, the persistent fantasy that he has, in the spirit world, a sisterly double: "Betsey Trotwood Copperfield was for ever in the land of dreams and shadows, the tremendous region whence I had so lately travelled" (p. 60). That this shadowy world is associated with his longing for his dead father, above whose grave the light that lights such ghostly travelers shines its mysterious nocturnal light (p. 60). That David's father left David a collection of novels that he avidly read and reread, "reading as if for life" (p. 106). That Dickens, in his Preface to the novel, speaks of his own sorrow at finishing the novel, comparing the entire world of the novel to David's imagined spirit world: "An Author feels as if he were dismissing some portion of himself into the shadowy world, when a crowd of the creatures of his brain are going from him forever" (p. 45). (I regard this less as an autobiographical statement than as a part of the fiction: Dickens in this way puts himself into his own text as a character.) That David Copperfield expresses, at the novel's close (a novel he has written) a similar sorrow – "subduing my desire to linger on", he dismisses "the shadows" (p. 950) until only Agnes's solid reality remains.

We now add to these several further facts. That David's relationship with James Steerforth casts him both as a storyteller and as the inhabitant of a world of moonlight and shadows, of enchantments and spells, in which David becomes first the Sultana Scheherazade (p. 145), who is "cherished as a kind of plaything" (p. 146) and, later on, the equally cherished character "Daisy", whose innocence is his seductive power. That Steerforth links David from the beginning with David's unborn sister, his ghostly female double:

> "You haven't got a sister, have you?" said Steerforth, yawning.
> "No", I answered.
> "That's a pity", said Steerforth. "If you had had one, I should think she would have been a pretty, timid, little, bright-eyed sort of girl. I should have liked to know her. Good night, young Copperfield". (p. 140)[28]

And Copperfield, or his shadowy sister, gazing at Steerforth as he sleeps in the mysterious moonlight, loves him from that moment:[29]

> I thought of him very much after I went to bed, and raised myself, I recollect, to look at him where he lay in the moonlight, with his handsome face turned up, and his head reclining easily on his arm. He was a person of great power in my eyes; that was, of course, the reason of my mind running on him. No veiled future dimly glanced upon him in the moonbeams. There was no shadowy picture of his footsteps, in the garden that I dreamed of walking in all night. (p. 140)

The "reason" of course is no reason; it says, in effect, that there is no reason, only a great power. He loves because he loves, and he thinks nothing, in his dreams, for morality. In the sensuous rhythm of the prose itself, we feel that he has entered the other world, the world of moonbeams and shadows, of mysterious ease and delight, the world of a particular turn of the imagination, where reasons come to an end.

Two gestures frame this novel. The first is the gesture of Steerforth's arm here, as it curves easily along the pillow, supporting his "fine face" with its "curling hair" (p. 139).[30] The second is the gesture of Agnes, on which the novel closes, as she stands by him, her arm pointing upward. The first gesture becomes Steerforth's leitmotif, just as the upward gesture is Agnes's. As his Good Angel and his other angel (for only Agnes calls Steerforth a "bad angel", p. 426),[31] they take up their positions beside his heart, beside his bed ("You belong to my bedroom, I find", p. 137), contrasting guardians, beckoning to him from their different worlds. Steerforth's gesture returns at two crucial moments later in the novel, as a hauntingly concrete vision, in which sensuous perception and emotion-infused memory join together. The last time David sees Steerforth before the seduction of Emily, the last time he sees him alive and as a beloved friend, it is this gesture, once again, that arrests him:

I was up with the dull dawn, and, having dressed as quietly as I could, looked into his room. He was fast asleep; lying, easily, with his head upon his arm, as I had often seen him lie at school.

The time came in its season, and that was very soon, when I almost wondered that nothing troubled his repose, as I looked at him. But he slept – let me think of him so again – as I had often seen him sleep at school; and thus, in this silent hour, I left him. – Never more, oh God forgive you, Steerforth! to touch that passive hand in love and friendship. Never, never, more! (pp. 497–498)

Notice that the gesture here is made a part of the remembering novelist's present life, as his art of writing takes him again to his vision of Steerforth, and his love. And years later, when the body of the ship-wrecked sailor is washed up, dead, upon the Yarmouth shore, David recognizes it, not by its form or feature, but by that same gesture:

The old remembrance that had been recalled to me, was in his look. I asked him, terror-stricken, leaning on the arm he held out to support me:
"Has a body come ashore?"
He said, "Yes".
"Do I know it?" I asked then.
He answered nothing.
But, he led me to the shore. And on that part of it where she and I had looked for shells, two children – on that part of it where some lighter fragments of the old boat, blown down last night, had been scattered by the wind – among the ruins of the home he had wronged – I saw him lying with his head upon his arm, as I had often seen him lie at school.

No need, O Steerforth, to have said, when we last spoke together, in that hour which I so little deemed to be our parting-hour – no need to have said, "Think of me at my best!" I had done that ever; and could I change now, looking on this sight! (p. 866)

(We have already been told that this entire episode, in addition to being a frequent dream of the narrator/novelist in later life, is seen vividly before him as he writes: "As plainly as I behold what happened, I will try to write it down. I do not recall it, but see it done; for it happens again before me" – p. 855).

We can begin our investigation of the tension between love and morality in the novel by thinking about these two gestures. Agnes's upward-pointing gesture is clear, unambiguous, conventional, literal.

What it means, it says – and in a way that anyone who sees can understand: "Strive to be more morally upright, more worthy of heaven". It is the gesture famous from Jacques-Louis David's portrait of Socrates, from, indeed, countless religious paintings and sculptures in many periods. (Agnes, in her "tranquil brightness", has already been compared by the narrator to a figure in a stained glass window – p. 280.[32]) It is the gesture of moral discourse, reason-giving, and advice: "'Everyone who knows you, consults with you, and is guided by you, Agnes. . . . You are so good, and so sweet-tempered. You have such a gentle nature, and you are always right'" (p. 333). It is a gesture that is not personal to Agnes; anyone, we feel, might use it to say the same. Nor is it personal in its directedness toward David: just as she gives advice to everyone, so she points out, for everyone alike, the moral path. It would not be stretching a point to say that it is the gesture of the sympathetic and judicious spectator, a gesture that represents, in the novel, the nonshadowy public world of morality and reason-giving moral discourse.

Steerforth's gesture, by contrast, signifies nothing publicly communicable. Its only meaning is that he is there. It is mysteriously, sensuously, his, his beyond explanations and reasons. Its power to haunt comes not from the public world of reason-giving (in fact, it distracts David from that world, making moral judgment upon Steerforth's actions impossible), but from the private world of personal emotion and personal memory. It is irreducibly particular, characteristic of him and no other. It is what David recognizes him by. And its easy charm and erotic grace are for David part of a world of shadows and moonlight, not of the world of reasons and justifications. He cannot explain its power. He can only repeat the description, in haunting and almost incantatory language, as if the description, and the gesture, were, for him, for us, a magic spell. Above all, the gesture, and the language used to describe it, are erotic. Agnes uses the bodily as an instrument of the moral; and we know that as he writes the novel David sees her with him, "journeying along the road of life" (p. 946) – a metaphor typical of Agnes in its lack of sensuous freshness – surrounded by children, emblems of a moral use of the body. In Steerforth's gesture we feel the mystery and excitement of a body animated by a unique spirit, pointing to nothing but itself and the bed on which it rests.

Agnes's gesture moves us, insofar as it does, because it reminds us of aspirations for the good life that we can articulate to ourselves and to others. Steerforth's gesture stirs us, as it hauntingly does, not because we see beyond it into something else, but because it is made, for us, a sensuous reality, because, by the spell of erotic and incantatory language we are brought, ourselves, into the charmed world of love. The emotion we feel when that language stirs us with its own magic is something akin to David's emotion. We feel toward that arm some part of the inexplicable erotic excitement, the stir of tumultuous feeling, and the sheer indefeasible devotion to a particular person that are present in David's love. And in that gesture we are led, as David is led, beyond morality. The hand curves along the pillow, fingers pointing onwards.[33]

Dickens' opposition of gestures disturbs us, making us aware (as we pass from one point of view to the other) of many of the problematic features of erotic love that we have already mentioned here in reflecting on Smith. And we are all the more disturbed because we respond to the gesture against our will, so to speak, against our expectation even. Just when we thought we were most morally secure in our judgment upon Steerforth's character, there we are, watching that bed in the moonlight, ready to weep. We notice love's mysterious character of inexplicable intimacy. We notice how, caught up in that moment, we don't see out for others, and we won't be seen by them. We don't care to attend to the injustice done to poor Mr Mell; we suspend all general sympathy. We don't even care for Ham Peggotty, since we know, with Emily, that he is indeed a "chuckleheaded fellow" and that we too would gladly have followed Steerforth wherever he beckoned. And we certainly won't permit Agnes to look in at us in these moments, telling us what a bad angel he is and speaking of moral uplift. The minute we, like David, hear Steerforth's footsteps, we react as David did when he says that they made "my heart beat high and the blood rush to my face" (p. 485). And Agnes, though we don't exactly dismiss her, is closed up for the time being in a sanctuary from which she is not permitted, so to speak, to look out or look on. As David says:

> I was never unmindful of Agnes, and she never left that sanctuary in my thoughts – if I may call it so – where I had placed her from the first. But when he entered, and stood before me with his hand out, the darkness that had fallen on him changed to light, and I felt confounded and ashamed of having doubted one I loved so heartily. I loved her none the less; I thought of her as the same benignant, gentle angel in my life; I reproached myself, not her, with having done him an injury; and I

would have made him any atonement if I had known what to make, and how to make it. (p. 485)

Much of this novel takes place in the daylight world, a world of social and other-regarding concern, a world in which the good heart cares for each part of its context and strives, with active sympathy, to do good. This world is also a world in which David can explain to us *why* each thing is good or bad, a world in which his feelings are always in proportion to these reasons and play an active part, we might say, in compassionate reason-giving social discourse. But we have already been made aware, from the beginning of the novel, that there is a darker world in this book as well, a world of shadows and spirits – and that the narrator presents himself to us not only as a person who has access to that other world, but also as someone who has a female double, pretty and susceptible, dwelling in that world. He has, then, access to that double, that realm. And it is in this counterworld – set over and against, or rather around the margins of the world of sympathetic morality – that the love of Daisy and Steerforth (of the Sultan and Scheherazade) is situated.

David's love for Steerforth contains, certainly, a great deal that the spectator could see: admiration for Steerforth's strength and boldness, his courage and intelligence, his power to do almost anything without apparent effort, his outspokenness and geniality, the way he protects and cares for David. And Steerforth's love for David (for I think we may really speak of love here) can, though more obscure, be similarly understood, in part: it addresses itself to Daisy's freshness, brightness, and innocence, his trust, his intelligence, his loyalty. David often gives expression to the communicable admiring side of his love, as if he were trying to satisfy himself that it could be explained to others, that reasons could be given, bringing it out into the public world.[34] But the shortcomings of his attempts only convince us the more that it is not entirely an articulable relation.[35]

We are aware, then, from the beginning, that there is, as well, in this love much that the spectator could not enter into – and that, insofar as we can and do, we are being led by the novel outside of the spectatorial role. The physical erotic attraction of the pair is only a part of this mysterious side. But it is stressed, in David's frequent remarks about Steerforth's good looks,[36] in his account of his physical reaction to Steerforth's presence, heart beating and blood rushing, in his jealousy of Steerforth's other friends (p. 416), in his response to the sensuous gesture of head and arm. In the punctiliousness, too, with which he informs us that he and Steerforth "parted with friendly heartiness at his door" (p. 347), slept under separate roofs at Yarmouth, and so on; in his obsessive thought of the touch of Steerforth's hand; in Steerforth's wish to be acquainted with David's shadowy sister, in the "dashing way he had of treating me like a plaything" (p. 358), in the flirtatious use of the name Daisy.

But the erotic/romantic relation goes beyond both liking and erotic flirtation. We have a sense of a secret world, dense with conversation, story-telling, ease, and laughter, with magic spells and the charm of being understood and loved. From the first, Steerforth beckons to the part of David that has access to the shadowy world: "Whatever I had within me that was romantic and dreamy, was encouraged by so much story-telling in the dark" (p. 146). His first meal with Steerforth initiates him into a universe of moonlight and magic, the blue glare of the phosphorous box shedding over everything its strange alluring light:

> How well I recollect our sitting there, talking in whispers; or their talking, and my respectfully listening, I ought rather to say; the moon-light falling a little way into the room, through the window, painting a pale window on the floor, and the greater part of us in shadow, except when Steerforth dipped a match into a phosphorus-box, when he wanted to look for anything on the board, and shed a blue glare over us that was gone directly! A certain mysterious feeling, consequent on the darkness, the secrecy of the revel, and the whisper in which everything was said, steals over me again, and I listen to all they tell me with a vague feeling of solemnity and awe. . . . (p. 138)

Steerforth, in this world, is the magician, shedding his strange light; and David is again in his presence, even as he brings us there. This love is at home in the night, in the bedroom; and its power of enchantment seems almost to have created around David the moonlit world. For we are made uncomfortably aware, always, of Steerforth's inexplicable power to charm:

> There was an ease in his manner – a gay and light manner it was, but not swaggering – which I still believe to have borne a kind of enchant-ment with it. I still believe him, in virtue of this carriage, his animal spirits, his delightful voice, his handsome face and figure, and, for aught I know, of some inborn power of attraction besides (which I think a few

people possess), to have carried a spell with him to which it was a natural weakness to yield, and which not many persons could withstand. (p. 157)

It's this, of course, that Agnes finds so objectionable. The essence of this love, we have to say, is an enchantment that cannot be explained, that is too particular to be explained. The enchantment constitutes a mutual relationship of intimacy, in which David is "nearer to his heart than any other friend",[37] and Steerforth inhibits David's dreams (p. 347).

Furthermore, we are, as readers, led by the novelist's art (by the vividness of perceptual memory that is, David tells us, at the heart of his own narratorial gift) to enter, ourselves, the shadowy world and to feel its enchantment through the enchanting power of David's poetic use of language. Led into the imaginings and habits characteristic of love, we, too, recognize the body by its posture on the beach and participate, mourning, in David's final farewell to the hand he has touched so often:

> I went through the dreary house, and darkened the windows. The windows of the chamber where he lay, I darkened last. I lifted up the leaden hand, and held it to my heart; and all the world seemed death and silence, broken only by his mother's mourning. (p. 873)

The chapter ends; the silence is also ours.

This romantic and participatory conception of readership is not only built into the structure of the novel, into the erotic ways in which it beckons to the reader. It is also explicitly described in the novel as David's own experience of readership in early life. Reading novels is his refuge from the gloomy religion of the Murdstones and his renewal of contact with his father in the world of ghosts and spirits. His reading is passionately, generously involved, as he enacts in fantasy his favorite plots and their relations:

> My father had left a small collection of books in a little room upstairs, to which I had access (for it adjoined my own) and which nobody else in our house ever troubled. From that blessed little room, Roderick Random, Peregrine Pickle, Humphrey Clinker, Tom Jones, the Vicar of Wakefield, Don Quixote, Gil Blas, and Robinson Crusoe, came out, a glorious host, to keep me company. They kept alive my fancy, and my hope of something beyond that place and time, – they, and the *Arabian Nights*, and the *Tales of the Genii*, – and did me no harm; for whatever

harm was in some of them was not there for me; I knew nothing of it.
... It is curious to me how I could ever have consoled myself under my
small troubles (which were great troubles to me), by impersonating my
favourite characters in them – as I did – and by putting Mr and Miss
Murdstone into all the bad ones – which I did too. I have been Tom Jones
(a child's Tom Jones, a harmless creature) for a week together. I have
sustained my own idea of Roderick Random for a month at a stretch, I
verily believe. I had a greedy relish for a few volumes of Voyages and
Travels – I forget what, now – that were on those shelves; and for days
and days I can remember to have gone about my region of our house,
armed with the centre-piece out of an old set of boot-trees – the perfect
realization of Captain Somebody, of the Royal British Navy, in danger of
being beset by savages, and resolved to sell his life at a great price. The
Captain never lost dignity, from having his ears boxed with the Latin
Grammar. I did: but the Captain was a Captain and a hero, in despite of
all the grammars of all the languages in the world, dead or alive.

  This was my only and my constant comfort. When I think of it, the
picture always rises in my mind, of a summer evening, the boys at play
in the churchyard, and I sitting on my bed, reading as if for life. Every
barn in the neighbourhood, every stone in the church, and every foot of
the churchyard, had some association of its own, in my mind, connected
with these books, and stood for some locality made famous in them. I
have seen Tom Pipes go climbing up the church-steeple; I have watched
Strap, with the knapsack on his back, stopping to rest himself upon the
wicket-gate; and I *know* that Commodore Trunnion held that club with
Mr Pickle, in the parlour of our little village alehouse.

  The reader now understands, as well as I do, what I was when I came
to that point of my youthful history to which I am now coming again.
(pp. 105–106)

This is an important passage; for it tells us clearly how powerful
novel-reading is in and for life, how surely it forms the life of fantasy, how
surely fantasy shapes, for good or ill, the reader's relations with the
world. David, as reader, is in no sense detached or judicious, as Adam
Smith seems to recommend. He is a romantic and passionate participant.
He peoples the world with the characters he loves, and puts his whole life
into enacting the story. And the habits of desire formed by the novels he
reads are kinetic and erotic, conducive to falling in love in life.

  We have spoken of falling in love with Steerforth. Now we can see that
this is the sort of novel-reading David knows and cultivates. The love of a
fictional character can be love because it is an active and interactive relationship that sustains the reader for many hours of imagining, of

fiction-making, beyond the time spent with the page itself; and because, in this relation, the mysterious and ineffable charm of interaction with a powerful presence can be experienced in much the way it is in life because, too, the reader is at the same time a reader of his or her own life; bringing to the imagining the hopes and loves of real life. Of course this interaction takes place in fantasy. But David insists upon the closeness of its links to love in life: its activation of the same generous, outgoing, and erotic impulses, its power to transform the texture of the world. And he also indicates that the loves we find in life owe, themselves, a great deal to the storytelling imagination and to romantic projection. This does not mean that they are based upon *illusion* in any pejorative sense, as we shall see; the way one thing is associated with another, the richness of the intersection of one image with many others, all this is not mere deception but part of the texture of life, and a part of life's excitement. Part, too, of our ability to endow a perceived form with a human life: in that sense, all sympathy, all morality, is based on a generous fantasy. Without "fancy", Mr Gradgrind's pupils cannot see truly, cannot love.

Now, however, we are prepared to notice something further about the novel's portrayal of storytelling. Steerforth is not only a character and an episode inside this novel; not only an object of love for its readers; he is also unmistakably linked with the novelist's craft. Most obvious is the fact that, whereas Agnes is associated with school books (historical and philosophical and religious, presumably, not literary[38]), Steerforth and David meet to tell stories. It is David's ability to re-create the world of his favorite novels, to be Scheherezade, that first draws Steerforth to him. His love of Steerforth has been prepared, as we have suggested, by novel-reading; and he links Steerforth with the protective father who gave him novels to read, and who lives in the shadowy world. The onward erotic movement of storytelling is the movement of their love – whereas we associate Agnes, on the other side, with stained glass and sermons, rest and immobility.[39]

This connection is brought out very clearly when David meets Steerforth again after the years of absence. He has just seen his first professional stage production of Shakespeare, and the mystery of that event prepares him for romantic love:

> But the mingled reality and mystery of the whole show, the influence upon me of the poetry, the lights, the music, the company, the smooth

stupendous changes of glittering and brilliant scenery, were so dazzling, and opened up such illimitable regions of delight, that when I came out into the rainy street, at twelve o'clock at night, I felt as if I had come from the clouds, where I had been leading a romantic life for ages, to a bawling, splashing, link-lighted, umbrella-struggling, hackney-coach-jostling, patten-clinking, muddy, miserable world. (p. 344)[40]

He now sees his own past life through the play, as if it is "a shining transparency, through which I saw my earlier life moving along" (p. 345); and into this charmed picture enters "the figure of a handsome well-formed young man dressed with a tasteful easy negligence which I have reason to remember very well" (p. 345). Steerforth has returned; the mystery of literature opens onto the other mystery.

What is more, the literary association is unmistakably linked with the generous and loving feelings that draw him to Steerforth:

At another time I might have wanted the confidence or the decision to speak to him, and might have put it off until next day, and might have lost him. But in the then condition of my mind, where the play was still running high, his former protection of me appeared so deserving of my gratitude, and my old love for him overflowed my breast so freshly and spontaneously, that I went up to him at once, with a fast-beating heart, and said: "Steerforth! won't you speak to me?" (p. 345)

Here David shows that love in life interacts in complicated ways with fantasy memory, and projection. That, indeed, insofar as it involves endowing a perceived form with a mind and heart, in this way going beyond the evidence, it is always a kind of generous fiction-making. All love is, in that sense, love of fictional characters; and literature trains us for that element in love. This fiction-making, we clearly see here, need not be pernicious or self-deceptive. His fantasy has led David outside himself to see Steerforth with love and to focus generously on his actual presence. Fantasy and a genuine relatedness are mutually supportive, as the imagining of the play makes him more keenly aware of what is outside him, and prompts a generous outpouring of feeling.[41]

These are only the most obvious links between erotic/romantic love and literary narration in the novel. What we need now to record is that, through very many hints, the character and effect of Steerforth himself are linked with the novelist's task, until we cannot help asking who wrote the text we are reading, and what is happening to us as we read.

Steerforth makes his first appearance in the novel as writing: "There was one boy – a certain J. Steerforth – who cut his name very deep and very often" (p. 131). Writing and an erotic romanticism are unmistakably linked; writing itself is eroticized and romanticized as bold, deep, cutting onward movement, dedicated to the particular, to a proper name. And consider the attributes of Steerforth as romantic charmer. "He is such a speaker . . . that he can win anybody over; and I don't know what you'd say if you were to hear him sing, Mr. Peggotty" (p. 196). "Steerforth could always pass from one subject to another with a carelessness and lightness that were his own" (p. 349). We know of "his natural gift of adapting himself to whomsoever he pleased, and making direct, when he cared to do it, to the main point of interest in anybody's heart" (p. 367). "How lightly and easily he carried on, until he brought us, by degrees, into a charmed circle" (p. 375). He "could become anything he liked at any moment" (p. 402). He charms even Rosa Dartle with "the fascinating influence of his delightful art" (p. 495). Aren't these all traits of a good novelist? And aren't these, as well, the arts that are being practiced on us, even as we read? The novel is written, for a great part of its length, from the moral point of view, clearly, the point of view of the compassionate spectator. But now we see, too, another art that writes it; and we are made to ask whether it isn't that art that is, somehow, more organizing, more fundamental.

One strange exchange makes the connection more complex still. Shortly before Steerforth departs for Yarmouth, he makes of his Daisy a singular request:

> "Daisy", he said, with a smile – "for though that's not the name your godfathers and godmothers gave you, it's the name I like best to call you by – and I wish, I wish, I wish, you could give it to me".
> "Why so I can, if I choose", said I. (p. 497)

This extraordinary response reminds us of the novelist's power to give names to things, to transform evil to good, guilt to innocence – or to move altogether beyond that distinction, if he so chooses. The novel can, if it chooses, fulfill our hopes for innocence and the ubiquity of morality; or, if it chooses, it can simply love Steerforth as he is and allow his charm to remain, as it does remain, untouched, at the novel's heart. David has neither changed Steerforth to Daisy nor simply condemned him; and yet he might have done either had he so chosen.

And there is something more. We are made to recall that, as so many other suggestions have indicated, Steerforth is in a sense the author of this novel, the creator of its erotic charm. Perhaps, then, this author has, in writing the novel, called himself David or Daisy, has separated out, given separate representation to, a strain of innocence and purity in his complex head. Dickens' Preface, read as a part of the narrative, reminds us of the complex relation of the passionate and tumultuous Dickens character to his own many-sided creation. For he has, after all, made himself into Daisy – but into a Daisy so wrapped up in Steerforth that he sees him and loves him without condemnation, despite the allure of morality. And he has made as well, in this scene, a Steerforth who wishes to be Daisy, whose selfishness is qualified by a real love of Daisy. He has made, then, in the relation of the two, a love that lies beyond strict morality and the distinction between guilt and innocence, and yet at the same time a love that moves us as something whose human value is not to be dismissed because it cannot be seen from the spectator's viewpoint. (And, if Steerforth is Daisy, he cannot, as we know, be killed at sea – so the identity question raises, for us, the possibility that Steerforth in some sense lives on.) The exchange continues:

> "Daisy, if anything should ever separate us, you must think of me at my best, old boy. Come! Let us make that bargain. Think of me at my best, if circumstances should ever part us!"
> "You have no best to me, Steerforth", said I, "and no worst. You are always equally loved, and cherished in my heart". (p. 497)

He keeps the bargain, even to the end of his writing. This novel, we now begin to see, contains the writing of J. Steerforth; it contains, as well, the writing of sympathetic morality. It is written by and in the tension between these two apparently irreconcilable viewpoints. But it also contains something further, something not precisely equivalent either to the charms of romantic/erotic love or to the judgments of morality – a movement of the loving heart that mediates between those two worlds, and insists on joining them in a coherently, if complexly, loving work of art. There is a profound question in fact – the question asked in the novel's opening sentence – about who the novel's hero is, and who its author.

But before we try to answer that question, and to describe the mediating attitude, we must return to the gesture of Agnes, examining the limits of moral spectatorship as the novel presents them. The failure of Agnes to inspire love in the reader is one of the novel's most insistent problems. One tends to suppose that it is inadvertent, a defect of Dickens' craft. But Dickens has given us enough hints about the subversive and Steerforthian character of novel-writing and the imagination of the writer that we are motivated to question this first judgment. The novel's final lines strike us at first as merely cloying and not terribly effective:

> O Agnes, O my soul, so may thy face be by me when I close my life indeed; so may I, when realities are melting from me, like the shadows which I now dismiss, still find thee near me, pointing upward. (p. 950)

But there is a chill behind the sweetness. And the hand that points upward is, we sense, as cold as death. For, unmistakably and quite deliberately, Dickens has made the gesture of morality equivalent to the gesture of death. In the one previous appearance of this gesture in the narrative, the one on account of which David remembers the gesture, thinks it as characteristic of Agnes, and projects it onto the Agnes who is standing at his side, it means, quite simply, that Dora, his frivolous child wife, has died. Agnes comes downstairs from her patient's bedside to David, who is staring with grief at the dead body of Jip, Dora's little dog.

> "Oh, Agnes! Look, look, here!"
> – That face, so full of pity, and of grief, that rain of tears, that awful mute appeal to me, that solemn hand upraised towards Heaven!

As Agnes displays the proper emotions of the judicious spectator, her hand points upward, both toward heaven and toward Dora, lying dead upstairs. Her gesture connects death and uplift. In the ascent to heaven we see the death of romance, of playfulness, of childhood, of trifles (and "trifles", as David has just been thinking, "make the sum of life" – p. 838). And, since good angels make it their business to vanquish bad angels, it is the death, as well, of Steerforth, of erotic romance.

In the chapter that follows, David makes the connection between Agnes's moral role and death explicit: for he suggests to us that the figure she represents in the stained glass window of his imagination may be none other than the Angel of Death:

> And now, indeed, I began to think that in my old association of her with the stained-glass window in the church, a prophetic foreshadowing of what she would be to me, in the calamity that was to happen in the

> fullness of time, had found a way into my mind. In all that sorrow, from the moment, never to be forgotten, when she stood before me with her upraised hand, she was like a sacred presence in my lonely house. When the Angel of Death alighted there, my child-wife fell asleep – they told me so when I could bear to hear it – on her bosom, with a smile. (p. 839)

Here, there is a movement of thought from Agnes's upraised gesture to the idea that she is a "sacred presence"; but this figure is closely associated, more or less elided, with the thought of the Angel of Death who visits the house. And the "her" on whose bosom Dora falls asleep is, in the narrative, Agnes; but in David's sentence the pronoun most naturally refers to the Angel. In this complex and ambiguous passage, we see how closely David links Agnes with death. Furthermore, at the close of the novel, David once again, and this time explicitly, imagines Agnes presiding at a death – in this case, his own. And she presides with that same gesture, "pointing upward". The gesture represents morality, and represents it as a death in the heart, a cessation of generous outward movement.

This ambivalence toward Agnes (characterized, always, with images of composure, rest, stained glass, tranquillity, as contrasted with Steerforth's restless horizontal movement) is deliberate. And even though the internal plot of the novel ends with a moral marriage, children, and the victory of Agnes, the real plot has a more complicated ending. For it ends, we must realize, with the writing of the entire novel; with the adventures of thought, emotion, and memory that take the hero as author into the shadowy world. It ends with the victory of the novel-writing heart.

It is made abundantly clear that this heart and its activities are concerned with morality. And yet we know perfectly well that Agnes would not approve of this book, or of her husband insofar as he occupies himself as its author. For the activity of memory brings the author, once again, into the living presence of James Steerforth, as in the present tense, again and again, he relives their evening adventures in the moonlight. In those moments he does not reject Agnes; he keeps her in a sanctuary in his heart. And yet he significantly departs from her and from her judgment – and in a way, we feel, in which he does not depart from himself, from his own morality and his own heart.

For we feel that there is, somehow, morality in the willingness to enter into that world of love, loving Steerforth without judgment. The book is not simply displaying to us a tension or even an oscillation between two viewpoints that it shows as irreconcilable – but it shows us, as a coherent movement of one and the same heart, David's movement from the one to the other. David is himself in all his adventures. There is romance in his morality, morality in his romance.

To get clearer about this coherence, we can return to the novel's opening, where David tells us in no uncertain terms that there is a certain cast of imagination that is characteristic of him as novelist, and that this is also a morally valuable way of confronting the world:

> I believe the power of observation in numbers of very young children to be quite wonderful for its closeness and accuracy. Indeed, I think that most grown men who are remarkable in this respect, may with greater propriety be said not to have lost the faculty, than to have acquired it; the rather, as I generally observe such men to retain a certain freshness, and gentleness, and capacity of being pleased, which are also an inheritance they have preserved from their childhood. (p. 61)

David tells us that he is not like most grown men in his childlike attention to and memory for the particularities of the world, in the freshness and susceptibility with which he confronts things. Adult life is seen as blurring the sensibilities, dulling the capacity for pleasure and delight. To write this novel, David has had to escape that blurring. It is clear that this perceptual freshness and this gentleness are what has permitted him to see the entire world of the novel as he wonderfully sees it. And so in this way, insofar as the novel has, through its vividness, a moral power, this childlike imagination has shown itself to be supportive of morality and moral responsiveness. It sees all around, with an intensity that brings sympathy to our hearts.

And yet we know perfectly well that it is this same susceptibility to delight and to the sensuously vivid, this nonjudgmentally loving attitude to the world, that has permitted David to fall in love and to be led outside of morality.[43] What I believe David indicates here, and shows in the construction of the novel as a whole, is that the posture of the heart that is best for morality – most vivid, most gentle and generous, most active in sympathy – is also more susceptible and less judgmental than Agnes's heart is, and is bound, in its mobile attention to particulars, to fall in love, and to feel for the object that it loves a nonjudgmental loyalty that no moral authority, however judicious, can dislodge. (Agnes, we recall, was never really a child. Substitute for her dead mother, guardian of an alcoholic father, she makes her first appearance with keys at her side, "as staid and discreet a housekeeper as the old house could have" – p. 280.)[44] Love is, in a sense, outside of morality, in the sense we have described. And yet it is a natural movement of the most truly human morality, and its fitting completion.[45]

In the act of writing this book, an act of which neither Steerforth nor Agnes would have been capable, David achieves a human completeness that they both fail to attain. His moral spectatorship and his love are, though in tension, all of a piece. His love is full of sympathy and loyalty, his sympathetic spectatorship of loving susceptibility to the particular.

There is one more arm in this novel that we must now consider. And its gesture shows us, I think, how the novel understands the mediating link between the other two. For the third arm that recurs prominently in David's memory is the arm of Peggotty, who lovingly supports his dying mother's head. Peggotty foresees, long before, that she will want that arm, and at the end she takes it:

> Daybreak had come, and the sun was rising, when she said to me, how kind and considerate Mr Copperfield had always been to her, and how he had borne with her, and told her, when she doubted herself, that a loving heart was better and stronger than wisdom, and that he was a happy man in hers. "Peggotty, my dear", she said then, "put me nearer to you", for she was very weak. "Lay your good arm underneath my neck", she said, "and turn me to you, for your face is going far off, and I want it to be near". I put it as she asked; and oh Davy! the time had come when my first parting words to you were true – when she was glad to lay her poor head on her stupid cross old Peggotty's arm – and she died like a child that had gone to sleep! (p. 186)

The gesture, connected with the reflection that a loving heart is better and stronger than wisdom, is, above all, a gesture of loving attention, support, and connection. It is different from our other two gestures, in that it cannot be imagined, even as a gesture, without imagining two people; it is a relation. It is different, too, in that, rather than pointing to or standing for something – even for the presence of someone uniquely loved – it actively *does* something. Agnes's static gesture of uplift, Steerforth's sleepy gesture of erotic presence, neither of these in itself does good for someone in this world. They are, merely, gestures. But this gesture is also an action, an action of love and unquestioning unjudgmental loyalty, of attention and responsiveness to a beloved particular. By being connected with Peggotty, the gesture is linked with the gentle childlike imagination that neither she nor David has ever lost. By being connected with the advice of David's father, it is also connected with the father's love of novels. And the fact that the gesture is a gesture of love and support toward David's mother shows us, even more fundamentally, its significance in his imagination, a way in which he understands, through that gesture, the link between his own delight in particulars and the two worlds of romance and morality.

For David's childlike imagination is not only drawn to the world by a general delight in the perception of the particular. It is drawn, from the first, by a very passionate perception of one particular above all. David's mother is the first particular thing he loves, the first object of the fresh delight, the gentleness, and the pleasure of which he tells us. And his connection to his mother combines, from the first, in a coherent way, perceptions of her beauty and kindness with incipient moral attitudes – above all tenderness, gratitude for support, and a corresponding desire to support and protect; and combines both of these, clearly, with intensely romantic feelings. (This is dramatized in many ways: in his remembrance of his mother's grace and beauty; in his jealousy of Murdstone even before his villainous character is known; in his developing fantasy of himself in the role of his mother's rescuer and true support, a fantasy deeply involved in his novel enacting – for we are told whom he casts as the villain, whom as the hero, and the identity of the heroine can hardly elude us; and finally in the extraordinary fantasy, before his mother's grave, in which he imagines (wishes) that the dead baby in her arms "was myself, as I had once been, hushed forever on her bosom" – p. 187.)

Romance, morality, and a mediating attitude of loyal support and connection are linked for him because they have been linked from the start. The pattern of all his relationships, however various, contains these basic ingredients, the ingredients that mark his earliest fantasies and encounters. And love conquers retentiveness and stern judgment in his heart because loving support, linked with novel-reading, from the first got ahead of the fear of punishment, linked for him with the Murdstone's religious moralism.[46]

David's movement from morality toward Steerforth, and his refusal to judge the person he loves, are, then, motivated not only by romantic desire but by a complex attitude in which desire is linked with active loyalty and support, fantasy with the true perception of the particular. (Steerforth is, to be sure, a parental figure, protective and supportive; but David also, clearly, supports and protects him in his recklessness.) And this active love is linked strongly with susceptibility to romance and erotic desire, through the portrait of the childlike imagination as delighting in the sensuous world. If Agnes, in the novel, represents wisdom – as there is much reason to think she does, learned and religious as she is – David's love emerges as the love that is "better and stronger than wisdom". If Agnes is the judicious spectator, he is, as a mobile participant, stronger than the spectator. His very susceptibility to extramoral danger is part of his strength, and part of the strength of his love. Morality, at its most generous and best, is something mobile and even volatile, something actively caring and sustaining. Its gestures will be nothing more than gestures of death if it does not retain its capability to move beyond itself into love.

In this way, the novel powerfully criticizes, as morally limited and ungenerous, an image of moral judgment dominant in the Scottish–English tradition, substituting for it a more romantic, yet, it is also suggested, a more deeply moral norm too. At the same time it continues, in its own way, the task that Smith assigned to the novel: the task of constituting its readers as moral subjects, according to this new and broader conception of morality. Only now, instead of surrendering romantic fantasy before the judgment of judicious perception, instead of dispelling the shadowy world by calling in the daylight of judicious spectatorship, the reader is encouraged to bring that fantasy and mysterious excitement into the world of reality, and to use the energy of fantasy toward a just and generous vision.[47]

The novel gives us no assurance that a single love, a single human relationship, can by itself contain and combine the sympathy of the spectator, the mystery of the erotic/romantic, and the mobile love of particulars that mediates between them. For, although David's complex attitude seems to have its origin in a single relationship, he represents himself, in later life, as finding the mediation only in the act of novel-writing itself. Like other novelists with tumultuous or problematic personal lives (I think, among others, of Proust), Dickens too – insofar as he makes himself, for us, a character – represents himself as finding only in his craft the moral synthesis he imagines. But the reader is shown, nonetheless, a paradigm and a possibility. If we do not cling rigidly to the ideal of the judicious spectator, but allow ourselves a more kinetic sympathy, susceptible to the fresh perception of the particular, we may find less tension and discontinuity than Adam Smith did between the romantic/erotic and the moral. And we might even discover that in a single adult relationship all of these attitudes could be more or less coherently combined, and could even support and sustain one another, constructing among them a world in which general sympathy, erotic moonlight, and active generous loyalty live together in conversation. Something like the world of this novel.[48]

NOTES AND REFERENCES

1. The sections in quotation marks are taken from *David Copperfield*: see below. The paragraph as a whole is in the spirit of the novel, and contains many paraphrases and allusions.

2. In this essay I use the word "moral" rather than "ethical" as the generic word, following the usage of the moral sentiment tradition. Adam Smith's own terminology (see below) is more complex: for he describes his task as the analysis of the "moral sentiments", but frequently also uses the terminology of virtue and the virtues, probably under the influence of the Stoics.

3. I. Kant, *The Doctrine of Virtue* (Part III of *The Metaphysics of Morals*, Berlin, 1797), trans. M. J. Gregor, Philadelphia, 1979, Akad. 500–1, 447ff; see also *Critique of Practical Reason* (Berlin, 1788), trans. Lewis White Beck, Indianapolis, IN, 1956, Akad. 83ff.

4. B. Spinoza, *Ethics*, Parts III and IV, esp. "Definitions of the Emotions", Def. VI.

5. An effective general criticism of the Kantian position on the emotions and the other sentiments is in Larry Blum, *Friendship, Altruism, and Morality*, London, 1980.

6. There are, of course, many varieties of love, and even of romantic love; the rubric "romantic/erotic", and the descriptions and discussions to follow, will make more concrete the type I have in mind.

7. Adam Smith, *The Theory of Moral Sentiments*, (1st edn, 1759; 6th edn, extensively revised, 1790), ed. D. D. Raphael and A. L. Macfie, Oxford, 1976. Hereafter TMS.

8. TMS, esp. Part I, Sections i–ii. "... the spectator must ... endeavour, as much as he can, to put himself in the situation of the other and to bring home to himself every little circumstance of distress which can possibly occur to the sufferer. He must adopt the whole case of his companion with all its minutest incidents; and strive to render as perfect as possible, that imaginary change of situation upon which his sympathy is founded" (I.i.4.6).

9. The Stoics are referred to prominently throughout, and Part VII contains extensive discussion (and some criticism) of their views. The cognitive nature of the view of passion is made clear from the start: see I.i.1.8, and many other places. Smith is critical of the Stoics for urging the extirpation of the passions, which he regards as elements in complete virtue.

10. Literature is first mentioned very near the beginning of the argument, in I.i.1.4

("tragedy or romance"), and these references form an important part of the account of the spectator throughout Part I.

11. TMS I.ii.1.1.
12. TMS I.ii.l.2.
13. Ibid.
14. TMS I.ii.1.3.
15. See, for example, I.ii.1.2, discussed above; there are many other such passages. But perhaps this is, after all, not such a confusion, since the moral world is, for Smith, the world of the publicly expressible, and whatever cannot with decency be publicly expressed would be ipso facto suspect; see below.
16. TMS I.ii.2.1.
17. TMS I.ii.2.2. Smith is here discussing the origin of our interest in pastoral poetry and other related literary works, and is arguing that we are drawn by the depiction of the lovers' wish for serenity and contentment, not by their love:

> We feel how natural it is for the mind, in a certain situation, relaxed with indolence, and fatigued with the violence of desire, to long for serenity and quiet, to hope to find them in the gratification of that passion which distracts it, and to frame to itself the idea of that life of tranquillity and retirement which the elegant, the tender, and the passionate Tibullus takes so much pleasure in describing; a life . . . free from labour, and from care, and from all the turbulent passions which attend them. Even scenes of this kind interest us most, when they are painted rather as what is hoped than as what is enjoyed. The grossness of that passion, which mixes with and is, perhaps, the foundation of love, disappears when its gratification is far of and at a distance; but renders the whole offensive, when described as what is immediately possessed.

18. TMS I.ii.2.3.
19. Smith has spoken of the disproportion between the passion and the value of the object, as seen from the spectator's viewpoint. But this and other passages depicting the intimate habits of loving exchange and conversation indicate, I think, that the problem is not an *illusion* on the lover's part; it is, rather, a strong response to what cannot be justified as admirable in the public world – to glances, gestures, habits of intimacy. What we are dealing with is a "peculiar habit" of the lovers' imaginations, entrenched ways of seeing and valuing that are idiosyncratic and not publicly communicable. It is not that the lover makes these things up when they aren't there; rather he or she endows them with an importance that the spectator cannot find in them.
20. R. Descartes, *Les Passions de l'Âme*, Part II, Art. VI; Spinoza, *Ethics*, "Definitions of the Passions", Def. VI. For Stoic definitions, see *Stoicorum Veterum Fragmenta*, ed. I. von Arnim, Vol. III, 397–420.
21. Aristotle, *Nicomachean Ethics*, VIII–IX; cf. M. C. Nussbaum, *The Fragility of Goodness*, Cambridge: Cambridge University Press, 1986, ch. 12.
22. On Aristotle, see *Fragility*, ch. 10, pp. 311–312; there is an excellent discussion of this question in unpublished writing by Christine Korsgaard.
23. There are many passages that point in this direction. Consider especially I.ii.1.12, where the fact that the spectator enters little into another's bodily pain is called "the foundation of the propriety of constancy and patience in enduring

it". If the spectator were merely heuristic, he would be not the "foundation" of propriety here, but only a clue as to where propriety (specified in some independent way) was to be found. Similarly, when Smith asks what we ought to feel in a case where our own response to a personal calamity is inclined to be much more violent than that which the spectator would feel, he simply answers without further remark that we should keep our feeling down to that which the spectator would experience (rather than pointing to some independent moral value that the spectator helps us discover); and he specifies the desire of the agent for "a more complete sympathy" with others as the reason why he will be right to leave aside the special involvement he has with his own case (I.i.4.7–8). The passage culminates in a praise of "society and conversation" (I.i.4.10). Similarly, in asking what we should feel for the dead, Smith grants that there is no independent thing there to inquire about – for the dead are dead; but it is the fact that the judicious spectator will grieve that makes such grief appropriate.

24. By asking for the "deeper significance" of the spectator stance I am not returning to the first (heuristic) sort of view. What I am asking is why this particular stance, described as Smith describes it, should be thought to be constitutive of moral appropriateness – why he has built up the spectator in this and not some other way.

25. Other authors who should be considered in this connection are Jane Austen and George Eliot.

26. Henry James, *The Art of the Novel*, New York, 1907, p. 62.

27. All references to *David Copperfield* will be taken from the Penguin edition, ed. Trevor Blount, Harmondsworth, 1966.

28. There may also be a forward reference here to Steerforth's involvement with Emily, who is depicted as similar in age to David, and in some sense his double.

29. Strictly speaking, the love has already begun. For just before this, reflecting on the school rumor that Miss Creakle is in love with Steerforth, David remarks, "I am sure, as I sat in the dark, thinking of his nice voice, and his fine face, and his easy manner, and his curling hair, I thought it very likely" (p. 139).

30. Of Steerforth's preference for pillows, see p. 347, where he arranges for David a room with "pillows enough for six". Curling hair is also a salient trait of Steerforth elsewhere – see pp. 346 and 863. In this way, the concerned reader, staging the scene in imagination, draws in details from other parts of the novel.

31. Here David repeatedly calls Agnes a Good Angel (see p. 436), but denies that Steerforth is correctly called a bad angel: "Agnes, you wrong him very much".

32. See also p. 289: "I feel that there are goodness, peace, and truth, wherever Agnes is; and that the soft light of the coloured window in the church, seen long ago, falls on her always, and on me when I am near her, and on everything around".

33. For the association of Steerforth with horizontal movement "on", see pp. 488 and 489, and the descriptions of him as sailor. See also p. 377: "I knew that his restless nature and bold spirits delighted to find a vent in rough toil and bad weather".

34. See especially his praise of Steerforth to Mr Peggotty (p. 196): praise of Steerforth is David's "favourite theme".

35. In this same scene David tells Mr Peggotty that "it's hardly possible to give him as much praise as he deserves". And the excitement that is, he tells us, in his whole manner as he speaks of Steerforth excites little Emily, who begins to fall in love from this moment.

36. On Steerforth's good looks, see, for example, "very good-looking" (p. 136); "his nice voice, and his fine face, and his easy manner, and his curling hair" (p. 139); "what a noble fellow he was in appearance" (p. 151); "the clustering curls of his hair" (p. 346); "the figure of a handsome well-formed young man" (p. 345); his "handsome head" (p. 488). At p. 345, he wishes to hug Steerforth, but is held back "for very shame, and the fear that it might displease him"; instead "I grasped him by both hands and could not let them go". Here we may have a clue as to why David, in recalling his fascination with Steerforth, and in the scenes of fascination themselves, tends to focus on the *sleeping* Steerforth: shame impedes acknowledgment of his strong feelings at any other time.

37. Strictly speaking, this records David's belief; but it seems, so far as we can tell, to be true; Steerforth values Daisy in a unique way, and blesses him.

38. See p. 288, where she shows him how to study from his schoolbooks. Since David has to be shown how to use them, it is clear (as it is in any case, given the educational methods of the day) that they are not novels.

39. For descriptions of Agnes as "calm", "placid", "quiet", "tranquil", see pp. 279, 280, 288, 326, 430, etc.

40. The play is *Julius Caesar*, significant for the way in which it, too, links love and morality. And notice that David finds something altogether new and better in the historical events, when they are displayed as literature, than he found in them before from his history lessons: "To have all those noble Romans alive before me, and walking in and out for my entertainment, instead of being the stern taskmasters they had been at school, was a most novel and delightful effect".

41. Compare Richard Wollheim, *The Thread of Life*, Cambridge, MA, 1984, on projection and love. On endowing a bodily form with life, see Stanley Cavell, *The Claim of Reason*, New York, 1979, Part IV.

42. Rosa Dartle is the one other character in the novel who both passionately loves Steerforth and sees him as a whole. But her self-absorbed jealous vindictive love is strongly contrasted with David's nonjudgmental generosity. Like Miss Wade in *Little Dorrit*, she shows how a preoccupation with resentment and judgment undercuts the generous outward impulse to love that is for Dickens essential to the moral life. And in the scene in which Rosa harshly confronts Emily we are made to understand how thoroughly her stern judgmental morality, which has its origins, unmistakably, in the fantasy of persecution and injury, differs from David's morality, which has its origins in a different sort of fantasy, loving and concerned with the projection into the world of images of the figures who are most loved. Dickens clearly links the latter sort of imagination with the power to write a novel; and through Miss Wade's narrative in *Little Dorrit* he shows us that imagination of the former sort is incapable of constructing a narrative in which the reader can participate as a friend. In the present passage, in which narrative art charms even Rosa, Dickens indicates that the generous impulses

involved in fiction-making have the power to overcome the angry impulses connected with revenge.

43. As a child, David, we recall, played the role of Tom Jones "for a week together" (p. 106). And he has much in common with that hero, in his combination of warmth and goodness with erotic susceptibility. David is at pains to insist that he played "a child's Tom Jones, a harmless creature"; and in general that the "harm" that was in some of the books "was not there for me; I knew nothing of it". But we are encouraged by his later eroticism to be somewhat skeptical of these protestations – especially since the narrator plainly knows very well what "harm" there is in *Tom Jones*. And it would indeed be a strange reader of Fielding's novel who did not notice its physical, earthy, and erotic content. The entirety of *David Copperfield* is in many ways a continuation of *Tom Jones*, but with the more romantic understanding of love that it now recommends.

44. The portrait of Agnes captures in a striking manner the features of a certain sort of child of an alcoholic parent, as these are emerging in the recent clinical literature. The inability to play or to enjoy childhood, the difficulty in feeling and expressing strong emotion, a judgmental attitude to self and others, a fear of vulnerability – all are striking similarities. In this connection, we can perhaps understand why Agnes is so drawn to David, who has an emotional robustness that she lacks and needs. And though for the most part Agnes remains in her ambivalently drawn moralizing role, the narrative permits her one expression of nonjudgmental individualized love. When she is about to confess her love for David, she repeatedly insists, "I am not myself" (pp. 934–935). And when they do embrace there is, in Agnes's life, a moment of childhood: "And O, Agnes, even out of thy true eyes, in that same time, the spirit of my child-wife looked upon me, saying it was well". Does this single moment produce a more lasting evolution? The descriptions of Agnes at the end of the novel allow us to doubt this. And indeed, since David speaks of the fresh imagination as something preserved from childhood, it seems unlikely that someone who had to that extent been completely deprived of a childhood could ever securely or stably attain it.

45. Dora shows, however, that the childlike imagination is insufficient, without further development, for adult morality. Frozen in early childhood, she lacks both dimensions of David's further development: the erotic and the moral.

46. Dora, by contrast, is shown to lack the particular type of relationship to her parents that would promote onward movement toward adult erotic and moral attitudes. Her determination to go on playing and to refuse responsibility is encouraged by those around her.

47. The novel itself represents itself as a true vision of reality propelled by fantasy of a particular sort.

48. This paper was first presented at a conference on Love at the National Humanities Center; I am grateful to Jean Hagstrum for organizing the conference and inviting the paper. At the conference it had the benefit of stimulating comments by David Halperin, whose Proustian skepticism about the romantic attitudes expressed here produced a lively discussion and provoked me to develop more fully the parts of the paper dealing with the generosity of fantasy. I am also grateful to Amelie Rorty, to Michael de Paul, to Henry Richardson, and

to Christopher Rowe for helpful comments, and to audiences at the Tri-College Colloquium at Amherst College, at Randolph-Macon College (Ashland), at Furman University, at the University of Illinois at Urbana-Champaign, and at Whitman College, for their helpful remarks. Above all I am grateful to Rachel for reading the novel well and getting me to read it again.

Chapter 9

"I–Thou" and "Doctor–Patient": A Relationship Examined

R. S. Downie and Harald Jodalen

The doctor–patient relationship is commonly seen as the central feature of medical practice; it is by means of this relationship that a doctor exercises professional skills and pursues the aims of medicine. The analysis of this relationship is the main concern of this essay.

The Bonds

We can use the word "relationship" in two ways: to stand for the bond which links two or more people, or to stand for the attitudes which bonded people have to each other.[1] As examples of the first kind of relationship we might mention kinship, marriage, business association, or teacher–pupil. As examples of the second kind we might mention fear, pride, respect, envy, contempt, etc. Thus someone seeing an adult with a child might ask what the relationship is between these two, and receive an answer in terms of the first kind of relationship: "teacher and pupil", "father and son", etc. Or he might ask "What sort of relationship do Jones and his son have?" and receive an answer in terms of the second kind of relationship: "Jones loves his son but his son can't stand him."

The two kinds of relationship are connected in various complex ways. For example, if the situation is a business transaction then the attitude of the parties would not characteristically be one, say, of affection or friendship. There are of course no logical impediments to such an attitude developing out of the business transaction, and indeed it is material for romantic comedy when the attitude in the relationship is inappropriate for the bond. What, then, are the special characteristics of a doctor–patient relationship?

Let us begin by examining the bond in the doctor–patient relationship. Typically in the relationship there is inequality of power. It can be argued that because of the dominant position doctors occupy in the relationship with their patients and because, as doctors, they must supply a service, and often assess its success as well, they must be governed more than many other people by principles of ethics. In particular, in this context they must be governed by a desire to be of assistance to their patients, often called "beneficence". The ethics are formalized in a special "bond", which usually takes the form of an institutional role relationship. The need for a formal bond is evident if we consider the significant interventions which doctors can make in the lives of their patients. We could approach this point in another way. We can characterize the doctor as someone who necessarily aims at health. It follows that the doctor's activities intimately bear on human good and harm, and therefore the state will take an interest in them. For example, the state will lay down broad conditions for the qualifications of doctors, or specify when a patient has a legal right to medical care, to hospitalization, and so on. There may even be cases, perhaps of certain infectious or psychiatric disorders, where the doctor has a duty to commit the patient to care against her wishes. In the latter case, the authority by which a person may be compulsorily detained in a hospital obtains legally in Britain from an Act of Parliament. The professional bond is constituted, additionally, by rather vaguer sets of rules, or even expectations, which doctors and patients have of each other. Doctors also refer to this as the "ethics" of their professions, and the medical profession is very strict about enforcing its own discipline on these matters.

It is important that the doctor–patient relationship should be constituted, at least partly, by these legal and quasi-legal institutional bonds, for at least the following reasons. First, doctors and all health and welfare workers, by the nature of their job, intervene in existentially crucial ways in the lives of others. This is a serious matter and its consequences for a patient can be enormous. It is therefore in the interests of patients that there should be some sort of professional entitlement to intervene. In other words, if they are not simply to be busybodies, doctors must have the *right to intervene*, and if they have the right to intervene they must have duties and responsibilities; the concept of an institution encapsulates these ideas of rights, duties, and responsibilities.

A second reason is that doctors must ask about many intimate details of people's lives, for example about their marriages; and they also may conduct examinations of people's bodies. Questioning of this sort, far less physical examination, can create situations in which people could be exploited, or which could be embarrassing even to doctors themselves. The fact that it is an institutional bond which brings doctors together with their patients provides *emotional insulation* for both parties in such situations. Moreover, there must be some assurance that no untoward use be made of the information, that it will not be passed on to neighbours, etc. But the idea of an institution entails that of rules, and the rules can, thirdly, impose *confidentiality* on the doctor and provide security for the patient.

Fourthly, doctors are given a measure of *security* by virtue of the fact that they work inside an institutional framework. There are various aspects to this. For instance, it is good for all professions to have ways and means whereby new skills and knowledge can be shared, and in general whereby members of a profession can support and encourage each other. Again, doctors require legal or similar professional protection from exploitation, unfair criticism or legal action against them by their patients. Reciprocally there must be some institutional mechanism whereby the professions criticize themselves and look for ways of improving their services to the public. These then are some of the reasons for which a complex legal and institutional structure has grown up governing directly and indirectly the relationships between doctors and their patients.

There are various desirable and undesirable aspects to this. For present purposes the relevant point is that when the doctor or other health worker appears to be acting as an individual she is also acting as a *representative* of her profession, and to a lesser extent also of the state. In other words, the individual action of a doctor or other health worker expresses also the collective values of her profession; individual responsibility becomes collective responsibility since it is through individuals that their professions are represented. We might say that individual doctors represent their professions in two senses. First, they are the ascriptive representatives, in that the profession authorizes their actions, having sanctioned their training. Second, they represent the values of the profession insofar as they act in terms of its ethics, and its ethics is all pervasive in the actions and attitudes of the individual doctor.

The aspects of the professional relationship which I have been discussing can be expressed through the concept of a social role, understood for this purpose as being a set of rights and duties to be analysed in terms of institutional concepts. When individuals have accepted a role they are authorized to act in certain ways. This, the traditional view of the doctor–patient relationship, depicts it as a role relationship with the features we have noted; it is through the role so described that doctors and patients are bonded.

We have so far used the concept of a role as a way of linking medicine as an institution with the interests of *specific* patients, but it also enables us to refer to a broader social function which involves the doctor's duty to speak out with authority on matters of social justice and social utility. For example, doctors have a duty to speak out on broad issues of health; for example, they might speak out against cigarette advertising. In this kind of way the professions can be seen to have the important social function of regulators in the interest of general utility and justice. This is another aspect of the doctor–patient relationship, one in which doctors are concerned with categories or broad classes of patients rather than with specific patients.

In sum, then, the traditional view of the doctor–patient relationship depicts it in terms of a set of institutional bonds, legal and quasi-legal, which can be united in the concept of a social role.

Attitudes

To describe the doctor–patient relationship in terms of the institutional bonds which unite doctor to patient is to tell only half the story, and perhaps the less important half. As we have said, relationships also involve attitudes, and it is to that aspect of the relationship that we now turn.

Before we can say anything specific about the doctor–patient relationship, however, it is necessary to analyse more generally some key features of attitudes. The most important point about any attitude for our purposes is that it is what philosophers call "intentional": the attitude is necessarily directed at an object seen in a specific way. This is what can be called the "formal object" of the attitude. For example, the formal object of the attitude of hope is an imagined good. It is the formal object of the attitude which determines its structure and content, as "an imagined good" gives structure and content to the attitude "hope". In order to understand the nature of a doctor's attitude to patients we must therefore consider the formal object of that attitude, which will be a patient seen in a certain way, or range of ways. It will be of interest to consider what these ways are, and whether some are more desirable or morally appropriate than others. As a preliminary to this we shall draw Martin Buber's[2] distinction between an "I-Thou" relationship and an "I-It" relationship. It will be helpful for our purposes to use his extended example of the range of attitudes one may adopt towards a tree.

I consider a tree.
I can look on it as a picture: stiff column in a shock of light, or splash of green shot with the delicate blue and silver of the background.
I can perceive it as movement: flowing veins on clinging, pressing pith, suck of the roots, breathing of the leaves, ceaseless commerce with earth and air – and the obscure growth itself.
I can classify it in a species and study it as a type in its structure and mode of life.
I can subdue its actual presence and form so sternly that I recognise it only as an expression of law – of the laws in accordance with which a constant opposition of forces is continually adjusted, or of those in accordance with which the component substances mingle and separate.
I can dissipate it and perpetuate it in number, in pure numerical relation.
In all this the tree remains my object, occupies space and time, and has its nature and constitution.
It can, however, also come about, if I have both will and grace, that in considering the tree I become bound up in relation to it. The tree is now no longer It. I have been seized by the power of exclusiveness.
To effect this it is not necessary for me to give up any of the ways in which I consider the tree. There is nothing from which I would have to turn my eyes away in order to see, and no knowledge that I would have to forget. Rather is everything, picture and movement, species and type, law and number, indivisibly united in this event.
Everything belonging to the tree is in this: its form and structure, its colours and chemical composition, its intercourse with the elements and with the stars, are all present in a single whole.
The tree is no impression, no play of my imagination, no value depending on my mood; but it is bodied over against me and has to do with me, as I with it – only in a different way.
Let no attempt be made to sap the strength from the meaning of the relation:relation is mutual.
The tree will have a consciousness, then, similar to our own? Of that I have no experience. But do you wish, through seeming to succeed in it with yourself, once again to disintegrate that which cannot be disintegrated? I encounter no soul or dryad of the tree, but the tree itself.
If I face a human being as my *Thou*, and say the primary word *I-Thou* to him, he is not a thing among things, and does not consist of things.
This human being is not *He* or *She*, bounded from every other *He* and *She*, a spe-

cific point in space and time within the net of the world; nor is he a nature able to be experienced and described, a loose bundle of named qualities. But with no neighbour, and whole in himself, he is *Thou* and fills the heavens. This does not mean that nothing exists except himself. But all else lives in *his* light.

With this extended quotation from Buber as a background let us now consider the range of possible attitudes a doctor may adopt towards a patient. Notoriously, but perhaps not uncommonly, the formal object of the doctor's attitude will be the patient seen as a set of symptoms – the fracture in bed three, or the neurotic who is always complaining, or the 20th patient who has come in complaining of feeling dizzy and sick. These ways of seeing patients will be perfectly familiar to most doctors, and no doubt there are many similar ways in which patients can be seen. Clearly they correspond to Buber's attitude to the tree when it is seen as the object of a range of possible sciences. When doctors see patients in such ways they are seeing the patient in terms of a range of medical sciences. The patient is being identified with a range of physical, psychological, or behavioural symptoms and the understanding which doctors have of a patient seen in this way is technical. Doctor and patient are in an "I–It" relationship because the doctor's attitude is characterized by, or its formal object is, the patient seen as sets of typical symptoms.

Now received wisdom in medical ethics over the past few decades would condemn this way of seeing patients. We have been reminded by scores of writers that "the patient is a person". Yet it is surely essential that the patient should be seen as a set of symptoms if the doctor is to provide any effective treatment. There has been a huge volume of literature about "deep caring" and the like, so that it is easy to forget that most patients are in the clinic for medical treatment and therefore must be seen in terms of their symptoms. But nothing Buber says excludes this. He is quite explicit that when he enters into the special relationship with the tree "it is not necessary for me to give up any of the ways in which I consider the tree". His suggestion is that it may be possible at the same time as he sees the tree scientifically or aesthetically to see it in another manner. We can now ask how, in addition to through the filter of their technical attitude, doctors can see their patients.

One answer might be that the doctor can see the patient as an individual. This does not mean discarding what might be termed the "medical model" of the doctor–patient relationship, for to see patients as individuals may just be to see them in terms of their case histories. For example, a given patient, Mr X, might be seen as presenting with a *typical* set of symptoms – high blood pressure, high cholesterol, a smoker, and so on – and the doctor might see him in terms of *typical* biological and statistical probabilities as likely to have an infarct. But the doctor may *also* see him in terms of his individual case history, as someone who is anxious about his family, his job, and possible redundancy, who is working too hard, and so on. Does this individuating of the doctor's attitude – from seeing the patient as a set of generalized symptoms to seeing a patient who has this case history – change the doctor's attitude from the mode of "I–It" to "I–Thou"? The second attitude certainly adds something of importance, both medically and morally, but it is not clear that the *mode* of the attitude has changed. As a result of looking at the patient through a case history the doctor does not seem to be "bound up in relation to [him]". The doctor, as it were, is still on the outside of the relationship, and the patient is still an "It", even if a specific "It".

It might be suggested that what is missing is the element of the human. Symptoms and case histories are for the doctor objective data, but for the patient they may well be a source of pain, discomfort, and anxiety. Additionally, the patient will be worried about what treatment, if any, the doctor can prescribe. In a word, what might be said to be lacking from the symptoms and the case-history models of the doctor–patient relationship is the awareness that the patient is *vulnerable*. We have already noted, in discussing the bond, that there is institutional and legal protection for patients because of their vulnerability, and it now seems reasonable to argue, that if the doctor sees the patient as vulnerable, the appropriate attitude towards this formal object is one of compassion or beneficence.

Something of importance has certainly now been noted. In particular, it has been recognized that the doctor must acknowledge the patient's humanity, and it is possible to do this through the adoption of the attitude of beneficence or compassion without losing any of the essential technical elements in the doctor's attitude already noted.

Nevertheless, there are two reasons why this suggestion falls short of the "I–Thou" relationship. These reasons come, as it were, from opposite directions. The first is that a doctor may see a patient as vulnerable but not feel compassion, or anything at all. This does not mean that the doctor is emotionally stunted, but perhaps means only that he is very busy, or has found that feelings interfere with clinical skills and judgement. The second reason, which is perhaps the more fundamental, is that to see patients as vulnerable, suffering, or the like is to see them in terms of only half their humanity, and perhaps the less important half. Even vulnerable patients have a dignity in their suffering and this must be acknowledged as much as or more than their suffering. Indeed, when this dignity is ignored, we may find creeping back into the doctor's attitude elements of the paternalism for which doctors were much criticized a generation ago. Paternalism is a dangerous virus, and it is easily communicated via attitudes such as "deep caring". But even if the doctor can avoid falling into the trap of paternalism there is still something missing in the beneficent attitude of the doctor towards the vulnerable patient, that is, if we wish to think of the doctor–patient relationship as a form of "I–Thou" relationship.

It might be said that what is missing in the analysis is the point that patients have *rights* to a doctor's services, and the doctor's awareness of the patient's rights is the missing element in the attitude as so far analysed. But this suggestion must be treated with great caution. If we really mean that the patient has rights to *require* treatment from the doctor, we have transformed the doctor–patient relationship into a salesperson–customer relationship. Now there are a number of problems arising from this approach, but for our purposes it is not a helpful move for the obvious reason that a salesperson and a customer view each other as links in an "I–It" chain. This model, then, will not help us, even if we ignore the many problems of seeing the professional doctor–patient relationship as a commercial one.

It might be said, however, that to admit that patients have rights is not be forced down the commercial road. The rights which patients have may be not to require the doctor to deliver certain services or treatments, but rather to have their views considered and their consent or refusal of treatment respected. Concepts such as "patient autonomy" are in the background of this approach and give rise to "partnership" or "contractual" models of the doctor–patient relationship. Let us consider briefly these slightly different models.

The contractual model, as the term suggests, is based on a legal analogy. It certainly limits paternalism, but it has serious drawbacks for our purposes. First, a legal contract contains specific undertakings, whereas a medical relationship tends to be more open-ended. Secondly, the point of contracts is to remove the need for trust between the contracting parties but, if trust is withdrawn from the doctor–patient relationship, very little is left of it. We have certainly not thereby created the "I–Thou" relationship.

The partnership model does better. Trust is essential to partnership, and partnerships have a much wider remit than contracts. Partnership suggests working together to plan care and to share responsibility for decisions. Above all it suggests the mutual respect which is essential to a true relationship between persons. It therefore seems to be the model which opens the door to the "I–Thou" relationship.

Unfortunately, it has some features which mean that it does not fit all aspects of the doctor–patient relationship. A partnership presupposes that there are two or more autonomous persons respecting each other in a relationship of equality. But in the doctor–patient relationship equality does not exist. The relationship is inevitably unequal in terms of its total power. The doctor knows more, and decides what to communicate to the patient and what to withhold. The patient is sick, vulnerable, perhaps in hospital or in a clinic, and as a result insecure. Moreover, the doctor will have a team of other professionals to back up her decision. For these reasons and others, the doctor–patient relationship cannot be one of equality. It therefore cannot be a partnership in the full sense, although elements of partnership ought to be present. If therefore the "I–Thou" relationship is one of equality then the doctor–patient relationship cannot in principle be of that kind.

But is the "I–Thou" relationship necessarily one of equality? Buber did not seem to think so. Certainly in the passage we have quoted he seems to think that it is possible to enter into that special relationship with a tree, and of course he holds that we can enter into such a relationship with God, and there is not exactly equality there! It seems then that, even if doctors and patients are not always in a relationship of equality, and even if through illness or serious disability a patient is not fully autonomous, it might still be possible for the doctor to see the patient as a "Thou". Note too, in support of this approach, that the "I–Thou" relationship need not be mutual. Buber enters into the relationship with the tree but he denies that the tree has a special consciousness. He encounters no "soul or dryad of the tree, but the tree itself". Pulling together the threads we might seem to be on the verge of a solution. We have argued that a patient can be seen as a set of symptoms, as a case history, as one who is vulnerable, and as one who has rights to be respected. It is tempting to say that to see the patient as a "Thou" is to see him in an organic unity of all these modes. If the doctor can hold all these together in a single attitude, she will have succeeded in seeing the patient as a "Thou". We said that an attitude is characterized by its formal object. Is the "I–Thou" relationship the outcome of the doctor seeing the patient as an organic whole? Holistic care is certainly a fashionable term!

Unfortunately there is a serious drawback to this analysis. When Buber entered into the "I–Thou" relationship with the tree it was precisely when and because he responded to the *treeness* of the tree, to its being a tree. But *patients* do not in a comparable way have a being. The concept of a patient is an abstraction from the totality of the person. In a similar way, we might enter into an "I–Thou" relationship with Mr X but not with a business man, even though Mr X is a business man.

Many philosophers would agree with this and argue that it is for exactly these reasons that patients should be seen as persons, because we can certainly enter into the "I–Thou" relationship with persons. But what is being here proposed? Is it that the *doctor–patient* relationship should be replaced by a *doctor–person* relationship? This is an absurd view. The doctor must deal with patients, or in other words with persons in certain restricted aspects of their total existence. Medical practice would become impossible if doctors and patients saw each other as persons in the full sense. It is the role relationship - the bond we have earlier discussed - which is the essential condition of medical practice. Have we then ruled out the possibility of the doctor–patient relationship being an "I–Thou" relationship? Is the best we can expect that the doctor should be technically competent, compassionate, and respect the patient's consent and refusal of treatment? Well, if that were the relationship it would be a good one. But it would barely be the "I–Thou" relationship. Is there more to be said?

We could say that, *in addition* to seeing the patient as a patient, the doctor could see the patient as a person. What does this mean? We must draw a distinction between a "medical good", the promotion of which is the intrinsic aim of medicine, and the patient's "total good", which will include the medical good but much else besides about which only the patient is aware. There is a tendency in any profession to read the whole of someone's personality in terms of the limited aspects which one may be professionally concerned with. For example, a university tutor may see a student entirely in terms of her performance in essays or discussions, whereas for the student this may be comparatively unimportant.

Likewise, there is an inevitable tendency for a doctor to medicalize every aspect of life and to forget that a medical good is only one among a range of goods. Certainly doctors must concentrate on promoting the medical good of their patients - that is the essence of their aim as a profession - but they must see this medical good in a larger context.

Let us take an analogy. Imagine a musical child who plays the Chopin D flat Nocturne at a music competition. The adjudicator says to the child: "You have played the Nocturne accurately and have observed the phrasing and dynamics faithfully, but you will play it much better when you have had three love affairs and two disappointments!" The adjudicator means that, although the Nocturne was played well technically, and the performance was even a musical one, it nevertheless lacked something. It was played in an emotional vacuum; it lacked a human context, or it was played from the outside, or the inner meaning was missing. In a similar way, a doctor could treat a patient in a way which was technically excellent, and the doctor might also show compassion and respect the patient's autonomous decision. Yet there might be something lacking, although not anything the patient has a right to complain about, and indeed the patient might not detect its absence. What might be lacking is the doctor's awareness of the total context of the patient, the awareness that the patient has a wider life. How can this awareness be shown? It can be shown in quite simple ways, such as through a comment on matters unconnected with the patient's illness – a football match, a book the patient happens to be reading. Such incidental comments can show an awareness that the patient has a *history*, a before and after beyond the medical relationship, and a *geography*, places and areas of life which have nothing to do with the clinic. Through such simple means the patient will, momentarily, cease to be "a nature able to be experienced and described, a loose bundle of named qualities. But with no neighbour, and whole in himself, he is *Thou* and fills the heavens. This does not mean that nothing exists except himself. But all else lives in *his* light".

We shall look at three further questions: theoretical, ethical, and educational. The theoretical question concerns the nature of the attitudes involved. We said that attitudes are intentional – directed towards formal objects. We have also said that, to the extent that the doctor sees the patient as a patient, and he logically must do that, the attitude will be an "I–It" attitude or range of attitudes, even if this "I–It" attitude is also humane, governed by ethical principles, and so on. But we have also mentioned that if the doctor has both "grace and will" she can become "bound up in relation" to the patient. In other words, the doctor may also, at times, have an "I–Thou" attitude to the person who is, among other things, a patient. How is it possible for the doctor to switch modes from one sort of relationship to another and back? There seems to be a problem here if we become fascinated by a misleading analogy. It is easy to think of the intentional attitude as being like a searchlight, either on or off. But perhaps (to continue the lighting metaphor) it is more like the flickering and varied coloured lights of a disco. It is possible for human beings to switch among a range of different technical attitudes, and then to a range of personal attitudes. It is this facility which makes it possible for the doctor–patient relationship to be at the same time an "I–It" and an "I–Thou" relationship.

The ethical point is that not all patients will choose to have in any sense or at all an "I–Thou" relationship with a doctor. They may wish to keep their personal lives entirely to themselves. This is their right and it is no personal failing on the patients' part if they should wish to exercise it. Patients, even terminal patients, may not wish to reveal themselves to anyone in the health care professions. And they should be spared the attentions of the whole tribe of counsellors and pseudo "experts" in emotional care. There is no expertise in the "I–Thou" relationship.

The educational point concerns the question of raising the consciousness of medical students and doctors to the possibility of these wider issues. Medical training is long; medical students tend to be taught together, without being much in contact with other students; doctors' friends tend to be other doctors. It is not surprising then that life for doctors becomes exclusively medicalized. Over the past two decades an attempt has been made to broaden the attitudes of medical students by teaching medical ethics. Now this discipline may help with decision-making, but to the extent that it is *medical* ethics it does not help with consciousness-raising. How, if at all, can the latter be done?

One way might be for medical students to be encouraged to take subjects other than medical ones as part of their medical curriculum. This happens to some extent in the USA, where medicine is a postgraduate degree and some medical students have first studied non-scientific subjects. It will happen in the near future in the UK, where the General Medical Council has insisted that a medical curriculum must contain "Special Study Modules", which need not be medical. It is possible for such modules to be "humanities", and texts for such courses already exist.[3] At the end of the day, however, this wider consciousness can come not from books but only from life itself. Perhaps medical schools should follow the lead of the adjudicator at the music competition and encourage their students to have "Three love affairs and two disappointments"!

Conclusion

We have argued that the term "relationship" has two aspects: it is a bond and an attitude. In the doctor–patient relationship the bond consists of the formal, quasi-legal links which safeguard the roles of doctor and patient. The attitudinal side to the doctor–patient relationship is much more complex. The relationship must always be a technical one, in which case the attitude must be an "I–It" attitude. And this may be all that is possible or desirable for some patients and some doctors. But it may be that through "will and grace" it is possible for at least some doctors and some patients to be additionally in an "I–Thou" relationship. This possibility requires the doctor to have a heightened consciousness, which may come from a counter-culture such as the arts, but may also come from a broad experience of the non-medical aspects of human life.

NOTES AND REFERENCES

1. R. S. Downie and B. G. Charlton, *The Making of a Doctor*: Oxford: Oxford University Press, 1992.
2. M. Buber, *I and Thou*, 1923, trans. R. Gregor Smith, Edinburgh: T. & T. Clark, 1937, p. 78.
3. R. S. Downie, *The Healing Arts: An Illustrated Oxford Anthology*, Oxford: Oxford University Press, 1994.

Chapter 10
Is Man a Moral Being?

Arne Johan Vetlesen

If another were not counting on me, would I be capable of keeping my word, of maintaining myself?

Paul Ricoeur

I

Is man a moral being?

The question is seldom posed in this straightforward manner. Yet our philosophical tradition suffers from no lack of attempts to come up with an answer to it. Man is not a moral being, but he may become one – asserts Hobbes. His becoming a moral being is a choice, an option he may pursue or decide not to. There is first man as he "is": a primitive being, a brute among brutes, a presocial creature busy keeping himself alive from one day to the next. Survival is a tireless struggle. Not only is Nature a severe master; her riches as scarce as they are precious. To make matters worse, other men will appear on the scene to take away from each man what he, laboriously, may have succeeded in extracting from Nature. The struggle for survival is a struggle against other men. In this "state of Nature", the mere existence of others means a threat to each man's existence.

There is a way out, however. Man is a being endowed with the gift of reason. When he reasons, he realizes that all men share the same fear of death. The threat to my life that the other man is to me, I am to his. Since our fate is common, a common way out must be found. As long as all men fight each other, no one will ever be safe. What each man wants for himself is security. Now reason asserts that security can indeed be attained – on the condition that each man agrees to cease threatening the lives of others. To end the fight of all against all, a covenant must be joined by all men alike. Thus is the sovereign, the Leviathan established: by the free consent of all men, by the parties who recognize that their self-interests – to secure for each his life, liberty, and property – are best served by swearing obedience to the Leviathan.

What Hobbes portrays, then, is a shift: Man "is" a presocial creature; his capacity for reason however convinces him that his need for security can be met provided he leaves the "original" state of Nature behind and willingly joins other men in a "social contract".

The shift implied means also a shift from a premoral to a moral existence. It is only within the juridical framework set up by a social contract that obligations and rights are properly ascribed to men, and likewise that goods admit of a distribution deemed just or unjust among the subjects affected by it.

In short, even if man "is" not a moral being, he may choose to become one. Man can be moralized. However, when man is moralized in the sense entailed in Hobbes, he is so inasmuch as he himself freely allows for it. To leave a premoral order behind in order to participate in a moral one is a choice man is free either to make or not to make. And when he does make it, he does so because reason informs him that his need for security is better served within a social contract than outside of it. Thus the path from the premoral to the moral is a path *chosen* on the grounds of being *advocated* by the voice of enlightened self-interest.

Hobbes' answer to the question, Is man a moral being? is starkly opposed to that given by Aristotle. In his *Nicomachean Ethics*, Aristotle is quick to point out that, when we study ethics, we study what man is. Ethics, properly understood, is preoccupied with what man does, with *praxis*; and to know what man does, and how, we need to know first what kind of a being man is. There is no doubt in Aristotle that man "is" a moral being; only as such are his ways, his deliberations and deeds, intelligible to us, susceptible to our evaluation and thus to our praise and blame. Man is an actor because he is a centre of motion and rest; an actor is a being who contains within himself "a principle of motion and change"; and what we are up to as agents is to "deliberate about things that are in our power and can be done".[1] Insofar as the agent is the origin of initiative and of changes brought about in the world, his actions are to count as voluntary and, furthermore, they are something for which the agent must be prepared to assume responsibility.

That man is free in the sense of having a capacity for voluntary action is not denied by Hobbes. The difference between Hobbes and Aristotle turns not on the issue of man's freedom but on that of man's social nature. Man, says Hobbes, starts out as an egoist. Man is a loner; his being-for-himself precedes his being-with as well as his being-for-others. When men appear in the plural, they do so under conditions of mutual enmity. Man is a suspicious being, and in the state of Nature he has every reason to approach other men with distrust. Since each man knows his own egoism only too well, he entertains no illusions about the motives of others, no matter what they may say to lure one into relaxing one's guard. In these presocial circumstances, man may be brutish; nonetheless, he is him*self*, that is to say, he does not await any not-yet-erected social order in order to realize his essence or his being *qua* man.

The latter, of course, is the view taken by Aristotle. It is not only that man's sociality is part and parcel of his being *qua* man; it is also that his being a social being is what truly makes him a moral one. To be just, declares Aristotle, we have to do just actions; and this holds for all the moral virtues. To become virtuous, we need to cultivate and thereupon to exercise certain dispositions in our selves; and, significantly, such cultivation, habituation, and exercise can take place only in the medium of interaction with others. Hence a virtue such as justice is other-oriented in a twofold sense, involving the moment of genesis as well as that of extension: justice is fostered by interacting with others and taking just persons as one's model; and it is exercised towards others, not towards oneself. Interpersonal interaction is therefore a *sine qua non* for the realization of man's nature *both* as a social and as a moral being. The individual prior to or somehow outside of any social setting is unintelligible to Aristotle; such a being, he tells us, not quite able to conceive of it, "can only be a monster or a God".

Aristotle's point is that the individual is never in a position to seek for the good or to exercise the virtues only *qua* individual. His or her belonging to society will be recognized by the individual as a good in itself without which all other goods would be unattainable. The "self" in Aristotle is not in any way detachable from its social and historical context.

The Aristotelian notion of selfhood is brought into particularly sharp relief if contrasted with an existentialist doctrine such as Sartre's. The self as portrayed by early Sartre believes itself to be radically free. The

Sartrean self is free to question, negate, or "transcend" what it typically takes to be the merely contingent features of its social existence. The individual of which Sartre speaks does not view himself or herself as belonging to a community, let alone as having any obligations whatsoever to a larger social world. Belongingness and obligations are viewed as wholly negative, as artificial constraints that would only restrict the agent's zone of operation and so more fundamentally what has come to be understood as the agent's freedom.

This connects with the question concerning man as a moral being. In Sartre's conception, to be a moral agent is to be able to *stand back* from each and every situation in which one may happen to be involved. Accordingly, moral agency is located not in socially defined roles or practices but in the *self* – a self, that is, having no teleologically conceived essence to actualize and no necessary or inescapable social content to help guide its deliberations. For this self, identity is not something socially derived and fixed; identity is nothing substantial. Rather, identity is freely chosen, and the more it is chosen by way of opposing and questioning what is expected by socially upheld conventions, the more "authentic" will be the choice of identity. Moreover, such a choice is not binding; it is always an open option to change one's mind about who one is and who one wishes to be. It is precisely because this self is in and for itself nothing that it can "be" anything, assume any role, or take any point of view. Fundamentally unsituated and uncommitted, this "democratized" self can slip into, drop out of, and move between an endless series of unconnected situations, roles, and identities; belonging nowhere, this self sees itself as realizing its *freedom* precisely to the degree that it is entirely unbound by and set over and against the social world, the latter being not something to which it belongs but an arena spanning the plurality of selves and on which they all pursue their more or less conflicting projects.

In Aristotle, the individual is nothing without others. It is thanks to the presence of others around me that I become a person, someone accountable for his actions and, moreover, someone identifiable as the "same" person throughout the entirety of his life. In Sartre, by contrast, the other is a threat. The world was my world; however, with the appearance of the other the world ceases to be centred around me and the projects I pursue in it. The other brings about a restructuring of the world to the effect that my freely projected possibilities turn into arrested, "dead" possibilities. Brought about by the presence of the other is a modification of my very being-in-the-world. Now this modification is not something I welcome as an enrichment of my being, let alone as something indispensable for my becoming what I truly am, namely a human among humans, to allude to Aristotle. On the contrary, the modification in question is something I *suffer* as imposed upon me: thanks to the other I am furnished with an "outside" from which I shall forever remain alienated, even though – nay, more subtly, precisely because – the outside in question is *mine*. The being that I am and cannot choose to not-be for the other is indubitably *my* being. Yet this peculiar new thing, this being-for, is not my making but the other's. I have not asked for this being, I have no need for it to become what and who I am, or wish to be, once "being" it, all I desire is to get rid of it, to break free from it; this, however, proves an impossible project. No wonder, then, that the other is experienced as threatening.

So whereas in Aristotle the others sustain and help preserve my very being as a human and moral being, in Sartre the emergence of the other causes a transformation of my being perceived as threatening insofar as the other undermines my freedom. On Sartre's premises, the appearance of the other will fill me with ambivalence. On the one hand, the other is a promise, a reason for hope, since I realize that only an other, a free consciousness, can possibly yield the recognition I seek. Only another freedom can do justice to myself *qua* free being. On the other hand, this promise is never fulfilled in reality by the other in her relations with me precisely because she is a free other, a subject just like me, and thus capable of imposing upon me an outside and so frustrate the undistorting recognition *qua* free subject I was hoping to receive from her. The dialectic between free consciousnesses each desiring that the other yield a recognition that leaves the for-itself unaltered in its being, adding nothing to it but quite simply affirming it – this dialectic cannot but run into an impasse.[2]

On Sartre's analysis, the *look* of the other signifies the ultimate expression of his power – his objectifying power over me. The look of the other transcends my transcendence, is the limit to my freedom, and therefore threatens to nullify all my projects. To be exposed to the other's gaze is to be exposed absolutely. In the look, the other's freedom devours mine. No escape route is available. I am not supported in my being by the fact that there are others, as Aristotle holds. And even though in Hobbes the others are approached with distrust as posing a threat to my life and liberty, my encounter with others does not signify a modification or metamorphosis touching my very being. Hobbes depicts others as affecting me merely in my material being; driven by fear of continued fight all-against all on the one hand and the prospect of attaining security for my life on the other, I am motivated to take the step from a presocial state of nature to membership in a social contract. But in Sartre the change brought about by the other is not at all to be located on a material plane, as involving me in a struggle for survival under conditions of need and scarcity (only in his late work *Critique of Dialectical Reason* does Sartre include this material dimension).[3] The change brought about by the other, contends early Sartre, is not material, it is not even social; it is ontological. In Sartre's terminology, "being-for-others is not an ontological structure of the for-itself";[4] it is *added* to the for-itself. Explains Sartre:

> If there is an Other, whatever or whoever he may be, whatever may be his relations with me, and without his acting upon me in any way except by the pure upsurge of his being – then I have an outside, I have a *nature*. My original fall is the existence of the Other. Shame – like pride – is the apprehension of myself as a nature although that very nature escapes me and is unknown as such.[5]

Neither supporting nor affirming my being, the other in fact undermines it. I am not enriched by the other's imposing a "nature" upon me, by her conferring upon me a peculiar being-for-him, that is to say, a being-for-others. Sartre tells us that the other steals my world, robs me of my being, constitutes the death of my possibilities, in short, marks an absolute limit to my freedom. The message is expressed in the same negative spirit, by way of summing up all the investigated concrete relations with others: "Conflict is the original meaning of being-for-others".[6]

II

Let us turn now to Levinas. We shall find in Levinas an altogether different picture of our relations with others from that witnessed in such thinkers as Aristotle, Hobbes, and Sartre. The latter three thinkers representing such a variety of outlooks, one would perhaps assume that between them they exhaust the principal positions available. Levinas' ethics is testimony that this is not so.

Levinas' other is sheer weakness, not sheer force. He appears precisely not as a power marking the boundaries of my pursuits. My encounter with the other does not spell conflict. The encounter does not take place according to some stubborn logic of antagonism. No contingently "given" condition of material scarcity and hence human hostility (Hobbes), no inescapable because ontological structure dictating conflict over mutual recognition among "free" consciousnesses (Sartre) lays the ground on which the encounter occurs. The look is not the paradigm for the entire repertoire of relations with others. Rather, says Levinas, the other is a *face*.

What does this mean? For a start, the other's appearing as *face* instead of as *look* means her coming to my attention in an ambiguous, twofold manner: as a master commanding me *and* as a being that is utterly defenceless, vulnerable, nude. Instead of stealing my freedom from me, the other gives it meaning in presenting it with a task: the face of the other issues an appeal to me to assume responsibility for his fate, first and foremost *to choose not to kill him*. In this reversal of Sartre's portrait, it is the Other *qua* destitute, weak, and frail that commands me. Hence there is non-symmetry here too, only now I am not paralysed in my freedom through the other's transcendence of it from a position of assumed superiority. Rather the other precisely *qua* destitute, meaning incapable of putting up resistance, meaning "an easy match" if I so wish, is what spurs me to act.

> The face is exposed, menaced, as if inviting us to an act of violence: At the same time, the face is what forbids us to kill. . . .The first word of the face is the "Thou shalt not kill". It is an order. There is a commandment in the appearance of the face, as if a master spoke to me. However, at the same time, the face of the other is destitute . . . There is here a relation not with a very great resistance, but with something absolutely other: the resistance of what has no resistance – the ethical resistance.[7]

Hence for Levinas "the force of the Other is already and henceforth moral".[8] The vulnerability of the face, not the look *qua* challenge to my freedom, is what issues an appeal producing awe instead of violence.

The face is not given to us as a product of knowledge. Writes Levinas, "the relation with the face is not an object-cognition".[9] To appreciate the importance of this, we must note that Levinas holds of knowledge in general that the goal of comprehension is to approach the known being in such a manner that its alterity with .regard to the knowing being vanishes: "The process of cognition is . . . identified with the freedom of the knowing being encountering nothing which . . . could limit it"[10]. Accordingly cognition fulfils its objective when the knowing being succeeds in depriving the known being of its otherness. In this way, says

Levinas, "the other is reduced to the same". What was met upon by consciousness as exterior to it, other to it, is taken into it, is turned into yet another element contained in the "interior" that is the homeground of consciousness *à la* Cartesian *cogito*. To "know" something therefore is to suspend and annul its character as not-yet-known, as residing in the exterior rather than in the interior. Knowledge succeeds as accommodation of the originally other, as accomplished containment.

Having rejected the path of knowledge, we may ask how on Levinasian premises it is possible to enter into a relationship with the other. A relationship, that is, where the otherness of the other is not violated but done justice to by the subject.

Levinas' answer is to point to what happens in language, in conversation with the Other. "Language institutes a relationship irreducible to the subject–object relation: the *revelation* of the other. In its expressive function language precisely maintains the other – to whom it is addressed, whom it calls upon or invokes".[11] Whereas the object of knowledge is always a fact, already happened, taken in and duly recorded by the knowing being standing over against it, the encounter with the other as face is an event, unfolding at this very moment. In the here and now of this event there is a uniqueness, a quality disobeying the logic of knowledge-cum-containment. There is a dignity worthy of the event, a dignity not to be wrestled away from it by the effort of the knowing being. Language obeys a different – for lack of a better word – logic altogether. Language allows the other to unfold before me without my cancelling his otherness from me. The I and the other who speak with each other do not border one another, do not merge into a whole, but persist in their separateness. Language is fundamentally non-monologic; indeed it presupposes that there be a plurality of interlocutors. Moreover, language is universal because it is "the very passage from the individual to the general, because it offers things which are mine to the Other. To speak is to make the world common".[12] Therefore "the world in discourse is no longer what it is in separation, in the being at home with oneself where everything is given to me; it is what I give: the communicable, the thought, the universal".[13]

Hence language succeeds where knowledge fails – in doing justice to the otherness of the other. To be more precise, we should say that knowledge fails here precisely to the extent that – on its own premises and according to its own criteria – it succeeds. Knowledge aims at totalization;

in all its modalities knowledge must convert everything it comes across into an occasion for generalization. Since its project is to subsume everything to be known under the already known, knowledge has no patience with otherness. Otherness remaining otherness would count as the ultimate failure of knowledge. The knowing I does not want to receive from the outside anything which would resist its attempt at containment within its interior. The openness towards what is other, what is novel, what is unique, is categorically ruled out in knowledge the way Levinas defines it.

Curious, then, that language is picked out to secure success where knowledge, so to speak, is the hallmark of failure – that is, in doing justice to the otherness of the other. To be sure, if cognition is recollection (Plato), I need not receive anything of the other but what is (already) in me; all I need to do is exercise my powers of introspection to the point of perfection. Now Levinas presents his critique of knowledge as, more basically, a critique of *ontology*. For it is in ontology – as elaborated in the great tradition of Western philosophy – that, exceptions not permitted, "the other is reduced to the same".

We gather from what has been said that Levinas is advancing two rather bold claims. The first claim is that knowledge according to its very structure must strip the moment of otherness and alterity from every object it brings within its totalizing view. The second claim is that language possesses the very openness towards otherness that is so desperately lacking in knowledge.

As far as I can see, Levinas' first claim succeeds, at best, in exposing what I for lack of a better term shall call the narcissism of idealism. Idealist epistemology and ontology, to be sure, can be said to proceed according to the formula of reducing the other to the same, the unknown to the known, the foreign to the familiar. Here the logic is obeyed according to which to know something is always to return (it) back to oneself *qua* knowing consciousness. However, non-idealist doctrines do not conform to the formula criticized by Levinas; hence they resist his claim. In particular, epistemology and ontology of a *realist* kind grant the world outside the knowing subject a quality of otherness from the latter such that no reduction to the same or to inferiority is – or can ever be – undertaken.

Levinas' second claim is no less problematic than the first. Not content to contrast knowledge with language, Levinas presents them as diametrically opposed alternatives. Hence language fulfils the promise of preserving otherness that is inevitably frustrated in knowledge or ontology. But this claim seems to depend on an understanding of language to the effect that, in speaking, the interlocutors engage themselves in some non-objectifying activity. Now, to be sure, language may possess the feature of openness and flexibility whose absence in knowledge-ontology Levinas – unjustifiably – so laments. However, for language to operate in accordance with the aim of reaching understanding among the speakers, it is necessary that the speakers intend and understand the same when they employ the same words and refer to the same entities or phenomena. Such referring or pointing-to is objectifying; what is intended and meant as "being *that* entity or phenomenon as opposed to *that*" is something pointed-to by way of identification; and the latter is inseparable from and not to be accomplished without objectification. True, this immediately implies that the old problem of how to speak of the particular, let alone the unique, without subsuming it under the general or the universal props up again. In other words, language is not "in itself" less committed to objectification than is knowledge, if we are to accept Levinas' description of knowledge. But, again, this state of affairs does not amount to the scandal contended by Levinas. For Levinas has not convinced us that to identify and hence objectify something for the purposes of knowing and being able to speak about it is tantamount to doing violence to it.

III

We started by asking the question, Is man a moral being? Three quite different answers were indicated. If the question were to be put to Aristotle, he would respond by declaring it incomprehensible, if not downright scandalous. An individual's action may be immoral, she may fail to cultivate a virtuous character and thus fail to give to others what is due to them according to the demands of justice. Or she may suffer from *akrasia*, professing always to seek what is good and just but failing constantly to realize her intentions in practice. Now all of this may occur, and does occur, and is judged as blameworthy when it occurs, because man is a moral being. Man is always already within the domain of morality – or else he is not a man at all, someone intelligible as a human among humans.

Hobbes gives a different answer. The anthropological makeup of man may be fully and exhaustively described without any reference being made to morality. In the material circumstances of life that are "given" and elementary, man finds himself *outside* morality, not already partaking in it. Man may shift his position, however. Guided by self-interest, by an insight supplied by reason into the gloomy prospects entailed in a prolonged war of all against all, he may decide to make the transition from a premoral to a moral order, that is to say, to an order committing him to obligations as well as granting him rights. In short, man makes a choice as to whether to enter into the moral domain or to stay outside of it. It is as if man stands at the threshold between the premoral and the moral; leaving the former behind and joining the latter is a free choice. Hence "moral" is not a predicate of "man", as in Aristotle. Outside of any moral order, man is no less man, even if he leads there what may prospectively be thought a harsh and uncivilized way of life. What matters in Hobbes is that the *moralization* of man is an individual option – an option, that is, not touching man in his very essence, in his being.

For Sartre, options are plentiful, choices are always and everywhere to be made, and responsibility is never to be relinquished. And yet there is something that is *not* a choice of mine – namely, the fact that there are others, and that each and every other marks a limit to my possibilities, stronger still, to my freedom. The encounter with the other, highlighted in his look at me, touches me in my very being: it is an ontological event, bringing about a transformation in my being-in-the-world by adding to it the dimension of being-for-others. This transformation is not wanted, it is suffered. I am fixed, a transcendence transcended. However, and significantly, my being as a *moral* being is not at issue for Sartre. The other touches me in the depth of my being – but his doing so is an ontological event, an ontological transformation, not a moral one. My gaining – inadvertently, reluctantly – a novel and, in a profound sense, forever alien dimension of being by way of the presence of the other is described by Sartre as an existential drama; yet this description is oddly neutral as far as its moral aspects are concerned. I believe that this is so because morality has entered only halfway in the scenario depicted in early Sartre. "Halfway" because the ethically informed notion of *responsibility* elaborated in *Being and Nothingness* is throughout taken to bear on the individual's relation to himself, not to others. The responsibility Sartre talks about is my responsibility for myself. What he terms "bad faith" is the strategies employed by a free consciousness to conceal from itself its freedom understood as its unlimited responsibility. To live authentically is to be true to oneself, to assume responsibility for the endless series of choices one's life is made up of. The criteria establishing what is to count as "authentic" and "true to oneself" are the making of the individual making the choices; the criteria are not the handed-down product of tradition, of shared and commonly recognized practices, in short, of some Aristotelian *ethos*. So, whereas the other touches my being, he does not join me – nor do I join him – in some larger meaning truly intersubjective moral domain. Rather I am myself my own moral universe; I am still my own moral judge, the only one laying a claim to be summoned.

Levinas paints a different picture. There is no hesitation on the threshold to morality over whether or not to join in on it. Rather, man is thrown into the domain of the moral. Such throwness, however, does not refer back to some original choice. The commitment to morality, in the sense of bearing responsibility for the fate of others, is precisely not an upshot of choice. Morality is not an option. It is a predicament.

That we are moral beings in Levinas' sense means that responsibility for the other is inseparable from the human predicament. Since my relation to the other is shot through with responsibility, everything that affects the weal and woe of the other will be a matter of non-indifference to me. Responsibility does not require that I myself be the one whose doings affect the other's lot: I am responsible for the other's pain even when I do not cause it. Responsibility as mine does not await my wrongdoing, my causing harm. Responsibility is not distributed between parties according to the roles assigned to them by the logic of cause and effect; responsibility is not the offspring of causality, nor does it serve what qualifies as functional. Both models or types of logic fail for the same reason: responsibility is not in terms of more or less.

So responsibility does not come in degrees. It is, period. The human condition is a moral condition. This is so because our lives are intertwined with each other; human lives are interdependent lives. A person steps into my room, a perfect stranger perhaps, or someone dear to me. It does not matter. By the sheer fact of having entered my room, that person will matter to me and I to her. As Knud E. Løgstrup says, each of us holds part of the other's fate in our hands. My movements, my look, my words; my patience, my haste; the softness of my voice overtaken by sudden sternness: none of this escapes the other, all of it contributes – however inconspicuously, however subtly – to the way the other is touched by me, by my appearance before her, by my every act, every word, every gesture.[14]

"Living decently" and refraining from harm will not therefore relieve me of bearing responsibility for the Other. To repeat our warning, responsibility is not the privilege of the offender. What is more, responsibility has not even awaited the event of offence, violation, affliction. Responsibility is prior to the deeds committed by the parties who meet upon each other. Hence there is no qualification to the sense in which responsibility is non-optional; it is what we – everyone of us – cannot flee, regardless of what wrongs we have or haven't done.

It follows that there is no interhuman relation which is not a moral relation. No relation with others is such that it falls outside the ambit of morality and so of responsibility. We said above that responsibility doesn't come in degrees. We now add that responsibility is not situational: there are no responsibility-free situations as between humans. In short, being-with-others and moral responsibility are equi-primordial; the one is never to be encountered without the other. To say that being-with-others is moral *sui generis* is, once again, to contradict Hobbes. It entails that the distinction between premoral and moral relations with others is blatantly false. The "threshold" metaphor applicable to Hobbes and representative of crude versions of contract theory badly misconstrues morality: there is no point available for man from which he can hesitate between being or not being a bearer of responsibility for others.

We may be tempted to protest that Levinas' doctrine – there being no interhuman relation which is not a moral relation – is tantamount to moral totalitarianism of the worst kind imaginable, eliciting in us a pervasive feeling of claustrophobia. Levinas' likely response is that the protest badly misses the mark. This is so because the protest is premised on ethical voluntarism, that is to say, the view that the only morality worth talking about must be one *acceptable* to us, and for this to happen morality must be of our making. Levinas' protest is that this is not so: that it is *hubris* to view morality – in particular the commitment that goes with responsibility – as being of our making.

The depiction of an interpersonal encounter given above suggests that *moral responsibility resides in human proximity*. In circumstances of proximity, in the closeness of face-to-face encounters, moral responsibility loses the abstract air of being equi-primordial with the human predicament. What happens in proximity is that moral responsibility gets individuated. Responsibility is absolute, unconditional, and – we are wont to say – universal; yet, *in concreto*, responsibility comes into being as *mine* and as *yours*. For Levinas, being responsible means being irreplaceable: "no one can take my place when I am the one responsible: I cannot shrink before the other man, I am I by way of that uniqueness, I am I as if I had been chosen".[15] Hence responsibility is non-transferable; Levinas deems it "ethically impossible to transfer my responsibility for my neighbour to a third party. My ethical responsibility is my uniqueness, my election, and my 'primogeniture'".[16] The shared humanity of the two parties involved in responsibility – the subject and his or her addressee – does not mean that they disappear behind the grey anonymity of simply being human and as *such* responsible beings. Far from obscuring individuality and blurring the distinction between persons, responsibility throws both into sharp relief. In the ethical relation between subject and addressee, both parties appear as irreplaceable to each other. So, whereas responsibility is universal in the (no doubt theoretically crude and leaving-a-lot-to-be-desired) sense of allowing no limits and tolerating no exceptions, responsibility is individual (or should we say personal?) in the sense that it always and everywhere rests with a particular agent.

Moral beings, ineluctably and existentially so: this is what we are. Writes Zygmunt Bauman:

> To say that human condition is moral before it is or may be anything else means: well before we are told authoritatively what is "good" and what is "evil" (and, sometimes, what is neither), we face the choice between good and evil; we face it already at the very first, inescapable moment of encounter with the Other. This means in turn that whether we choose it or not we confront our situation as a moral problem and our life choices as moral dilemmas.[17]

So Sartre is right that responsibility resides always in me. However, although unmistakeably *mine*, responsibility is just as unmistakeably *for the other*. To see where Sartre and Levinas part company, we need to consider the issue of freedom.

The responsibility Sartre attributed to the for-itself rested on the all-important condition of freedom: the for-itself is free owing to the negating–transcending power of consciousness, which separates it from everything by way of a nothingness; and responsibility is the essence of the being of the free consciousness, i.e. of the for-itself. I realize my freedom in the choices I make; I cannot choose not to choose. In a word, I cannot decide not to be free – lest I choose to live in bad faith. To do so is exactly to flee the responsibility that I am.

To "trace freedom back to what lies before it" for Levinas is to show the way to the encounter with the other, the entry of the other. "To welcome the Other is to put in question my freedom".[18] This is not what we are used to hearing from moral philosophers. We are used to conceiving freedom, hence the possibility of choice (Sartre), hence autonomy and rational self-legislation (Kant), as the *sine qua non* of responsibility, indeed of morality as such. Opposing this received wisdom, what Levinas asserts is that in responsibility we are without a choice. To be without a choice here "precedes the freedom non-freedom couple". It thereby "sets up a vocation that goes beyond the limited and egoist fate of him who is only for-himself, and washes his hands of the faults and misfortunes that do not begin in his own freedom or in his present. It is the setting up of a being that is not for itself, but is for all".[19]

Prior to freedom yet constitutive of subjectivity and responsibility alike is a going to the other without concerning oneself with his movement toward me. It is a fact, says Levinas, that in existing for another I exist otherwise than in existing for me. This fact he designates as "morality itself". We can now appreciate what Levinas is up to when he finds for morality a deeper and more primordial origin than that provided by freedom – be it Sartrean or Kantian. Levinas denies freedom the priority commonly granted it. In doing so he turns the tables: the Thou – the other, the neighbour, the stranger – is *before* the I, therefore also before the freedom of the I. It follows that the I stands not in the nominative but in the accusative, addressed by the other before any chance to address him. "The neighbour assigns me before I designate him. I am bound to him before any liaison contracted. He orders me before being recognized".[20] Before wanting to – also before not-wanting to, for that matter – we stand here in a relation of kinship "against all logic". The relation is not of an ontological order, nor is it a modality of knowledge, of cognition: it is prior to both. Prior to embarking upon the project of knowing the other, he comes to me as an intruder as it were and catches me unawares. He comes as a face, whereby he signifies for me "an unexceptionable responsibility, preceding every free consent, every pact, every contract".[21]

The face has authority but no force. Still it summons me to assume absolute responsibility for the fate of the other. This is what morality is all about – what my being a moral being is about. I am not driven into morality by force, or by threats of any kind. And neither am I socialized into it, Aristotelian way or some other. Moral dispositions, conceived as virtues of character or of the intellect, are not cultivated in me so as to make me moral too, thus a human among fellow humans. There is no learning by doing, no trial and error within the safe walls of some shared *polis* and socially upheld *ethos*. There is no symmetry. Morality does not obey the cherished logic of reciprocity. The relation between I and other is shot through with lack of reciprocity, that is, with asymmetry. Responsibility amounts to being always "one step behind" the other for whom I am responsible.

It is tempting to state that for Levinas there is no I, no real subjectivity, prior to the encounter with the other as face. But this would be an erroneous depiction. There *is* an I before this I is addressed by the other. So subjectivity is not after all coextensive with responsibility for the other; it is not constituted in the act of assuming such responsibility.

Now if there is, according to Levinas, an I before the event of being addressed by the other, the question arises: what is the relation between the I "before" the encounter with the other and the I that emerges as (morally) addressed by the other?

Levinas devotes a large part of his work *Totality and Infinity* to developing a phenomenology of enjoyment and need. Surprisingly, there seems to be a premoral mode of existence in Levinas, as there is in Hobbes; yet, unsurprisingly, the two pictures drawn are highly divergent. Existence is not harsh, it is enjoyment. I do not start out as a foreigner in the world, thrown – without warmth, without security – into a life of scarcity, a life dictated by that severe and cruel master, Nature. There is instead immediate belongingness in the world; it is mine, I am at one with it, and at one with myself in being so. There is dwelling; I have a home, I am surrounded by things. They are familiar and dear to me by way of my employing them, using them, wearing them out, mending them, needing them. *I live from* the elements of my existence in the world; I live from "good soup", air, light, spectacles, work, ideas, sleep. These are not so many things perceived first as objects of representations. Nor are they (as we might have expected) tools or implements in the sense known from Heidegger's *Being and Time*. Their utility neither defines them nor exhausts their existence. Instead they are always in a certain measure "objects of enjoyment, presenting themselves to taste, already adorned, embellished".[22] Thus things are always more than the strictly "necessary"; they make up "the grace of life". Life is *love of life*; the reality of life is "already on the level of happiness", a relation with contents that are "not my being but more dear than my being: thinking, eating, sleeping, reading, working, warming oneself in the sun".[23] True, life is not pure happiness, pure enjoyment; we are also beings having *needs*. But needs do not spoil happiness, do not frustrate enjoyment. It is the other way around. "What we live from does not enslave us; we enjoy it." The human being "thrives on his needs; he is happy for his needs". Before anything else, therefore, there is complacency and pleasure. "Living from . . . is the dependency that turns into sovereignty, into happiness – essentially egoist".[24]

So there is happiness and enjoyment precisely because there are needs. Life is abundance of sources of life, of reasons for man to love life and experience living as equal to enjoying. "The primordial relation of man with the material world", maintains Levinas, "is not negativity, but enjoyment and agreeableness of life".[25]

What matters to the question posed above is this: "In enjoyment I am absolutely for myself. Egoist without reference to the Other, I am alone without solitude, innocently egoist and alone. Not against the others, not 'as for me . . .' – but entirely deaf to the Other, outside of all communication and all refusal to communicate".[26]

The I as portrayed here is thus perfectly self-sufficient, preoccupied with enjoying things in the very act of needing them, using them. It is an I immersed in the primordial positivity of enjoyment, a positivity opposed to nothing and therefore sufficient to itself from the first. This, then, is the I as it exists, depicted here in the primordial mode in which it exists, before the entry into its existence of the other. We wish to know: How does this I receive the other? Does receiving the other require a *different* I from the one portrayed above? In short, is there buried in Levinas a Hobbesian problematic, insofar as the I is required to *shift* from a pre-moral mode to a moral one, from primordial egoism to genuine other-orientedness?

Put in this somewhat provocative fashion, the meaning of this question is not to smuggle into Levinas some dubious Hobbesian anthropology that is not present, or presupposed, in what Levinas in fact is saying. The "egoist" Levinas speaks about is no fighter in a war of all against all. It is rather that the other does not (yet) matter, and that – coming as an intruder at night – he suddenly does so – start to matter, that is, and more than anything else. The other passes from irrelevance to primacy; and we wish to know what kind of shift this process involves, nay calls for, in the I.

Levinas tells us that "The surpassing of phenomenal or inward existence does not consist in receiving the recognition of the Other, but in offering him one's being. To be in oneself is to express oneself, that is, already to serve the Other. The ground of expression is goodness".[27] The other is thus received by the I in the mode of goodness. Elsewhere Levinas speaks of gentleness: "The Other precisely *reveals* himself in his alterity not in a shock negating the I, but as the primordial phenomenon of gentleness." He adds: "The welcoming of the face is peaceable from the first, for it answers to the unquenchable Desire for Infinity." This "peaceable welcome is produced primordially in the gentleness of the feminine face, in which the separated being can recollect itself, because of which it *inhabits*, and in its dwelling accomplishes separation".[28]

The other is welcomed, the other is received, and this occurs in an atmosphere informed by the goodness and gentleness of the welcoming I. If there is at all a transition undergone by the I here, it appears to be a thoroughly undramatic one. There is no metamorphosis. It is rather as if the life experienced as innocent, in the so-called primordial positivity of enjoyment sufficient to itself, helps prepare the I to open itself to the other and thus to the appeal emanating from the nudity of his face. All peace here.

We could put this otherwise by saying that what Levinas describes is indeed a far cry from Sartre's thesis that conflict is our original relationship with others. However, this does not hold for the Sartre who, in the years following his first major work, drafted what has been posthumously published as his *Notebooks for an Ethics*. Here Sartre offers an analysis of "help" and "the appeal" that is of immediate relevance to the question we have raised above as regards the "I" in Levinas' work.

Help, writes Sartre, is originally gratuitous. "One *first* has a tendency to help someone to pursue and realize his end, whatever it may be. This is a favorable prejudgment. *Afterwards*, but only afterwards, comes the idea that this end may be incompatible with my own ends or with a system of values to which I adhere. What we have is a *willingness to oblige*".[29] In this reversal of Hobbes, trust precedes distrust. My trusting the other does not ask for evidence, for guarantee. We may therefore call it a risk, yet it is a risk I am willing to take without ado: ill premonitions and the like are here conspicuous by their absence. Sartre is worth citing:

If I ask a passerby to indicate a street to me, it may be in order to steal something or to commit a crime. Distrust would have the passerby assure himself that my goals are not bad ones. He does not do so. Not because he necessarily assumes that these goals are *moral*, but because *a priori* he posits that it is good that a goal be attained. Better still, often *his* goal becomes my goal: I go back to see if he did "turn left", etc. People take an interest, intervene. A human goal has a value in itself.[30]

For this to be the case, a self-imposed restraint is required as far as the transcending powers of the I are concerned. This is what Sartre has in mind when he goes on to state that helpfulness necessarily implies a "refusal to transcend". Does this restraint mean that I give up my freedom? No. It is always a freedom that I want to help; and I can offer help only in my capacity as free. Indeed, the value of freedom is exactly what is affirmed in every act of help. "To want a value to be realized not because it is mine, not because it is a value, but because it is a value for someone on earth; . . . to replace the closed-off and subjective totality as the ideal of unity by an open diversity of outward movements building on one another is in every case to posit that freedom is worth more than unfreedom".[31] In help as well as in the appeal there is then a refusal to consider the original conflicts between freedoms by way of the look as "something impossible to surpass".[32] The refusal thus described – as *possible*, at that – can be seen as Sartre's refutation of the "conflict" thesis he took hundreds of pages to defend in his early work.

Does the "revised" Sartre come down on the same position as Levinas, then? No. In trying to see why, we shall appreciate the really instructive element of bringing in Sartre's analysis.

"The appeal", says Sartre, "is a promise of reciprocity. It is understood that the person I appeal to may appeal to me in return". Consequently "the appeal is itself a form of reciprocity from the moment it springs up".[33]

Now *reciprocity* is what Levinas is intent on ruling out. Remember that I am always "one step behind" the other. I will never catch up with the other. There is *absence* of balance, symmetry, reciprocity both as far as the ground and as far as the aim of Levinasian responsibility is concerned. Levinas' radicality lies precisely in his insistence that responsibility be completely dissociated from reciprocity. In "revised" Sartre no less than in early Sartre, the supreme status accorded to freedom makes for a dissimilarity with Levinas' position that has truly come to stay.

IV

We are now ready for a final look at Levinas.

In focusing on goodness and gentleness, Levinas in *Totality and Infinity* encourages the impression that the I who is to "welcome" and "receive" the other has *in himself* the resources called upon for meeting the other's appeal for absolute responsibility. The I seems prepared for the task awaiting it, prepared as it "is" and where it is – in the world of enjoyment. Hence, as we said above, the appearance on the scene of the other spells no Sartrean conflict, entails no big drama, requires no essential "shift" let alone conversion.

This being so, the event of the encounter with the other seems oddly underplayed. We wanted to know how this I is prepared to respond to the other's appeal for absolute (meaning unconditional and thus not reciprocated) responsibility. We were told simply that the I "is" prepared as it is. The capacities for *receptivity* in the I which, presumably, are needed here receive nothing of the close attention we are inclined to expect from Levinas, in order that his claim be substantiated. (This is a point finely raised by Paul Ricoeur.)[34]

But the drama that is conspicuous by its absence in early Levinas is all the more at the forefront of his theorizing in *Otherwise than Being or Beyond Essence*. Here we are told that "The recurrence of the self in responsibility for others, a persecuting possession, goes against intentionality, such that responsibility for others could never mean altruistic will, instinct of 'natural benevolence', or love".[35] Such rejection of psychologise is not novel in Levinas' reasoning; more to the point, we are prepared here for the stronger language, vor *allem* stronger claims, that follow: "Under accusation by everyone, the responsibility for everyone goes to the point of substitution. A subject is a hostage."[36] We read on: "The self is a *sub-jectum*; it is under the weight of the universe, responsible for everything."[37] So the other accuses me to the point of persecution; such persecution is now alleged to be constitutive of subjectivity. Because subject to the Other's "accucation", subjectivity is subjection. In pursuing this path, Levinas in the end advocates a "modern antihumanism", which "clears the place for subjectivity positing itself in abnegation, in sacrifice, in a substitution which precedes the will".[38] No recourse to intentionality, to psychological motives, to natural inclinations, to Aristotelian cultivation of dispositions, etc., is allowed for. In Levinas' view, these ethical doctrines are so many variations on the theme of auto-affection, by which he intends the position that, when affected, the I-subject is affected solely by itself. As against the model(s) of auto-affection, Levinas tirelessly reiterates that the I affected with regard to the other, by the other, is affected despite itself. "From the start", says Levinas, "the other affects us despite ourselves."[39]

Let us summarize this dense teaching by saying that, for Levinas, subjectivity is something the subject receives from the other. Subjectivity – *ethically* understood, because this is invariably what matters here – is not of the subject's own making. But neither is it a product of socialization, of engaging in interaction with others. "The openness 'to the other'", Levinas is at pains to point out, preventing the Hegelian scenario, "is not complete if it is on the watch for recognition."[40] But these are so many negations. Where is Levinas taking us here?

It is not easy to identify the direction taken by Levinas. On a programmatic level, his claims are easily rendered, his criticisms of rival doctrines easily conveyed. Levinas endeavours to make us grant ethical primacy to the other. That is his programmatic goal. In building his case, Levinas wages war starting, or better grounding, the ethical relationship in a concern with freedom and/or reciprocity. However, in the end Levinas so overemphasizes his case for the primacy of the other that he underplays the ethical status of the acting I-subject to the point of the wildly implausible. The Levinasian ethics of the other is attained at the price of surrendering the I. If the crux of ethical relationships lies in giving – giving conceived as an act facilitated by being able to respond to the appeal issuing from the face of the other – then, clearly, the one who gives is no less significant, ethically speaking, than the one who receives.[41]

Selflessness, one might argue, is admirable considered as an ethical ideal. But it is nothing on which to build an ethical relationship with others. True, likewise, that the model of auto-affection is hopelessly ill-suited to provide a basis for ethics. Here the other is surrendered, or, to be more accurate, fails to come properly into view in the first place. But unfortunately Levinas' warranted dissatisfaction with this model leads him simply to turn the tables and assert the converse position – the absolute ethical primacy of the other over the I. Levinas thereby replaces one extreme with another. It is as if the further one moves away from the viewpoint of the acting I, the better. We may talk here of a shift of focus from the I to the other. But great caution is called for: it is true that now everything that matters is the other; yet it is no less true that from now on everything depends on the I – or better on the me who, placed in the accusative, is addressed before addressing.

There is a dialectic between giver and receiver which is overlooked in Levinas. This dialectic is not of the symmetrical kind Levinas is intent on dismissing in ethics, and rightly so. We caught a glimpse of it when we referred to Løgstrup. A person steps into my room; instantly part of that person's destiny lies in my hands. To interact, to stand face to face, means to matter to the other. Not only that, however; it means to matter to *each other*. In human affairs, mattering is no one-way affair. I hold a part of your fate in my hands by the sheer fact of interaction; what I do, or fail to do, matters to your life, contributes to making it a successful or a failed one. But the same holds for what you do to me. Løgstrup therefore speaks of the human condition as one of interdependence: our lives are intertwined with each other. Hence, just as vulnerability is encountered on both sides, in both parties, so too is responsibility.

To hold, as I do, that man "is" a moral being, is not to imply that he has no need of others. Indeed, in the absence of others there would be no point to our being moral. On these premises, Levinas is right that ethical subjectivity is something – a capacity – I receive from the other. Now, to receive, there must be interaction. I grow up, I turn into a human in the full sense of the word, thanks to others who interact with me. What do they do? They assume responsibility for me – like others did for them – lest I die for want of nourishment, shelter, love. In this way, responsibility as received, as enjoyed, indeed as needed for life to be sustained, is prior to responsibility as taken up and assumed for the other, for my other. What is given to the other was originally received from an other – perhaps from a *different* other; but the point remains all the same. So every giver has enjoyed the experience of receiving what an other has given her or him by way of assuming a responsibility that, when acted upon, could not be reciprocated. It is this precious experience of having been at the receiving end of responsibility that is neglected in Levinas' account. Yet without this experience no concrete I will assume responsibility for a Thou. Having been cared for when absolutely helpness – a newborn child – is the *sine qua non* for caring. The process of growing from a new-born child to a responsible agent is truly interpersonal in that it requires others in the role of showing care; the process is the avenue to becoming a moral subject by way of having initially been an addressee. In neither instance is there symmetry between giver and receiver. Levinas, as we have seen, rightly stresses that responsibility is always a going to the other, a concern for the other without being concerned with his concern for me. But, for this to happen, concern for me there must have been. There is no first human – moral – mover who has not him- or herself been moved.

NOTES AND REFERENCES

1. Aristole, *Nicomachean Ethics*, 1120a 30.
2. See the chapter on "being-for-others" in Jean-Paul Sartre, *Being and Nothingness*, trans. H. Barnes, New York: Washington Square Press, 1956, esp. pp. 471–534.
3. See Jean-Paul Sartre, *Critique of Dialectical Reason*, trans. A. Sheridan-Smith, London: Verso, 1976, pp. 79ff. and 122ff. for analyses of "need" and "scarcity".
4. Sartre, *Being and Nothingness*, op. cit., p. 376.
5. Ibid., p. 352.
6. Ibid., p. 475.
7. Emmanuel Levinas, *Ethics and Infinity*, trans. R. Cohen, Pittsburgh: Duquesne University Press, 1985, pp. 86 and 89.
8. Emmanuel Levinas, *Totality and Infinity*, trans. A. Lingis, Dordrecht: Kluwer Academic Publishers, 1991, p. 225.
9. Ibid., p. 75.
10. Ibid., p. 42.
11. Ibid., p. 73.
12. Ibid., p. 76.
13. Ibid.
14. See Knud E. Løgstrup, *The Ethical Demand*, trans. T. Jensen, Philadelphia: Fortress Press, 1971, esp. ch. 1.
15. Emmanuel Levinas, *Outside the Subject*, trans. M. Smith, London: Athlone Press, 1993, p. 35
16. Ibid., p. 44.
17. Zygmunt Bauman, personal correspondence, 15 March 1994; cf. Bauman, *Postmodern Ethics*, Oxford: Blackwell, 1993.
18. Emmanuel Levinas, *Otherwise Than Being or Beyond Essence*, trans. A. Lingis, Dordrecht: Kluwer Academic Publishers, 1991, p. 85.
19. Ibid., p. 116.
20. Ibid., p. 87.
21. Ibid., p. 88.
22. Levinas, *Totality and Infinity*, op. cit., p. 110.
23. Ibid., p. 112.
24. Ibid., p. 114.
25. Ibid., p. 149.
26. Ibid., p. 134.
27. Ibid., p. 183.

28. Ibid., p. 151.
29. Sartre, *Notebooks for an Ethics*, trans. D. Pellauer, Chicago: University of Chicago Press, 1992, p. 275.
30. Ibid.
31. Ibid., p. 281.
32. Ibid.
33. Ibid., p. 285.
34. Paul Ricoeur, in his *Oneself as Another*, trans. K. Blamey, Chicago: University of Chicago Press, 1992, makes an important point when he states that, in Levinas, "the theme of exteriority does not reach the end of its trajectory, namely awakening a responsible response to the other's call, except by presupposing a capacity of reception, of discrimination, and of recognition that, in my opinion, belongs to another philosophy of the same than that to which the philosophy of the other replies" (p. 339). I agree. Levinas in the final analysis fails to account for the capacities – sensuous, emotional, cognitive – in the subject that enable it properly to receive and act upon the Other's appeal to it. Ricoeur puts the point like this: "Must not the voice of the Other who says to me: 'Thou shalt not kill', become my own, to the point of becoming my conviction, a conviction to equal the accusative of 'It's me here!' with the nominative of 'Here I stand'?" (ibid.).
35. Levinas, *Otherwise than Being*, op. cit., p. 111f.
36. Ibid.
37. Ibid., p. 116.
38. Ibid., p. 127.
39. Ibid., p. 129.
40. Ibid., p. 119.

Chapter 11

The Dialectic of Proximity and Apartness

Alastair Hannay

I

How can we be concerned with one another without sharing values and interests, without being relevantly similar or even the same? The answers seem too obvious for the questions themselves to be more than rhetorical. Yet there are other questions, just as rhetorical, whose obvious answers seem directly to conflict with these. How can I be concerned with you unless I regard you as the independent source of your own interests, as relevantly "other". And how can I regard you in that way without releasing myself from the hold upon me of the web of my own personal interests in which my concern with you is interwoven? How, in other words, can you come within the scope of my authentically moral concerns without standing before me as someone totally alien?

The dialectic of proximity and apartness I refer to here is not Hegelian. If it were, then the conflict would be merely apparent; it would be the result of seeing the terms – you and I – too abstractly and in isolation, of failing to appreciate that, in properly ethical contexts, closeness and apartness are related to each other internally. On the contrary, I shall suggest that the closeness required of the true ethical relationship presupposes genuine apartness. The philosophical affiliation here is not with Hegel but with Levinas, though it is in Kierkegaard that we find its first as well as its clearest expression.[1] A mind-catching but potentially misleading way of putting it would be to say that true sharing is the prerogative of mutual aliens. I am suggesting a sense of apartness in which the object of our moral concern eludes conceptualization. What is shared simply gets in the way, and only by removing it does the object become visible. Only then does the "other" come within moral reach.

II

That the object of moral concern should be nearby is a well-entrenched principle of European moral thinking. It finds its historical expression in the New Testament injunction to love one's neighbour as oneself.[2] Of course, "neighbour" need not refer to someone living next door; the word (*plesios*) as it occurs in the commandment (*ton plesion*) means "the one close by", and in the everyday marketplace that could be anyone. Yet it is clear that the settled contiguity implicit in the idea of one's neighbour had special moral significance in the history of the time. To be asked to love the one next door to you is to be asked to show, even feel, love just at that boundary where equitable relations with your fellow humans are exposed to their severest test, at the wall or fence where the distinction between what is yours and what the other's is most evident. The significance of neighbour relations for a society split between local and Roman allegiances is not hard to see; in the face of oppression from above there is clearly room for an alternative way of cementing social relations from below. That might be the origin of the ideal of neighbour love, but it is not how it has come down to us. For us it has the form of a universal principle; we are to love the neighbour as ourself be he friend or foe, at home, in the marketplace, and in the field of conflict. The question is whether the notion contains any ethically viable core that survives this radical de-contextualization.

For the modern world, the literal interpretation of the commandment to love one's neighbour as oneself has clear limitations. First, it is exactly that, a commandment, and Kant's question immediately arises, whether it is possible to obey it even in the case of those to whom one is not inclined by nature, or social habit, to extend one's loving concern.[3] Second, in the modern world the test of ethicality presented by nextdoor neighbour relations is more than outweighed by an even greater test, namely the challenge of distance: the physical and psychological distances which, because they remove the immediate perception of others as sharing in our lives, so easily cause moral concern for these others (or any others) to dissipate. Modern technological society, besides pressing individuals out of those community and other consolidating contexts in which moral intuitions were once traditionally fostered and reinforced, allows an enormous expansion of the possibilities of acting in contexts which are morally relevant but where one's acts of commission and omission have an impact on persons one never has to face at all, let alone across the garden fence. In our own day, moral indifference and callousness present a (to put it mildly) serious and special challenge, not least to our powers of moral imagination. Moreover, the causes of indifference and callousness are not confined to demographic distance; they extend, owing to dissolutional factors of the kind just mentioned, to various forms of psychological distance manifested in an inability or refusal to consider others as sharing in our life. An important inadequacy of the garden-fence analogy is that, besides assuming actual demographic contiguity, by presenting the parties as physical neighbours from the outset it prescinds from all those ethically relevant factors (racism, élitism, and other self-serving forms of partiality) which prevent such actual, social contiguity from occurring in the first place.

This is clearly a valid objection to any proposal to present the literal interpretation of the injunction to love one's neighbour as a viable vehicle for serious ethical reflection in our own age. The question then is whether we can find in the New Testament commandment some more far-reaching, perhaps universal ethical message, not its historical intention perhaps, but some insight which an original locally good idea has nevertheless spawned and, owing to the spread of Christianity, allowed to become an integral part of a moral culture to which large parts of the world pay at least lip-service. Clearly, a version of the homely metaphor which abstracts from its homeliness need not inherit objections which apply to it because of its homeliness. There may be something of general significance there after all. And indeed, at least one morally sensitive thinker in our time has fastened on the dialectic of proximity and apartness pinpointed by the nextdoor neighbour metaphor to construct the makings of a deep-rooted ethics which is advertised also as an ethics of love.

That thinker is Søren Kierkegaard. Kierkegaard's special perspective, from the point of view of the individual, brings certain aspects of the ethical relationship into sharp focus. Whether that perspective is sufficient, or the case for the commandment acceptable, is hard to decide and there will be no attempt to resolve the matter here. But a preliminary examination of Kierkegaard's views does help to throw light on questions fundamental to morality.

Granting that ethical concern is the active acknowledgement of the interests of persons, Kierkegaard's claim is in effect that it is not until a person whose concern it is has achieved a state of autonomous selfhood that that address becomes available. There are familiar, not least communitarian, objections to such a view. Let us first see what the view is and then what the objections amount to.

III

First, in order to lay bare the structure and implications of Kierkegaard's view, it is useful to contrast its apparently fundamental atomism with an opposed view which seeks to establish social ethics on the basis of a supposedly innate communality. Kierkegaard's "I"-based position can be compared with (or contrasted to) Rousseau's "we"-based position. The comparison with Rousseau is especially revealing since Kierkegaard and Rousseau both agree that group identities and distinctions impede advancement to the ethical situation, though in opposite directions.

For Rousseau the non-divisive standpoint of ethics is that of what he calls commonality. It is the notion of a concretely abstract "we", such that, in respect of myself, the other with whom I acknowledge my oneness in the first-person plural is seen in terms of a sameness, a shared generality. From the latter there grows a natural respect for beings capable of referring to themselves individually, that is, able to relate to themselves in the first-person singular. What we share at the level of greatest generality, and what distinguishes us from mere animals, is precisely this self-referential capacity. It is this capacity, therefore, that forms the basis of our commonality. The moral psychological basis for this claim is that the ability to refer to ourselves enables us by the same token to direct a sense of pity at others. A pity directed at others as such is a pity unmediated by the social, political, and economic differences which separate us from them. Thus Rousseau's "pity" is a spontaneous feeling of compassion; it is not a feeling evoked by comparison with others, as would be a pity directed from one or another position of superiority, which then slides so easily into contempt, just as easily as its counterpart, envy, stemming from a position of inferiority slides into resentment. That there is such an uncorrupted pity, based upon the use of the self-referential "I", is due to the alleged fact that self-identities are themselves "mediated", not of course by any social categories but by other self-identities, or rather by the sense of interacting directly with others at a level transcending that of social mediation. Why the operative sensation should be pity in particular is explained by Rousseau, in *Émile*, as follows:

> We are drawn towards our fellow-creatures less by our feeling for their joys than
> for their sorrows; for in them we discern more plainly a nature like our own, and
> a pledge of their affection for us. If our common needs create a bond of interest our
> common sufferings create a bond of affection . . . Imagination puts us more readily
> in the place of the miserable man than of the happy man . . . Pity is sweet because,
> when we put ourselves in the place of the one who suffers, we are aware, never-
> theless, of the pleasure of not suffering like him.[4]

Any view which can posit a "species-ability" as the basis of human unity has a considerable initial appeal. It provides a focus of ethical attention even where humanity is divided, so that it is possible, by appealing to something all humans have in common, to address one's fellows across present barriers and work together to eliminate them. There is a sense, then, in which even if universal respect could only reign unhindered in a society where that goal was achieved, it may also reign in the form of a good will in a world where actual distinctions still obstruct social, political, and economic unity.

There are nevertheless severe defects in any such view. In the first place, the unity posited is merely abstract: a species-function is selected, in this case that human beings are particulars in a special, self-reflective way. The ability of every human being to ascribe that same function to other human beings is made the basis of an innate or primordial sense of "we". But what is the ethical content of this notion? Indeed what content does it have at all beyond providing one means of differentiating the human species from others? In order to have ethical content, the notion would have to address the relations in which human beings stand to one another, yet all the notion can provide is a metaphor which represents humanity in all its plurality and division suspended as though from a single peg. Finally, even if that metaphor could be translated into a position with relevance for either politics or ethics, the implications of that position would not speak at all convincingly for it. Politically, it is exposed to the objection that society is of necessity differentiated (Hegel's objection to the abstract "citizenship" of the French Revolutionaries). It is also exposed to the same objection that can be levelled at Marxism, namely that it is uncritical, not to say naïve, to assume an innate but repressed first-person-plural unity whose spontaneous flowering waits only upon the removal of the institutions that divide people externally. Ethically, it is exposed to the objection that even were non-divisive political unity possible, ethics is directed in the first instance at fellow beings in their present divisions and differences.

Here Rousseau's pity, an ability vicariously to feel the other's sorrow, may seem to do service. But remember, this is no ordinary pity; it is a pity uncontaminated by relative positions in social space. The pityer is to conceive him- or herself and the pitied as sharers in a common humanity by virtue of a general characteristic beyond social differentiation. But what is it in that characteristic which counts as something actually being shared? The question is analogous to that posed of membership in Kant's kingdom of ends, and the only answer we seem able to give is an abstract defining characteristic of human being. No doubt pity and concern for human suffering and sorrow are an essential part of moral psychology, but regrettably they are not a universally defining characteristic of human being, and if the claim is that pity would not even be possible but for the special manner of human particularity, then the answer is that the very same is true of failure to show pity or concern, of callousness and every form of *in*humanity. Indeed, if we look more closely at this special manner of human particularity, the way in which human being becomes an object for itself, it may appear that it is not the notion of human being at all (a general concept) that first comes to light in this capacity for self-reflection but particularity (the self and its own interests). And not the general concept of particularity either, but particularity itself.

IV

It is just this that underlies Kierkegaard's contrasting view. For Kierkegaard, generalities are not merely modes of human differentiation and possible division; more fundamentally, they are protective devices shielding the individual from a desolate sense of its sheer particularity. Or, more to our point, they are psychological strategies shielding the individual from the unwanted insight into a fact which the ability to refer to oneself in the first-person singular brings with it, namely that the differentiating social and political categories in terms of which we fashion our self-images are pure contingencies and not the clothes of any lastingly true selfhood. Let us, in outline, note the main strands of Kierkegaard's thought here, first his criticism of the belief that one must always act as a member of a group or association on behalf of group aims, and the corresponding belief that human freedom and fulfilment are to be found in the idea of a universal affiliation.

This associational idea is by no means foreign to political rhetoric; it has formed the ideological underpinning for many a political movement. Kierkegaard refers to it as "levelling". This is not so much a refusal to accept exceptionality *per se*, getting everyone to step in line, as a refusal to see the ethical agent except under some socio-political category, so that one never acts on one's own beliefs and behalf. At bottom, then, levelling is an evasion, a refusal to accept the challenges and claims of individuality. It is a flight into abstraction, and levelling itself is, as a motivating factor, "an abstract power" and its influence "abstraction's victory over individuals".[5] In levelling, Kierkegaard writes, "the dialectic turns away from inwardness and wants to render equality in the negative; so that those who are not essentially individuals constitute an equality in external association".[6] The unity of association is a "negative unity" involving a "negative mutuality". It is negative because, in Kierkegaard's categories, it places sociality in the external and temporal instead of in the subjective and eternal. Similarly, negative mutuality is the mutuality of an overriding commitment to common rules of association, of shared duties and rights, under an associative umbrella which covers associates indiscriminately and protectively. The most inclusive umbrella of all is the "higher negativity" of "pure humanity",[7] the association of all associations, which Kierkegaard considers the typical fabrication of an age of reflection. It enables people to suppose quite spuriously that they have a personal and social identity simply by being human beings.[8]

What precisely are the claims and challenges of individuality? *The Sickness unto Death*, Kierkegaard's main text on selfhood, talks of an "act of separation in which the self becomes aware of itself as essentially different from the environment and the external world and their effect on it".[9] There are several ways of reading this notion of separation, but it is clear that what Kierkegaard refers to is not simply the ability to refer to oneself in the first-person singular. The separation comes as a development *within* what is normally called self-consciousness. In general terms one might say it was a sense of an essential distinction, even an incongruity, between the "I" as possessor of all and whatever predicates make up its sense of a continuing identity and these predicates themselves. The incongruity could even be said to stem from the general capacity to refer to oneself in the first-person singular, simply because this capacity of the "I" is the continual possibility of reviewing, looking upon, the characteristics with which it is identified, but from a position which transcends not only them but the "I" itself. The "I" is always one jump ahead of the characteristics with which it would identify itself and systematically eludes its own glance. This is a Sartrean manner of expression but captures the general point. However, in Kierkegaard's case, the predicates in question are special by being those which define some respect or respects in which the project of personal fulfilment has been essayed. We may think of them in particular as being those predicates specifying social roles whereby, in sharing these predicates with others, we aspire to some form of human universality, or perhaps just respect and honour – as though that was what counted for fulfilment. The act of separation is then one in which it is acknowledged that personal fulfilment cannot be provided by any such predicate. The first consequence of the act of separation is the acknowledgement that the "I" is essentially bare. But then, since the appropriateness of ascribing a predicate to the self is the only way in which the "I" can be said to share any characteristic or property at all with other "I"s, in finding itself bare or naked ("naked and abstract, in contrast to the fully clothed self of immediacy"),[10] the "I" also finds itself radically alone, in the face not only of its peers but also of transcendent reality and, if he exists, God.

Here, then, we have one term in the dialectic of proximity and apartness. Aloneness is apartness. But what ethical implication has this? As the quotation above asserts, the difference in kind implied by the act of separation also means that the naked self sees that its nature, if it is to have one, is not the "effect" of the environment and the external world. Here we can detect a Kantianism in Kierkegaard's thought; the naked self, deprived of the fulfilments which seemed available in the state of its "immediate" consciousness through common, role-taking attribution, recognizes that in order to be itself, whatever that may be, it must at least prevent such attributions from motivating whatever activities are to be its fulfilling ones. So, the naked and alone "I" is also in a sense autonomous, but only in a negative sense. For, according to Kierkegaard, this is only the "first form of the infinite self", it is the "progressive impulse" which sets in motion the process of fulfilment, "the entire process through which the self infinitely takes possession of its actual self along with its difficulties and advantages".[11]

V

The kernel of Kierkegaardian ethics (not, be it noted, that of the quasi-Hegelian ethical life-view depicted in Part Two of *Either/Or*, in which the implications of the religious aspect have not been drawn out as they are in the works that followed) lies in this notion of taking possession of the "actual" self. But what does that mean? A comparison with Kant can help. Kant's categorical imperative is designed to guarantee motivation by the idea of membership of the association of all human associations. In acting morally you take the side of humanity in general and focus upon an ideal of impartial considerateness, and you do that by removing yourself in the moral moment from the push-and-pull of inclination. The categorical imperative is, as Kant says, a compass which the moral agent carries around so as to be able to chart the moral course in any event or situation.[12] There is no provision for the possibility that pushes and pulls of inclination can themselves be transformed in a way that would make the compass redundant. That, by contrast, is exactly what becoming, or taking possession of, the actual self is intended to amount to. Instead of the notion of a natural self, with its affections and partialities in the situation, being set aside in favour of an impartial but abstract ideal of agency, we have the notion of an actual self primed to respond impartially to its immediate environment.

At a pinch, the ideal of impartiality might be called love, love of one's neighbour, or loving one's neighbour as oneself. If we ignore the emotive overtones of the term "love" for a moment, we can see that the notion of love and of an ethical relationship coincide. Or at least we can see this if we allow that ethics is primordially an interest in the interests of others. Further, and still retaining something of the form of love, if not yet admitting any clear foothold for its content, an ethical concern for the other is a concern that is not hedged about with conditions. Of course there are forms of love which are so hedged about. You love the other because you are attracted to the other, so that if the other or your own susceptibilities changed significantly then the love would cease. Preference, clearly, is an expression of such a condition, the condition under which you prefer, or are attracted by, one person in preference to another. Preferential love, then, is self-regarding at least in the sense that it does not address itself fully to the other. Kierkegaard claims that "to love the one who is preferentially nearer one than all others is self-love".[13]

What would it be fully to address the other? What or who *is* the other? Any individual is a continuous, finite subject of experiences, with a sense of identity through experiences, and with a focus of its own interests for the future. How do you address such a person? What is it to love *them*? Surely it is to consider the whole history as it has been and how it may be, subject to whatever changes may occur. Suppose the one you love preferentially suffers a transformation, disfiguration perhaps, plus some significant personality change, as in Alzheimer's disease, perhaps acquiring characteristics by which, in Kant's words, you are no longer attracted but "repelled by a natural and unconquerable aversion".[14] Love will require that none of this makes any difference; for, if it did, your love would be shown to be conditional. It would by the same token be preferential, because, given the same susceptibilities, you would prefer another with the preferred characteristics to the one which once had them but, having now lost them, has lost also the ability to attract you.[15]

VI

The ideal of adequately addressed love of the concrete other is in effect a transformation of the abstract "we". Both it and the "we" of membership of the association of associations are specifications of the notion of "anyone". The difference is that, by bringing the notion of anyone to earth in the shape of the other, the "we" is now specified under the category of the particular and not of the universal. Instead of "we" being innately, primordially, even politically derivable from man's nature, we see it now as having to be constituted in and by the particular itself, the individual, in the relation it establishes to the other. "We" now embraces particulars not by virtue of accidents of affection or affiliation which abstract from the "I"s in the relation, but by virtue of being a relation between genuinely concrete "I"s. Your "neighbour" – the one hard by, on any morally relevant occasion – is such an "I", another "I" accessible or "visible" for the first time as such only when the veil of preference has been lifted.

The essence of the view is that the ethical sense of the universal is one of a commonality that must be established *by* human beings, and is not inherent in any given property whereby the beings that are human are picked out as such, or whereby those animals that are human are picked out as human animals. Establishing this sense of commonality is itself a task for the individual, the task of becoming ethical. Indeed, for Kierkegaard this is what selfhood means. Selfhood, becoming an "I", is for Kierkegaard therefore a rigorous concept. But until we have *this* "I", we cannot have a "we" either. For "we" does not express some characteristic innate to humankind, and if "we" has any ethical reference it is to any feature not of our social forms but of the individual will which may or may not be expressed in social forms. The primordial sense of "we" is the will to society and that will has to be cultivated and maintained. Before that intention can be acquired in its adequate form, the "I" must be wrested from immediacy in the face of the blandishments, subterfuges, and protective devices of association. One has to become an individual *apart from* other individuals before one can establish a relation *with* those other individuals, who in terms of their "actual" selves are also individuals apart and faced with the same task of realizing those selves so as to be able to will society.

VII

As one would expect, there are several objections to be raised. At this stage, however, I shall be mentioning just two, because these are based partly on misunderstandings and should be ignored. The first of these objections is that the conception of ethical relationships here is excessively, even maximally, atomistic; and the second is that the whole idea is based on an illegitimate extension of the notion of love, so that, even if a relation of the form described were feasible, "love" could never be the right word to describe its content. Limitations of space preclude my entering into detailed discussion of these questions,[16] but I shall offer some comments directed at the misunderstandings. The objections, and replies, fit quite neatly into a distinction between "affiliation" and "affection".

The first objection (today it would be called communitarian) is that affiliative "we" relations are of the essence of ethics or social morality, and therefore the claim that an "I"–"I" relation forms the basis of ethics is misconceived. In respect of Kierkegaard, however, the objection would itself be misconceived, because it ignores the way in which Kierkegaard's notion of taking possession of the actual self involves accepting the self as it is in its situation, in all its affiliative relations, but now addressing both itself and its relationships from an ethical point of view which focuses on the individuals *in* these relationships. Of course, from Kierkegaard's point of view, the objection would be misconceived in any case if it stemmed from the idea that ethical relations are to be understood on the model of affiliation. But, in denying that, Kierkegaard is not making the Kantian (or Rawlsian) mistake which communitarians point to, namely that the categorical imperative (or the veil of ignorance) is a compass designed to determine the ethical (or equitable political) course in defiance or ignorance of personal ties and reciprocal sympathies based on shared interests.[17]

This form of reply may not appease every communitarian scruple, for it may still be objected that, by making the unconditionality of one's address to the other itself so unconditional, even such ordinary yet ethically significant relationships as maternal and paternal love will fail the test. And Kierkegaard does indeed say things which might suggest that. Thus, because even the requirement that I might be the one to bestow love on the other is a condition on the love, this again means that the love fails to be addressed to the other.

But, if love has the form of an interest in the interests of the other (ignoring here how these interests are to be determined), there are surely cases where the interest of the other is exactly that I or perhaps you should be the one to bestow that love. Having the interest in question, that is, in the interests of the other, is subject to an appreciation of what the interests of the other are, and these may well be expressed in the expectations aroused in the other by the mores which would lead to a sense of desolation and abandonment if the love were not directed from the accepted source but came, for instance, in the form of a welfare cheque. Of course, in another society that might be the expectation and, if the legitimate interests of the other include not having such expectations disappointed, that would have to be known by the person intent on doing the loving thing. But, at a guess, in most societies the child's interests would include having its interests catered to by a parent or the *human* functional equivalent.

Kant concluded, when faced with the Christian commandment of universal love, that whatever the form of a moral intention its content cannot be what we call "love", for what we mean by that is by its very nature instinctual. Consequently acts of will are superfluous where love already exists, and ineffectual where it does not. He recommended, therefore, that in interpreting the commandment we replace the impossible duty to love one's neighbour with that of trying to like practising one's duties towards one's neighbour.[18]

One reply would be to say that it is tendentious of Kant to adopt as his model of love something which tends in the direction of infatuation. He might have done better to consider the "cooler" Aristotelian notion of friendship (*philia*), which Aristotle distinguishes from the "emotion" of liking (*philesis*), because unlike the latter it is based on a "fixed disposition".[19] We note that Aristotle's description of friendship conforms with our own proposal concerning at least the form of love; he says that it is "those who wish the good of their friends for their friends' sake who are friends in the fullest sense".[20] Since dispositions can be trained, why not propose that one's friendship can be trained to cover the "anyone" who fills the role of "neighbour"?

A difficulty with this is pinpointed by Aristotle's own remarks about what motivates true friendship. It has to be something that elicits the affection and, even though Aristotle allows there to be some absolute quality of goodness in a person that attracts the affection of friendship, it is still a *quality* of the person, whereas, as we saw, the ideal of universal love has to overcome, as Kant rightly says, the case where you are "repelled by a natural and unconquerable aversion". Also, it seems, as Aristotle also points out, that the affection of friendship has to be "prompted by similarity"[21] and, since the similarity here is not universal, in terms of universal love that would be just another manifestation of preference and therefore conditionality. A promising solution might be to say that universal love, and the feature that warrants the use of that word as an extension at least of the Aristotelian friendship model (but perhaps even more), is based not on any recognizable feature, not, that is, on any actually perceived goodness or whatever, but on the decision to *ascribe* some notion of autonomous value to every human being. The Kantian notion of "end in itself" comes to mind. But Kant believed the attribution to be backed by objective reason, which is just another form of cognitive realism, in this case a characteristically rationalistic form. The point, initially, is that the values people (and animals and things) have are not functions of the pleasure others derive from them, or their power to attract in others friendly relations of concern. Why? One reason is that pleasure and utility provide a poor perspective from which to discern inherent value. That would also be an objection to Aristotelian friendship based on what mutual friends took to be the instrinsic good that they both shared; the particular quality they find likeable in each other may not be the good that really resides in them. But according to the assumptions of the present proposal there would be no such value to be found residing there anyway. What the solution says is that the value is attributed on the basis of the idea that all things, including persons, have their own value and, in the case of persons, that this value belongs to what can be achieved from the position of particularity.

VIII

This may sound no better than the abstract feature which we criticized Rousseau for positing. Indeed, we may seem merely to have come full circle, the only change being – and it may not seem a gain – that now we have the ethical agent arbitrarily positing the feature in order to justify ethical performance, instead of deriving it as Rousseau himself did from some agreed aspect of human existence.

And yet, by positing this feature, we place the other, any other with whom we enter into a morally relevant relation, and however lacking in the properties that would normally elicit concern in us, in a context of mutual moral development. We add to his or her recognizable features a dimension our attribution of which to them is already, on our part, an expression of good will or love. In addition, this feature is still nevertheless one that "attracts" us to them in terms of what can be done to bring them, too, to the point of moral self-insight, from which they in their turn can posit this feature in others. This may not seem sufficient to attract us to them; but if not we can still add what in Kierkegaard's thought is clearly the real source of the attraction. In seeing the other in this light we are partaking in God's (distributive) love of mankind.

Whatever further objections arise at this point, and it is not hard to anticipate their tenor, there is at least something to be said in terms of the autonomy of moral discourse itself for a solution which posits, as a principle of ethical relationship, some property whose very positing is itself a moral act. A further fact in favour of the view is that deciding to treat others as autonomous centres of moral development is the exercise of a specifically human ability, just as much a feature of human being as the ability to refer to oneself in the first-person singular. And, when it comes to deciding, in terms of ethical relations, which of these two deserves to be called foundational, there is something to be said for preferring the former. After all, in the light of the view as we have outlined it, exercising this particular ability is the only way in which the world can actually manifest itself to human beings in genuinely moral terms, the only way in which there can *be* a world of which a disinterested regard for the other is a universally defining feature.

IX

But is that not an exaggerated and unnecessary demand? Perhaps morality should be seen instead as a Manichaean conflict in which basically good (or other-regarding) and basically evil (or self-regarding) people struggle for supremacy or survival. Many will object on post-Nietzschean grounds to a morality based on Christian compassion and might be willing to dispense with the notion of morality in any case, or at least under that loaded name. Others would not be seriously disturbed philosophically if the world betrayed no moral dimension but morality had to be worked out by humans contractually, or perhaps, as Habermas would have it, simply by living up to the ideals implicit in the very nature of their discourse.

Still, it would be wrong to dismiss the Kierkegaardian perspective too quickly, either on Nietzschean grounds or more generally. In the first place, Kierkegaard's insistence on the particularity of the individual brings several easily obscured aspects of the ethical relation into focus. One of these is the reality of the other as a separate subject of experiences, a fact easily lost sight of in traditional theories of ethics which, by marginalizing the individual's own sense of moral integrity, tend to denature rather than elicit the moral personality. Second, systems of law, political institutions, and social habits are usually assumed to be ethically effective, and necessary, *extensions* of private morality. They extend the scope of natural concern to morally relevant reference groups and serve as guarantees of the exercise of such concern where moral feeling is no longer present or, if present, no longer works. From a Kierkegaardian perspective, however, they appear in the guise of surrogate moral agents which, by relieving actual agents of their own responsibilities, allow those very dispositions to atrophy which motivated the laws, practices, and institutions in the first place, thus leaving political institutions to be steered by more sinister forces.

X

It is here, finally, that Kierkegaard's thought provides an interestingly particularistic, though undeveloped, parallel with Nietzsche. What they have in common is the idea that excellence is the outcome of struggle. The *agon* in Nietzsche is one in which Dionysian chaos is channelled into creative order; conflicting and mutually destructive forces are converted into constructive activity, and energies which otherwise work divisively, and in the ends of power, are harnessed into socially creative ends.[22] In Kierkegaard this motif appears in the ontogenesis of the ethical agent, first in *Either/Or* where the destructive aesthetic forces which "poetize" the other out of reality are brought under the stabilizing influence of self-hood,[23] and later where motivations that split the self are brought together under the unifying ideal of the eternal. Just as in Nietzsche the power play of politics is favoured because the social politics of pity serves merely to conceal lack of the strength and dignity to stand alone, so in the struggle out of which Kierkegaard's individual emerges there is a hardening against the pity one is disposed to feel for human suffering, and the emergence of an ethics in which suffering is accepted as an inescapable challenge. Pain and suffering then become part of the struggle out of which alone true individuality and ethical excellence can be sustained. Accordingly, as with Nietzsche, Kierkegaard too opposes prudentialism and social programmes which presuppose in their beneficiaries fear, insecurity, and self-interest.[24]

Unlike Nietzsche's, Kierkegaard's *agon* is decidedly moral. Its *telos*, or "excellence", is the formation of a genuinely social intention. His idea is that the latter implies treating others as autonomous generators of value, and this requires the would-be moral agent to struggle free of attachments to the other, since these reduce the metaphysically incontrovertible otherness of the other to a feature of the would-be moral agent's own world. Similarly, morality is not the immersion of individuality in common projects, but a devotion to being the kind of being a human being is, a being capable of individual and autonomous ethical reflection.[25] This devotion is expressed *in situ*, in daily dealings with one's fellows, the neighbour or the one close by. "Neighbour" means anyone with whom one stands in relations of responsibility. "Close by" means anything from visibly across the garden fence to invisibly at the receiving end of a ballistic missile.

NOTES AND REFERENCES

1. For informative discussion of the Levinas–Kierkegaard connection in this and other respects, see Merold Westphal, "Kierkegaard and Levinas in Dialogue", in Martin J. Matuštík and Merold Westphal (eds), *Kierkegaard in Post-Modernity*, Bloomington/Indianapolis: Indiana University Press, 1995, pp. 265–281.

2. Matthew 22: 37; cf. Luke 10: 25 and 27.

3. I. Kant, *Critique of Practical Reason*, in *Kant's Critique of Practical Reason and Other Works on the Theory of Ethics*, trans. T. K. Abbott, London/New York/Toronto: Longmans, Green & Co., 6th ed., 1954, p. 176.

4. *Émile*, *Oeuvres complètes de Jean-Jacques Rousseau*, ed. by Pléiade Bernard Gagnebin and Marcel Raymond, five vols, Paris: 1959–, vol iv, pp. 503-504, trans. Barbara Foxley, London: Dent, 1974, p. 182.

5. Søren Kierkegaard, *Samlede Værker*, ed. A. B. Drachmann, J. L. Heiberg, and H. O. Lange, Copenhagen: Gyldendal, 1962, vol. 14, p. 78.

6. Ibid., p. 37.

7. Ibid., p. 42.

8. This illusory supposition is supported by the myth of "the public", a "monstrous abstraction", for which Kierkegaard blames journalists (ibid., p. 43): it is the "phantom", or "mirage", which appears to give social substance to this airy "all and nothing" (ibid., p. 44), and which allows the most comprehensive and destructive form of levelling to take effect: "genuine, purely abstract levelling" (ibid., p. 45).

9. S. Kierkegaard, *The Sickness unto Death*, Harmondsworth: Penguin Books, 1989, p. 85.

10. Ibid., p. 86.

11. Loc. cit.

12. Immanuel Kant, *Fundamental Principles of the Metaphysic of Ethics*, trans. T. K. Abbott, London: Longmans, Green & Co., 1946, p. 24.

13. S. Kierkegaard, *Kjerlighedens Gjerninger* [Works of Love], *Samlede Værker* 12, p. 26. The essentials of Kierkegaard's account of love are anticipated in the *Nicomachean Ethics*, VIII, iii, 2, where Aristotle observes that "in a friendship based on utility or on pleasure men love their friend for their own good or their own pleasure, and not as being the person loved, but as useful or agreeable". Such friendships are "based on an accident, since the friend is not loved for being what he is, but as affording some benefit or pleasure as the case may be" (*Aristotle*, XIX: *The Nicomachean Ethics*, trans. H. Rackham, London: Heinemann/Cambridge, MA: Harvard University Press, p. 459).

14. Kant., op. cit., p. 18.

15. Just as Aristotle says that when the "motive of the friendship has passed away, the friendship itself is dissolved, having existed merely as a means to that end". (op. cit., VIII, Cf. William Shakespeare's "Love is not love which alters when it alteration finds" (Sonnett CXVI)).

16. There is a fuller discussion in my *Kierkegaard*, London/New York: Routledge, 1982, rev. ed. 1991, ch. 7.

17. See M. Jamie Ferreira's brief but timely "Kierkegaardian Imagination and the Feminine", *Kierkegaardiana* 16, pp. 79–91.

18. See note 2 above.

19. Aristotle, op. cit., VIII, v, 5. His reason for this is that friendship, as a reciprocal form of liking, involves "deliberate choice", and deliberate choice in his view must spring from a fixed disposition. I am grateful to Marianne McDonald for bringing this to my attention.

20. Ibid., VIII, iii, 6.

21. Loc. cit.

22. See Tracy Strong, *Friedrich Nietzsche and the Politics of Transfiguration*, Berkeley: University of California Press, 1975, pp. 192–202, and Keith Ansell-Pearson, *Nietzsche contra Rousseau*, Cambridge: Cambridge University Press, 1991, pp. 214–215.

23. Cf. Nietzsche's claim in his unpublished essay on "Homer's Weltkampf" of 1872 that natural talent must develop through struggle.

24. Cf. Nietzsche's unpublished essay of 1871 on "The Greek State".

25. Cf. *The Sickness unto Death*, op. cit., p. 86.

Chapter 12

Is and Ought
On Authenticity and Responsibility in Heidegger's Ontology

Joachim Renn

In this essay, I would like to examine Heidegger's contribution to ethics or, rather, moral theory. This contribution has to be termed "concealed", since initially, when we begin enquiring after a practical philosophy, Heidegger is silent. We hear nothing of the criteria, justification, or scope of moral principles, nor anything about procedures for reaching practical consensus or the normative resources regarding the legitimacy of social arrangements.

I

The first impression with which any attempt to understand Heidegger's *"Denkweg"* or "course of thought"[1] is confronted is the following: there is neither an ethics nor a moral theory to be found in Heidegger.[2] This first impression has its systematic justification: fundamental ontology – like both the analysis of *Dasein* and, especially, Heidegger's figurative language after the *"Kehre"* – avoids the classical trichotomy among spheres of reason, the rationally relevant employment of language in the theoretical, practical, and aesthetic or expressive dimensions. And this is not because the *Denkweg* has set itself up within one of these three spheres, neglecting the other two; rather, fundamental ontology and the philosophy of the history of Being claim to be working the soil out of which practical, theoretical, and aesthetic theory can grow apart in the first place. Heidegger's ontological fusion of a theory of subjectivity, knowledge, the work of art, and its normative character (initially found in the call for authenticity, then in the admonishment against the forgetfulness of Being) is methodologically justified by a hermeneutically uncovered difference. In Heidegger's view, before this division of faculties of reason could orient itself in accordance with the ontic structure of beings [Seienden] (that is, in accordance with the corresponding subject-areas), we initially give these areas a preliminary projection by the underlying understanding of Being.

The latitude for explicating the meaning of Being is understood as freedom, in the sense that, say, Kant's criterion for distinguishing between the fields of theoretical and practical reason (namely, the difference between the laws of nature and the freedom of the will) is itself not an *a priori* fact but rather the outcome of the basic preliminary projection of differing meanings of "Being".[3]

Heidegger views the hypostatization of the traditionally inherited distinction between "is" and "ought" as a normatively significant symptom: Heidegger's schematization of the relationship between basic concepts of metaphysics – which he works out in *An Introduction to Metaphysics*, but whose central point forms a thread that can be followed back along the "Denkweg" to *Being and Time*[4] – reconfirms the fact that, for Heidegger, the basic distinction between "is" and "ought" is to be considered the product of yet another misguided [fehlgeleitet] history of theory.[5] In Heidegger's eyes, the appropriate task of philosophy consists not in this metaphysical forgottenness of Being [Seinsvergessenheit], but rather in remembering the purportedly fundamental question about the meaning of Being [der Sinn von Sein]. Hence, whereas other philosophical projects tended to view the contribution of hermeneutics as limited to the "critique of meaning" [Sinnkritik],[6] Heidegger considers understanding – or, rather, the explication [Auslegung] of "Being"[7] – to be prior to the distinguishing of practical and theoretical philosophy. This meta-theoretical tack deserves some attention, at least to the extent to which, by means of hermeneutical themes [Motive], the central (that is, quasi *a priori*) significance of contingent world-disclosure has, for some time now, been enjoying a renaissance.[8]

Regarding the issue of Heidegger's possible contribution to ethics and moral theory, the somewhat abstract controversy over whether ontological difference should be promoted to the status of a methodological *leitmotif* can contribute little or, perhaps, only indirectly. The most that would be decided here is whether practical philosophy would have to be derived from a more fundamental discipline, but not what would have to be derived or how.

If, however, one starts by assuming, for the sake of argument, that there are good reasons for studying the ontological "dimension of depth"

[*Tiefendimension*] – that is, for assuming that Heidegger's hierarchicalization is worthwhile, if perhaps not in every detail of its execution[9] – then the ground has been cleared for a more precise appraisal of what Heidegger may have to offer practical philosophy. There are thus several normatively interesting basic components that can be identified here.

The fundamental ontology concerned with the analysis of *Dasein* is, in the first instance, a theory of action, an analysis of the basic structure of what is usually called the practical domain of reason, an analysis that has recently been related closely to pragmatism.[10] As such, it is also a theory (i) that asserts the priority of (pre-predicative) action to the rational faculty abstracted from it and (ii) that, as an existential analysis [*Existentialanalytik*] and under the banner of authenticity, ascribes normative implications to the analysis of that basic pragmatic structure. Hence, one could almost call it, quite vaguely, "fundamental ethics" [*Fundamentalethik*]. To say the very least, *Being and Time* is anything but normatively neutral.[11]

For the interlaced methodological perspectives of *Being and Time* – both of ontology and of the analysis of *Dasein* (the understanding of Being is always a question about *Dasein*'s manner of Being, in which it is concerned, in its being, with its Being) – can be related to an interest that guides any practical philosophy. Hence, Günter Figal devotes an entire book to trying to demonstrate that Heidegger's guiding intention was the search for a "philosophy of freedom".[12] At the same time, in accordance with the connection between ontology and the analysis of *Dasein*, this talk of freedom refers both to the freedom of human existence and to the relation of "Being" to freedom in the sense of the identification of Being as "possibility". This means, in turn, that the primacy of *Dasein*'s modal constitution – possibility as the "yet-to-be-given" [*ausstehende*] existing of "beings" [*Seienden*] that have yet "to be" – is also understood, ontologically, as prior to the branching of freedom of the will and natural causality. The freedom associated with the preliminary projection [*Vorentwurfes*] of the boundaries demarcating the ontologies of various domains precedes and underlies the tie to the faculty of perseverance of objects of knowledge and to the necessity of the laws of nature.

Furthermore, even if *Being and Time* fails to make a convincing contribution to social philosophy's question as to the conditions of possibility for intersubjectivity (indeed, as we shall see, it systematically excludes an approach that starts out from the rationality of communicative interaction), in this context the analysis of subjectivity-cum-*Dasein* still foregrounds a social component under the heading *"being-with"* [*Mitsein*]. The crucial feature here is the desubstantialization of the concept of a person, and one of the pillars of this desubstantialization is at least a suggested theory of fundamental intersubjectivity. It is not far from criticizing the Cartesian subjectivity of knowledge to relativizing the concept of the moral person. And thus, in the context of the desubstantializing of the *ego*, Heidegger can be said to provide, in terms of an analysis of *Dasein*, a commentary on personal autonomy.

II

Before turning to Heidegger's interpretation of personal autonomy (in the Kantian sense), it must be shown what "desubstantialization" means in *Being and Time*. In what way "is" *Dasein*, when it is not "present-at-hand" [*vorhanden*]? To begin with, *Dasein* is not a subject that encounters the world. The split between *res cogitans* and *res extensa* is replaced by "Being-in-the-world", in the sense that *Dasein*, exclusively engaged in pre-theor-etical, pragmatic "circumspection" [*Umsicht*], does not deal with things but rather makes use of "ready-to-hand" [*zuhanden*] tools in "concern" [*Besorgen*]. Heidegger's definitions of "Being-in-the-world" portray factic-ity as a concrete, already understood yet unarticulated relation to the world, one that precedes every form of the dichotomy of *ego* and world, subject, and object – or, rather, one that renders any approach that starts out from such a dichotomy abstract. *Dasein* and world comprise a pre-dichotomic unity.

Heidegger defines the mode of Being of human existence in terms of what he calls the care structure [*Sorgestruktur*], that is, the structure of a pragmatic, future-oriented, this-worldly [*innerweltliches*] interest that comprehends pre-linguistically.[13] This relation to the world is first described in the mode of everyday life, that is, in the dimension of a general interpretedness of the world into which *Dasein* finds itself "thrown". Heidegger then identifies the freedom of preliminary ontologi-cal projection with the free "resoluteness" through which an individual-ized *Dasein* arrives at its "own" [*eigentlich*] authentic *Dasein* in the mode of radical individualization [*Vereinzelung*] and in defiance of the everyday conventions in terms of which "they" [*man*] understand both themselves and the world pragmatically. In doing so, genuine and ontologically interesting *Dasein* must, as it were, tear itself out of the generality of this-worldly facticity and, "in anticipation of death" (that is, in the resolute appropriation of *Dasein*'s own, irreplaceable [*unvertretbar*] finitude), must choose its individual possibilities – its "to be" – in existential freedom.

Authentic *Dasein* thus "is" by seizing, in its freedom, upon possibilities, without, however, thereby eliminating [*aufheben*], within the positivity of traits, its modal constitution as "being" a possibility. In distinguishing possibility as a characteristic of human *Dasein* from the empty category of the "mere" possibility of something that is sometimes like this and sometimes like that, Heidegger is arguing that, although *Dasein* is characterized by possibility, as something that in fact exists and that pursues goals under the heading "for-the-sake-of-which", its realization is also endowed with a necessity of sorts. Hence, the modal characterization of *Dasein*'s manner of Being cannot be reduced to only one of the modal categories. *Dasein* is necessary, in that it seizes upon possibilities – that is, realizes the contingent – without thereby fully giving up the status of being possibility. This means that *Dasein*'s possibility is characterized by necessity in two ways: (i) as "thrown", *Dasein* cannot but exist – it is "condemned" (Sartre) to freedom, (ii) it is necessarily the case that *Dasein* must "be" in a particular, self-chosen manner – it must seize upon opportunities and not simply "leave everything open" – even though the choice of certain possibilities can never fully eliminate the latitude presented by a range of possibilities.

The composition of modal forms rests on the composition of temporal modi that mediate between the possibility and the realization of the contingent, and time, in this sense, is the temporal extension of actions in their "ecstatic" form. Heidegger defines the type of possibility that "is" existence – as opposed to the presence-at-hand of objecthood [*Gegenständlichkeit*] of this-worldly beings [*Seiendem*] – in terms of the pragmatic distance between action possibilities and realized actions. To say that *Dasein* "has to be" [*hat zu sein*] is also to say that it has to be ahead of itself with regard to its current action by anticipating the meaning and purpose of its action. The analysis of *Dasein* is thus a form of action theory. As a result, the distinction between "mere" possibility and *Dasein*'s form of possibility is linked to the practical dimension associated with the freedom of action. The extent to which Heidegger is actually thinking here of the difference between natural causality or causes, on the one hand, and the teleology of action or motives, on the other,[14] can be seen in *The Basic Problems of Phenomenology* of 1927. Here, Heidegger refers to Kant's *Metaphysics of Morals* and welcomes the distinction between persons (as ends in themselves) and things.[15] In discussing Kant, Heidegger has a dual agenda. First, he wants to use the distinction between persons as ends in themselves and things [*Dingen* or *Sachen*] as a way of answering the question about the *ego*'s mode of Being. Heidegger is here studying the transcendental theory of subjectivity with an eye to the analysis of *Dasein*, in the narrower sense. Second, he is trying to demonstrate signs of ontological difference even in the case of Kant. Ontological difference becomes noticeable in the distinction between things and persons as soon as the status of the person is understood in terms of the problem of freedom. If the understanding of Being projects and determines the meaning of Being, then ontological difference emerges only where Being can be understood or projected at all. Only if *Dasein* projects a meaning of Being is it possible to distinguish Being from that which is [*Seiendem*]. Thus, the condition for the possibility of the capacity for ontological distinction is the case in which *Dasein* relates to what is [*Seienden*], and this relation is defined as freedom. For Heidegger conceives of this relation not as distantiated knowing but rather as latitude for action. Hence, it is human freedom that makes ontological difference possible or, rather, "meaningful",[16] so that here Heidegger's first aim (the interest behind the analysis of *Dasein* in the Being of persons or, rather, of *Dasein*[17]) and his second aim (the ontological question) turn out to be one and the same.

In the interpretation of Kant, which is supposed to demonstrate the connection between *Dasein*'s mode of Being, freedom, and ontological difference, Heidegger refers in the first instance to the "*personalitas moralis*" and that speaks in favour of [*für*] the normative qualification of the neutral ontological foundation. With regard to both the empirical person (*personalitas psychologica*) and the transcendental subject (*personalitas transcendentalis*), he displays an interest only in distanciating them. This begins to make sense once one follows Heidegger's argument and recognizes, in the moral feeling of respect (the only such feeling, according to Kant), a clue to the ontological deciphering of human existence.[18] Within the horizon of fundamental ontology, the distinction between a person (which deserves to be called an end in itself) and a thing [*Sache*](which may be viewed as a means) comes to be a distinction between modes of Being: this differentiation between persons and things provides "the basis . . . for distinguishing ontologically between beings that are egos [*ichlich Seienden*] and beings that are not egos, between subject and object, *res cogitans* and *res extensa*".[19] The status of human freedom in the organization of Kant's three *Critiques* becomes a synonym for what Heidegger called "ontological distinctiveness" [*Auszeichnung*] in *Being and Time*. At the primary level of the understanding of Being, the depiction of the ontologically significant, action-theoretical mode of *Dasein*'s Being as freedom posits an *ontological* "ought" alongside the ontically understood "ought" of the everyday (empirical) acceptance and requirements of, for example, moral norms.

As is well known, Heidegger viewed Kant as only anticipating and not fully or consistently clarifying the ontological significance of this distinction.[20] Whereas for Kant the decisive distinction between these modes of Being remains that of subject and object, Heidegger was interested in the overcoming this split between the transcendental *ego* and the world in terms of the fundamental Being-in-the-world, by replacing this split with the distinction between Being and beings.

From a normative point of view, however, this replacement demands its price. The reinterpretation of human freedom as *Dasein*'s mode of Being as "factical" existence rather than the practical reasonableness of the autonomous subject entails a shift in the meanings of the expressions "respect" and "responsibility". For Kant, the subject of practical self-respect must appeal to the general form of the moral law as the only content of the *a priori* certainty of its practical quality; the subject respects the general moral subject in itself, in the sense of the dignity of "humanity in one's person",[21] without regard to any non-intelligible determining grounds of the "ought" (such as inclinations or drives), which is associated with the realm of the empirical and of natural causation. It is, however, only in this sensible realm – following Heidegger, one would have to say only in the facticity of the already interpreted world – that a person can distinguish himself or herself as the authentic individuality that, for Heidegger, becomes a central instance of the hermeneutical *a priori*. Hence, Heidegger's ontological "correction" consists precisely in recasting, in the course of the critique of the philosophy of the subject, the status of the moral person as the factical existence of an *ego* that is in-each-case-mine [*jemeinig*]. Once autonomy has been transformed into authenticity in this way, what can be the object of respect and responsibility?

Compared with *Being and Time*, what stands out in *The Basic Problems of Phenomenology* is Heidegger's emphasis on the sense of responsibility that a person encounters in feeling respect for the law and in discovering the intelligible freedom of his or her will. Initially, Heidegger remains faithful to Kant's text in presenting him as follows: "The specific having of a feeling for the law which is present in respect is a self-subjection. I subject myself in respect for the law to my own self as the free self. In this subjection of myself I am manifest to myself; I am as I myself. The question is, As what or, more precisely, as *whom?*"[22] The first answer to this question is still close to Kant: the subjection to the law that is motivated by respect, the "submissive self-elevation . . . discloses as such, me to myself in my *dignity*". And again: "The moral feeling, as respect for the law, is nothing but the self's being responsible to itself and for itself. This moral feeling is a distinctive way in which the ego understands itself as ego directly, purely, and free of all sensuous determination."[23]

In Kantian terms, there is no difference between the responsibility of practical subjects vis-à-vis themselves and respect for the moral law, insofar as this respect obtains [*die Achtung gilt der Form*] exclusively in its pure form, ultimately the form of the possible non-contradiction of an orderly system that generalizes the specific maxims of an action. For, in my dignity as a universal *personalitas moralis*, I respect myself for that which, disregarding all distinctions between empirical persons, links me as a human being to all other accountable persons (if not rational beings), namely, the capacity to recognize within myself, separate from all sensuous determinations and empirical inclinations, the moral law as a matter of both freedom and duty. This equation of recognition of duty or respect for the law, on the one hand, and the freedom and dignity of the person, on the other, presupposes the universality of the transcendental subject in its practical instantiation.

It is precisely this presupposition, however, that is ruled out by Heidegger's reinterpretation of the subject of practical reason as *Dasein*'s factical existence as in-the-world. As a consequence, he has to interpret the meaning of the phrase "responsibility of the self to itself and for itself" in a way that eliminates any reference to duty, the universal form of the law, or subjection to a form of practical intersubjectivity. Heidegger's wording two pages later confirms this: "Only in responsibility does the self first reveal itself – the self not in a general sense as knowledge of an ego in general but as in each case mine, the ego as in each case the individual factical ego."[24]

As a result, the meaning of the term "freedom" shifts from the idea of duty conjoined with the free recognition of the universal law – as in the case of Kant – to existential liberation from external constraints; one could perhaps even say that there is a shift here from a concept of positive freedom to that of merely negative freedom.[25] Hence, in contrast to the conception of the autonomy of the transcendental, practical subject, the subjection to the formal, abstract universality of practical laws that is required by the categorical imperative now counts as an imposition of heteronomy. Autonomy, in the sense of the free restraint of egocentric freedom of choice, becomes divorced from authenticity.

From a normative perspective, then, one's first impression is that the radicalization of the question about the *ego*'s mode of Being ends up breaking the link to the universality of the law's form and, ultimately, to the problem of justice. Does this mean that, as long as *Dasein* authentically [*nur recht eigentlich*] takes responsibility for itself and vis-à-vis itself, it can "do and omit what it wants to"?

Matters are not so simple, however. For not only does the practical *ego* get redefined, externally, as the individual (whose autonomy Kant would have termed "purely arbitrary will" [*reine Willkür*]), the transformation of its definition also takes, as we have seen, an ontological detour via the relativization of the division between practical and theoretical subjectivity. Heidegger thus characterizes the goal of his ontological work as follows: "Present in Kant is a peculiar omission: he fails to determine originally the unity of the theoretical and practical ego."[26]

However much it may suggest ontological difference, Kant's determination of the moral person remains inadequate, because he develops the concept of freedom by opposing it, on the one hand, to the sensuous determining grounds of action and, on the other hand, to the theoretical faculty of reason. Heidegger, by contrast, attempts to trace freedom and duty as well as knowledge and objectiveness [*Gegenständlichkeit*] back to a more originary basis in the projecting [*entwerfende*] understanding of the meaning of Being.

Heidegger connects two problems here: first, the impossibility of grasping the mode of Being of the theoretical *ego* in terms of the categories of the understanding, which synthesize the sensuous (that which occurs in time and space) and, second, Kant's "failure" to clarify the "I act" ontologically.

Whereas *Kant and the Problem of Metaphysics* is concerned primarily with temporality in connection with the question of the theoretical *a priori*, in *The Basic Problems of Phenomenology* the links between freedom, the understanding of Being, and, finally, temporality are more clearly visible: Heidegger writes here that Kant

> has not shown that the "I act" itself cannot be interpreted in the way in which it gives itself, in this self-manifesting ontological constitution. Perhaps it is precisely time which is the *a priori* of the ego – time, to be sure, in a more original sense than Kant was able to conceive it. He assigned it to sensibility and consequently from the beginning, conforming with tradition, he had in view natural time alone.[27]

Indeed, the *Critique of Practical Reason* contains only the dichotomy between a concept of temporal extension – an extension which the pure form of the inner intuition attributes to those things that, as objects, are subject to causal laws – and the atemporality of pure reason. This disjunction, which Heidegger considers incomplete, is itself dependent on a concept of causality, which can be saved from the threat posed by the antinomy of an unconditionally first cause only by the concept of a "supersensible" form of freedom.[28] Thus, Kant writes:

> The concept of causality as natural necessity, unlike the concept of causality as freedom, concerns only the existence of things as far as it is determinable in time, and consequently as appearances in contrast to their causality as things-in-themselves. If one takes the attributes of the existence of things in time for attributes of things-in-themselves, which is the usual way of thinking, the necessity in the causal relation can in no way be united with freedom. They are contradictory to each other . . . Since the past is no longer in my power, every action which I perform is necessary because of determining grounds which are not in my power. This means that at the time I act I am never free.[29]

On Kant's view, everything that can be determined in time strives for something determinate in order to become an empirical object, subject to the laws of nature and not those of freedom. Against this, Heidegger thinks that, in contrast to natural time, the authentic, ecstatic time of the hermeneutic horizon of *Dasein*'s [*daseinsförmigen*] self-understanding makes possible the unity of freedom of action and concrete temporal determination.[30]

Here, too, Heidegger thus lets the ontological cat out of the bag and at least implies that temporality – in the sense to be developed by *Being and Time* – comes up for consideration as the horizon of the mode of Being of *Dasein* (as the derivative separation of is and ought, knowledge and duty).

On the one hand, then, the distinction between is and ought is a question of time; on the other hand, as responsibility, the freedom of *Dasein* is already normatively charged, even before the division of is and ought. As an ontological foundation, not only does freedom thus have the theoretical character of a condition of possibility of the *a priori* of pure reason (as in the book on Kant); as responsibility, it is also a meta-practical conception.

Once the Kantian figure of the unity of justice – as law, along with the universal form of or respect for the law – and the autonomy of the moral subject (owing to the formal universality of the subjective faculty) has been eliminated from the perspective of fundamental ontology, it becomes important to attend to the way in which the fundamental mode of authenticity associated with *Dasein*'s use of its freedom can be re-translated as a substitute for what Kant called autonomy. The meaning of the formal concept of autonomy is in part a question about justice: as *personalitas moralis*, my interests do not conflict with those of other persons, since the differences between our interests are empirical and thus eliminated [*aufgehoben*] in transcendental autonomy. Factical authenticity (that which is made concrete in this world), by contrast, must be reconnected to the moral-theoretical issue of how my arbitrary will [*Willkür*] is to be restricted for the sake of another. Is it possible for there to be an equivalent figure, according to which authenticity (ontological) and autonomy (here one has to say, "ontical") do not conflict, or is this possibility ruled out by the fundamental decisions of Heidegger's proposal?

This question can be answered as soon as one considers how the normative dimension implicit in the concept of ontological authenticity is developed in the course of the analysis of *Dasein*.

III

The determination of *Dasein* as facticity as Being-in-the-world in advance of the dichotomy discussed above shares with Hegel's critique of Kant the opposition to the restriction of the reasonableness of universal intersubjectivity to the mere form of law. As Hegel says:

> In the Kantian definition of right, which is also more widely accepted, the essential element is "the *limitation* of my freedom or *arbitrary will* [*Willkür*] in such a way that it may coexist with the arbitrary will of everyone else in accordance with a universal law." On the one hand, this definition contains only a *negative* determination – that of limitation; and on the other hand, the positive [element] – the

universal law or so-called "law of reason", the consonance of the arbitrary will of one individual with that of the other – amounts simply to the familiar [principle of] formal identity and the law of contradiction. The definition of right in question embodies the view, especially prevalent since Rousseau, according to which the substantial basis and primary factor is supposed to be . . . the *particular* individual, as the will of the single person in his distinctive arbitrariness. Once this principle is accepted, the rational can of course appear only as a limitation on the freedom in question, and not as an immanent rationality, but only as an external and formal universal.[31]

This reminder of Hegel's position helps to clarify what can be expected from Heidegger's critique of a formal conception of duty and the restriction of arbitrary will: Hegel's concretization of the element of duty in a theory of the particular will that is mediated by the universality of civil society's universality does not have to give up the link to respect for the law. Hegel merely points out that this law is not distinguished exclusively by its pure form; rather, its particular instantiation contains the mediation of subjective and objective Spirit [*Geist*] in the concrete ethical life of the "System of Needs".[32] Can something comparable be hoped for from Heidegger's hermeneutical ontology, which appeals regularly to examples of working with one's hands and yet devotes not a single word to trade unions?

Although the abstract determination of individual practical interests as immediate data that are to be constrained by the universality of the form of human freedom comes in for criticism, it should be kept in mind that, in Kant, this abstraction is due to the relegation of individual inclinations to the realm of empirical natural causes. Once this is kept in mind, the bridge to Heidegger is clear. This abstract determination of individual interest is dependent on the assimilation of personal individuality to the individualizing synthesis of the empirically perceivable objects that belong to nature, to the extent to which they are governed by natural laws. For Kant, the qualitative determination of individuals (in the sense, found more recently in Strawson, of concrete phenomena) remains a matter of conjoining general predicates, and their identification remains a matter of localizing them in a similarly universal spatio-temporal coordinate system. It is this model of the determination of individuals that is undermined by the analysis of *Dasein*, and this in two ways. First, as an approach to the qualitative determination of personal individuality, existential mineness [*Jemeinigkeit*] is stressed over the conjunction of universal determinations, and the ecstatic temporality of self-determination is emphasized over the isotropic spatio-temporal continuum. Second, the notion that abstractly posited individuals are connected to the intersubjectivity of formal socialization by their obedience to the mere form of the law is challenged by the theory of Being-with [*Mitsein*].

Heidegger's reason for introducing Being-with here – in what seems, at first, to be a parallel with Hegel – is virtually to turn the relationship of the particular and the universal associated with personality on its head. *Dasein* is – in the first instance – intersubjectivity, even if the use of this expression to characterize the existential structure goes against the standard approach, which declares the predicatively differentiated universality of rationality – which Heidegger takes to task, using the example of statements [*die Aussage*] – to be the criterion for intersubjectivity. But what is at issue is the opposition of a conception of fundamental sociality to a theoretical perspective that – by abstractly overlooking mediation, as Hegel would have put it – makes the specific and particular interest, the definite and goal-oriented, rationally calculative arbitrary will [*Willkür*] the datum from which to proceed. To this extent, Heidegger is in agreement with a reconstruction of the intersubjective mediation of personal identity based on a theory of socialization. What Heidegger introduces as the medium of mediation is not, however, language but rather the prepredicative understanding belonging to the pragmatic relation to the world, which is first sketched in the analysis of equipment [*Zeug*] and then developed as the structure of care. Furthermore, we shall see that, for methodological reasons (i.e. owing to the necessary tie, in Heidegger, between ontology and an *ego*-logical analysis of *Dasein*), in the course of the analysis even the fundamental intersubjectivity – initially introduced as the originary mode of *Dasein* – loses its significance as soon as everydayness comes to be devalued, and is forced into decline and inauthenticity. At this point, Heidegger's opposition to moral formalism departs from Hegel's model.

The analysis of equipment and the study of "worldhood" develop in concrete detail the starting principle that, as *Dasein* and as the "performance" [*Vollzug*] of acts, persons are not something present-at-hand, like "other created things".[33] Later, Heidegger turns to the social dimension of the desubstantialization of the ego or "I": "In clarifying Being-in-theworld we have shown that a bare subject without a world never 'is' proximally, nor is it ever given. And so in the end an isolated 'I' without Others is just as far from being proximally given."[34]

Again the determination of this given – in this case, the Others –
acquires its contours through the contrast with presence-at-hand. The
givenness of Others differs in three ways from the presence of objects,
understood as external. First, this givenness is existential, such that even
the actual absence of the Other – "Being-alone"[35] – remains a mode of
Being-with, as the mode of care, Being-with is distinguished from the
objectivity associated with knowing something in a distancing way. And
this distinction, in turn, has two meanings: first, in inexpressible understanding, and then "thematically". In the first case:

> By "Others" we do not mean everyone else but me – those over against whom the
> 'I' stands out. They are rather those from whom, from the most part, one does not
> distinguish oneself – those among whom one is too. This Being-there-too [*Auch-da-
> sein*] with them does not have the ontological character of a Being-present-at-
> hand-along-"with" them in the world. This "with" is something of the character of
> *Dasein*; the "too" means a sameness of Being as circumspectively concernful
> [*umsichtig-besorgendes*] Being-in-the-world . . . The world of *Dasein* is *with-world*
> [*Mitwelt*]. Being-in is *Dasein*-with [*Mitdasein*]. Others . . . are encountered from out
> of the world, in which concernfully circumspective *Dasein* essentially dwells.[36]

The second stage is reached in the transition from pre-predicative understanding to explication, in which the Others still do not yet become
present-at-hand: "But even if Others become themes for study, as it were,
in their own *Dasein*, they are not encountered as person-Things present-
at-hand: we meet them 'at work', that is, primarily in their Being-in-the-
world."[37] Not only the tacit, detailed know-how of working with one's
hands but even thematizing explication allows the other *Dasein* to appear
as relating pragmatically to the world. Thus, in speaking of Others as "co-
workers" we can go beyond inarticulate understanding without necessarily having to "reify" [*verdinglichen*] them. One would like to have heard
more from Heidegger in this regard, for example as to whether what is
intended here is a distinction between speaking "about" someone and
speaking with one another (in the sense suggested by a hermeneutics
of dialogue) or rather a difference between first-person attitudes and
second-person attitudes (in the sense suggested by Habermas' theory of
communicative action).

One sees Others at work, even if only negatively, in mere "standing-
around".[38] Since what is here called "at work" involves a reference to
care, its determination must, in retrospect [*nachträglich*], also be characterized as Being-with. And Heidegger rightly concerns himself with

correcting the *ego*-logical connotation of the first determination of care. Indeed, in the analysis of equipment, the circumspection of *Dasein* was always discussed in the singular, whereas thrownness was related only to the facticity of existing [*bestehender*] constellations of equipment and hence without any explicit reference to the givenness – that is, the further explicating influence – of another *Dasein*.[39] (For "who", then, would have "already explicated" the world?) The correction of the *ego*-logical connotation occurs in the coining of the expression "caring-for" [*Fürsorge*]. One can expect that it is in caring-for that we find the fusion of the pragmatic structures of Being-with, which – if *Dasein* is concern [*Besorgen*] – has to be "caring-with" [*Mitsorge*], and from this point on one must think of the ontological foundation underlying the explicating and understanding projection [*Entwerfen*] of the meaning of Being as being extended to include what one could call an ontological division of labour. What is at stake here is not only the empirical or ontic industriousness in constellations of equipment but also the underlying ontological distinguishing of concern, so that, at this point, one would have to reconstrue what the explication of the meaning of Being achieves by way of constitutive, preliminary projection in light of the interconnection of the *Dasein* of various cooperating, "*jemeinig*" existences.[40]

IV

In addition, the suggestion of "caring-with" could be expanded into a reconstruction of a primordial form of obligation to others. Does not the insight that we cannot take care of anything ourselves in complete isolation from the care of others lead to the discovery of a fundamental obligation to make cooperative concern [*Gemeinsam besorgen*] possible and to keep it so – an obligation, as it were, to cooperation, not to mention *communication*?[41]

Revealingly, however, Heidegger sets his analysis on a different course here. Against the possible expectation just mentioned, the expression "caring-for" turns out not to be a matter of cooperative concern associated with the ready-to-hand but refers rather to the care that *Dasein* bestows upon others. At first, this sounds like the materials for an existential reconstruction of a primordial obligation to the Other, but it turns out that this specification merely serves the purpose of reducing Being-with to the *ego*-logical ascription of caring to a *Dasein*, in the singular. The mode of givenness of a being that is neither ready-to-hand nor present-at-hand but rather, as an Other, is *Dasein*-like deserves a name. Heidegger selectively narrows the concepts of care originally introduced with "care-with" to the problem of the care for the Other and unnoticeably occludes the question of shared concern. Consider the following passage:

> Concern is a character-of-Being which Being-with cannot have as its own, even though Being-with, like concern, is a *Being towards* entities encountered within-the-world. But those entities towards which *Dasein* as Being-with comports itself do not have the kind of Being which belongs to equipment ready-to-hand; they are themselves *Dasein*. These entities are not objection of concern [*Besorgen*] but rather of caring-for [*Fürsorge*].[42]

In this passage, one finds disappointed the above-mentioned expectation that concern-with-one-another is to be thematized here as a basis of co-operative ontological understanding. For the shift of perspective from the question of how *Dasein* shares concerns with other *Dasein* to the question of how it cares for another serves, first, to reconfirm the *ego*-logical perspective (about which more will be said in discussing "*das Man*") and, second, in the course of the analysis of everydayness, even to lead to the reduction of care for the other to the care of the self.

To begin with, however, caring-for is here distinguished into authentic and inauthentic modes. Caring-for can assume a form in which, by intervening or "leaping in" [*einspringen*], it fails to do justice to the Other; alternatively, it can succeed as caring-for that "leaps ahead" [*vorspringen*]. Caring-for can rob the Other of his or her freedom by taking away, as it were, the care of the Other and "put itself in his position in concern".[43] In this case, the other is intervened upon, not as a matter of responsible assistance but rather as a matter of "throwing the other out of his wn position". (The thrownness of *Dasein*, it is implied here, can also be a matter of being thrown by another *Dasein*.) To this extent, if one recalls Kant's connection between autonomy and dignity, the criticism of caring-for that "leaps in" or takes charge suggests a principled opposition to "humiliating" others, in which one catches sight of an existentially reconstructed concept of intersubjectively secured maturity [*Mündigkeit*].

The caring-for that "leaps in" is to be contrasted with that which "leads ahead", which "pertains essentially to authentic care – that is, to the existence of the Other, not to a '*what*' with which he is concerned."[44] The difference between these two modes of caring-for is connected normatively to the character of the analysis of *Dasein* as a philosophy of freedom: Heidegger refers explicitly to the "two extremes of caring-for – that which leaps in and dominates [*einspringend-beherrschend*], and that which leaps forth and liberates [*vorspringend-befreiend*]", referring to the opposition between domination and liberation, or – as one could say, with an eye to his interpretation of Kant – between heteronomy and autonomy. One must read precisely here. In what sense does caring-for "pertain" to authentic care? Heidegger avoids suggesting that authentic care would reveal itself as caring-for as soon as one pays attention to Being-with. A conceivable position – one taken recently by Levinas – would be that this central "final for-the-sake-of-which" [*worum-willen*] that matters to *Dasein* is the care of the Other. This reading seems to be suggested by Heidegger's claim that "[t]hus, as Being-with, *Dasein* 'is' essentially for the sake of Others."[45] In that case, authentic *Dasein* would have been discovered ontologically in its obligation to responsibility vis-à-vis the other *Dasein* who "is with". And that would mean that part of authentic existence would be the authentic fulfilment of one's genuine duty to ensure that "things turn out well for the Other". In light of the later arguments of *Being and Time*, an interpretation of caring-for as essentially obliged to "liberate" the other *Dasein* would be very unusual. Were that the case, indeed, the analysis of Being-with would contain the traces of the inter-subjective enabling of authentic *Dasein*'s existential genesis. For then the enabling of existential genesis, that is, the realization of existential freedom, would not (as in *Being and Time*) be declared to be a project of an individual liberating himself or herself from the Others, but it would be placed, at least in part, in the hands of *Dasein* that "is with" [*mitseienden Daseins*].

Moreover, the ontological foundation of the understanding of Being would become a set of tasks divided into perspectives, and the analysis of *Dasein* as the reconstruction of the origins of genuine "mineness" [*Jemeinigkeit*] or authenticity and the question as to the ontological constitution of the understanding of Being would become questions that would have to be treated separately.

Heidegger takes a different tack here, however. Caring-for "pertains" to authentic care only insofar as authentic [*eigentliche*] care (in the sense of one's own [*eigene*] care) is concerned with *Dasein* in the singular. In other words, authentic care is not caring-with. The enabling of care as authentic freedom of the other *Dasein* is not itself part of authentic care. This means that the path sketched above of the existential proof of the unity of in-each-case-mine freedom and duty is not taken.

In these passages, caring-for remains restricted to individual *Dasein*, which can be separated only forcibly from Being-with, but which is put right back into this isolation in the following steps, by way of the interpretation of *das Man*.

As a result, the purpose of the discussion of Being-with consists only in the rejection of the "theorems of empathy" and other models of intersubjectivity that presuppose the separateness of present-at-hand subjects who "appear along side each other".[46] The attempt to locate caring-for remains subject to the systematic tension inherent in Heidegger's attempt to put *Dasein*, care, and the ontological achievement of the authentic understanding appropriate to *Dasein* back into the *ego*-logical perspective.

There are thus two steps in Heidegger's argument that – despite his having tacked on the notion of Being-with – rob this existential of its relevance. First, caring-for remains the mode of care associated with a singular *Dasein*, even if the object of concern is a *Dasein*-like being [*daseinmäßig Seiendes*]; a term such as "caring-with", which would refer to an ontological division of labour, is still lacking. Second, caring-for serves to liberate *Dasein* to engage in authentic – that is, free – care, but it is not the case that, as Being-with, authentic care is always also "leaping ahead" and liberating caring-with that is responsible for others. This last move in particular is ruled out in principle, because the notion of Being has been introduced in the general mode, which is indicated by Heidegger's recurrent use of the term "always already" [immer schon]. Now, however, in the transition to the discussion of everydayness and *das Man*, Heidegger draws on another distinction between authenticity and inauthenticity and turns the "always already" into the "to-begin-with and for-the-most-part" [*zunächst und zumeist*], which reduces universality to everydayness, to merely empirical (ontic) validity [*Geltung*]. This strategy is announced already in the transition to paragraph 27: "One's own *Dasein*, like the *Dasein*-with of Others, is encountered to begin with and for the most part in terms of the with-world with which we are environmentally concerned. When *Dasein* is absorbed in the world of its concern – that is, at the same time, in its Being-with towards Others – it is not itself."[47] But if *Dasein* cannot be itself in Being-with, how can there then ever be liberating, "leaping ahead" caring-for? This question calls attention to a lacuna in the analysis of everydayness.

It is well known that the entire analysis of *das Man* can lead to only one conclusion, namely, that *Dasein* cannot attain authentic mineness unless it breaks with the "fall" into everydayness. Fear and the call of conscience become the instances that announce themselves from the hidden inner realm of *Dasein* that is "somehow" already individualized, sounding a call to radical individualization. Aside from the still-transcendental architectonics of *Being and Time*, the primary motivation for the solipsistic description of the existential genesis is the intention to describe individual existence as irreplaceability [*Unvertretbarkeit*]. This is why Heidegger elects to take the thanatological detour via the "anticipation of death" which alone is able to enable "potentiality-for-Being-a-whole" [*Ganzseinkönnen*], that is, the identity of *Dasein* in the sense of its constancy. A closer examination of the criticisms of the role that Heidegger attributes to death would lead us too far astray;[48] it should merely be noted that, if one takes it seriously, Heidegger's brief mention of "caring-for that leaps ahead" suggests the possibility of mediating between responsibility for the freedom of the Other and the impossibility of taking the place of the Other.

It is striking that the "distantiality, averageness, and levelling down" that "constitute what we know as 'the public sphere' [*Öffentlichkeit*]"[49] are attributed to a diminishing of responsibility: "Yet because *das Man* presents every judgment and decision as its own, it deprives the particular *Dasein* of its responsibility [*Verantwortlichkeit*]."[50] Once again, this involves an unmistakable reduction of the concept of responsibility to existential self-determination. The self that has responsibility for Others in "caring-for" is here equated with the "they-self" [*Man-selbst*][51] of the everyday condition of fallenness. Suddenly, caring-for – along with, certainly, Being-with – has become an inauthentic mode of existing. Whatever form of dialogically mediated support persons can offer each other – enlightening conversations with others, any form of solidarity, the search for advice from others – they succumb to the verdict of having fallen inauthentically to levelling, reifying everydayness. Thus, there is a phenomenon of responsibility for Others, but it is not something that can be "in each case one's own" [*jemeinig*]. The universal "*Man-selbst*" is always already intervening, according to whom "each is the Other, and no one is himself". But if this is the case, what can be the basis for Heidegger's earlier distinction between caring-for that "leaps in" and caring-for that "leaps ahead"?

Moreover, writing as if the modern lifeworld (introduced under the heading of "everydayness") did not include, for example, legal procedures for attributing individual responsibility, Heidegger draws a picture of the public sphere in which no one is ever held responsible for any action whatsoever, even in terms of the faulty model of the *"Man-selbst"*. Not only does this fail to do justice to the hardly artificial phenomenon of legal liability or custody [*Sorgerecht*]; it also demonstrates that the normative character of the ontological analysis of *Dasein* is a long way away from offering a specification of moral theory in terms of a philosophy of law. For even if legal liability could be considered an "inauthentic" mode of responsibility, the pejorative sense of the distinction between authenticity and inauthenticity would be mitigated as soon as one distinguished between context-specific instantiations of legal systems of liability, on the one hand, and "authentic" – that is, context-neutral – resources for the legitimacy of these systems, on the other.

The reference to the courts' attribution of responsibility raises objections to an exclusively positivist conception of law, and the Heideggerian [*daseinanalytische*] injunction to take authentic responsibility can capitalize on this. The difference between authentic responsibility and the responsibility of *das Man* (for whom everything is reduced to the level, for example, of criminal law) can be tied to the idea that, in the role of a legal person, a *Dasein* would have to recognize the responsibility juridically ascribed to it only in the case where it can view itself, in principle, as the author and not merely the addressee of particular legal norms.[52] It is, however, precisely this recognition, in principle, of determination by the law that requires the very universalizations – including, for example, that the same individual rights are granted by everyone – that, according to paragraph 27 of *Being and Time*, have to be seen indiscriminately as part of the general levelling that *Dasein* must break out of for the sake of authentic self-choice. In this way, the analysis of Being-with draws negatively [*partizipiert negativ*] on the basic principle introduced and criticized according to which "the rational can of course appear only as a limitation on the freedom in question, and not as an immanent rationality, but only as an external and formal universal".[53] Heidegger leaves untouched the distinction – criticized by Hegel – between formal universality and individual freedom and merely puts the affirmative accent on the other side, as compared with the *Critique of Practical Reason* (which only allows this freedom to be labelled *"Willkür"*). As a result, one ends up being forced to view the principle of equality before the law as an institution opposed to the freedom of authentic *Dasein*. (Incidentally, it is not at all clear, on the other hand, how this idea can be compatible with the *"Führerprinzip"* that Heidegger wanted to make the "guiding principle" of the University of Freiburg during his irresponsible acceptance of institutional responsibility.)

But is it not the case that the part of the legal system (however formally supported) devoted to individual liberties is, as it were, a public condition of possibility for existential freedom and the possibility of decision? This point makes its way into the analysis of Being-with only once the sphere of personal freedom defined by individual liberties is no longer suspected of being an indirect threat to the possibility of authentic choice. If he had ever taken up this discussion, Heidegger could of course have condemned the constraints on one's personal sphere of freedom that accompany one's freedom (lying essentially at the boundary with others' spheres of freedom) as levelling interventions in authentic existence. And indeed, both his own political conclusions during the Nazi period and the discussion of "historicality" [*Geschichtlichkeit*] in *Being and Time* – in which *das Volk* replaces personally individuated *Dasein* as the "subject" of authentic choice[54] – allow one to conclude that, from the perspective taken in *Being and Time*'s analysis of the public sphere, a crime only has to be major and successful enough to earn the laurel crown of responsibility. Thus, in the *Introduction to Metaphysics*, it is the authentic statesman who takes responsibility, as the advocate of a destined community [*Schicksals-gemeinschaft*] of *Dasein* that has fused into a monolithic *"Volk"*, by positing law. It is then "history" that decides which act of violence can subsequently claim legitimacy. Given these assumptions, someone who fears the dictatorship of the public is driven precisely to Hitler.

Even if one rightly takes offence at Heidegger's approach, a critique of the analysis of Being-with must still meet the requirement of speaking the *Dasein*-analytic language of *Being and Time*. It is not enough, then, to oppose the interpretation of the existential genesis as a Gnostic leap[54] to the unity of socialization and individuation in the symbolic reproduction of the lifeworld. The concept of the person must meet the claim to the desubstantialization of the person raised by the hermeneutic interpretation of *Dasein*. This means that it would merely reverse the situation if one were to withdraw entirely the conception of authenticity found in the analysis of *Dasein* in favour of a principle of intersubjective responsibility. A conceptual mediation between autonomy and authenticity must adhere to a conception of authenticity, in the sense of an account of authentic, possible, irreplaceable, and future-oriented *Dasein*. One must then anchor the appreciation of the public conditions of possibility for existential freedom in the conception of Being-with that precedes the discussion of *das Man*. What one is looking for here – and what gets lost in paragraph 27 – is a mode of Being-with that could generate, for example, the encouragement [*solidarische Anregung*] of others to seize authentic possibilities. The principle that no one can relieve another of existential decision may well be justified, and it is already raised as a critical reservation in the concept of caring-for that "leaps in". But the previous distinction between caring-for that "leaps in" and caring-for that "leaps ahead" makes possible a further distinction between imposing decisions and presenting a range of possible decisions among which one is encouraged to choose. In the analysis of *das Man*, however, the liberating form of caring-for has been forgotten.

In *Being and Time*, the analysis of *das Man* functions, so to speak, as a filter. After the initially singular *Dasein* has been augmented by the Others' mode of Being and the encounter with them, the devaluation of each and every form of public sphere counteracts the reference to an ontological division of labour. In the same way, the link between the authenticity of authentic *Dasein* and duty as responsibility for the other *Dasein* gets lost.

What remains is the identification of the ontological project with the analysis of the existence of a single, authentic *Dasein*. Thus, when Heidegger writes that *Dasein* comes to terms with itself, comprehending itself as itself, propelled by anxiety and the call of conscience, only in radical individuality [*Vereinzelung*], he thereby sacrifices the potential suggested by his prior development of the concept of facticity in favour of the methodological premise that fundamental ontology must be carried out within the perspective of the *ego*, however hermeneutically extended it may be. The hermeneutic transformation of the *a priori* remains, up until the book on Kant, committed to a philosophy of the subject. Hence, if the formalistic constitution of transcendental philosophy is to be corrected hermeneutically, the move to an existentialist "*ego*"-perspective cannot be sufficient, since it restricts the concept of freedom (to put it in terms of a theory of intersubjectivity) to the negative freedom of "irresponsibility" vis-à-vis others. Only by taking up the themes that are at least suggested by the concepts of "Being-with" and "caring-for that leaps ahead" [*vorspringende Fürsorge*] would it be possible to utilize the hermeneutic emphasis on the concrete facticity of the relations to the world specific to *Dasein* for a constructive critique of formalistic and cognitivistic moral theory. For only then could one draw a picture in which the problem of concretely applying abstract maxims could be circumvented by giving priority to the factically concretized division of labour with regard to explicating the meaning of what needs regulation. [!] The idea of an onto-logical division of labour among cooperating and co-responsible exis-tences would create bridges between the ineluctable [*unhintergehbar*] "mood"-based character of *Dasein*'s relation to the world, the practice of drawing boundaries between "is" and "ought", and communication ori-ented toward mutual understanding between bearers of equal individual liberties. Under such conditions, an existential analysis of the roots of the processes by which individuals come to normative agreements could con-tribute to an understanding of the role of emotions in moral judgement.[56]

Why, then, did Heidegger decide to pursue an existential "*ego*logy" instead?

This reluctance is not to be attributed to the inertia of his thought, as being still beholden to Husserl, Kierkegaard, and the "Freedom of Christianity"; rather, it is rooted in the very theme that became the central corrective to the orthodox explication of Being and that leads our interpretation back to Heidegger's encounter with Kant, namely, temporality.

V

As Heidegger's interpretation of Kant demonstrated, the hermeneutic interpretation of the *a priori* ought to reveal temporality not merely as the pure form of inner intuition [*Anschauung*] but rather as a primordial syn-thesis.[57] In *Being and Time*, however, the authentic temporality of *Dasein* – that is, the ecstatic unity of the past ("state-of-mind"), the present ("falling" or "moment of vision"), and the future (anticipation and under-standing) – is equated with primordial time as the ontological foundation of the preliminary projection [*Vorentwurf*] of the meaning of Being. Ultimately, the preliminary projection of the meaning of Being is dele-gated to the authentic disclosedness of *Dasein* that has left the everyday behind. This identification stems not merely from the quasi *ego*-logical perspective with which *Being and Time* approaches the analysis of the

mode of Being of singular *Dasein*; rather, it is forced upon Heidegger by
the problem of defining an authentic present. Heidegger assigns to temporal "ecstases" various existentials, and this ascription divides into
authentic and inauthentic modes. Thus, anticipation counts as the
authentic relation to the future, and that which is present [*Gegenwärtigen*]
is the inauthentic relation[58]; anxiety and fear separate a state-of-mind, as
an instance of that which has been into authentic and inauthentic orien-
tations to the past.[59] The present gets connected with "falling" [*Verfallen*],
which had previously been equated, as an existential mode of *Dasein*'s
manner of Being, with the fall into everydayness, thereby associating it
with inauthenticity. But if this "falling" is inauthentic in and of itself, how
can one distinguish here between an authentic and inauthentic mode?[60]
The way out that Heidegger proposes – somewhat inconsistently, since
authentic deterioration cannot be derived from the previously analysed
structure of care – is the equation of the authentic present with the
"moment of vision" [*Augenblick*]. We are not told much about this, except
that: "It brings existence into the Situation and discloses the authentic
'there.'"[61] Heidegger indicates which situation is meant here two pages
later, where he writes of a present that "gets brought back from its lost-
ness by a resolution, so that both the current Situation and therewith the
primordial 'limit-Situation' of Being-towards-death, will be disclosed as a
moment of vision which has been held on to."[62] The moment of vision
brings existence to the threshold of the realization of its authentic existential constitution, which means, however, that the entire horizon of
authentic time is present in the present. This has negative consequences,
however, for the theoretical distinction between authentic (*Dasein*-like)
time and primordial (ontologic) time, a distinction that Heidegger had
stressed even before *Being and Time*.[63] For wherever the horizon of authentic time cannot be analysed into individual modes of its performance
[*Vollzugsmodi*] in line with the schematization found in *Being and Time*,
one loses sight of the distinction between primordial time and its performance [*Vollzug*]. In this move, the authentic temporality of *Dasein* – as
existential, individual anticipation of death and seizure of inherited possibilities within the present of the moment of vision – is equated with the
meta-level of primordial time, as the synthesis of the hermeneutic *a priori*.
This reveals why it is that the mention of an "ontological division of
labor" in the concept of the form of "caring-for that leaps ahead" could
not establish itself and had to be forced, instead, into the devaluation of

everydayness as a result of the systematically necessary radicalization of individualization. Since the expulsion of primordial time – and thus of the basis for the preliminary projection of the meaning of Being – could be carried out only in concepts of temporality associated with radically individualized *Dasein*, this *Dasein* cannot be relativized by an authentic form of intersubjectivity. For this reason, the responsibility of resolute *Dasein* can never be more than "responsibility for itself and towards itself".

Here one can take the slogan Heidegger used against Kant and turn it against Heidegger: perhaps temporality is in fact the *a priori* of the projection of the meaning of Being, albeit in a more primordial sense of time than Heidegger intended, a sense that precedes the (*pace* Heidegger, necessary) separation of an individualized temporal horizon of *Dasein* and authentic primordial time. What could this be? It would have to be a form of temporality that privileges not resolute, radically individual *Dasein* but rather a type of *Dasein* that, as Being-with, always already relates to Others in the ontological division of labour; it would thus have to be a form of temporality that could not be read off of a single *Dasein* but only off of the complex structure of the ontological division of labour carried out cooperatively by various personal realizations of *Dasein*'s freedom.

In summary: Heidegger first relativizes the "ontic" distinction between "is" and "ought" and singles out *Dasein* as the performance [*Vollzug*] of the ontological understanding of the meaning of Being as "Being-free". In its Heideggerian version, however, the meta-practical qualification of *Dasein* as a mode of Being that is responsible in its freedom robs the concept of responsibility of its intersubjective dimension. *Dasein* is responsible only for itself and towards itself. Compared with a Kantian concept of personal autonomy, the existentialist concept of authenticity is less formalistic – authenticity consists in the concrete, factical, and attuned employment of freedom – but it is also poorer, since it lacks the moment of freely chosen and self-imposed obligation to Others. Although this moment is suggested in a rudimentary way in connection with caring-for that "leaps ahead", it is driven into the realm of the inauthentic in the course of the analysis of everydayness. The systematic reasons for this lie in Heidegger's identification of fundamental ontology with the analysis of *Dasein*, that is, in the identification of a radically individual understanding of Being with hermeneutic *a priori*. This identification is based, in turn, on the problematic identification of authentic temporality with primordial temporality. The problem of the authentic present forces everydayness and deterioration [*Verfallen*] into the position of the inauthentic present and mistakenly equates the contrasting concept, the authentic present, with the ecstatic horizon of time as a whole. As a result, primordial time and its passage [*Vollzug*] (the existential appropriation of the ecstatic horizon in the present) can no longer be distinguished.

The conclusion to be drawn from this series of impasses [*Engführungen*] is the following. If the question about the mode of Being of individual *Dasein* (that is, about personal authenticity) were to be distinguished from the question about the structure and genesis of hermeneutic *a priori*, it would be possible to liberate the concept of "caring-for that leaps ahead" – that is, the fundamental responsibility for the freedom of Others – from the devaluation of the intersubjectivity found in everydayness. As a result, it becomes possible to develop the unity of freedom and duty by supplementing *Dasein*'s authenticity with responsibility vis-à-vis the freedom of others, who cooperate with *Dasein* in "being-concerned-along-with" [*Mitbesorgen*]. Rather than leading into a heroic solitude accountable only to itself, authentic individualization leads to the voluntary acceptance of responsibility (or perhaps even the *discovery* of responsibility, which, as Levinas asserts, is always already there) and to the voluntary submission to obligations that are concrete and not merely formally justifiable. Such obligations would represent a concrete, context-specific expression of the institutionalization of everyday norms governing the reciprocal allotting of spheres of freedom. This would further allow the one ontic form of moral norms that we know as individual liberties to be derived from an existential interpretation of the mode of Being specific to *Dasein*. The freedom of religious faith and practice, for example, expressed not merely individual, negative freedom from universal impositions of faith but rather mutually recognized insight into the necessity of guaranteeing one another's freedom. To repeat, Heidegger's analysis of *Dasein* continues to be exemplary insofar as it succeeds in deciphering the meaning of this freedom in connection with the specific temporality of the Being of a person. As we have seen, however, this deciphering remains incomplete. In this connection, in order to "surpass" Heidegger's conception of primordial time, one would have to maintain the fruits of the analysis of *Dasein* (namely, the temporally and pragmatically developed concept of personal authenticity) while at the same time avoiding the solipsistic impasse, that is, by introducing the moment of normative responsibility associated with autonomy. With regard to the concept of time, this would mean correcting, in line with Heidegger, the Kantian disjunction between atemporal freedom and empirical within-time-ness [*Innerzeitlichkeit*] and tying this move to the notion of an ontological division of labour. Heidegger was able to show that the concept of "ecstatic" time allows one to think together two things that Kant's formalism had to keep apart, namely, the possibility of conceiving the moral person's mode of Being as freedom (of action) and the possibility of conceiving, within time, reasons for action.

This idea can be reappropriated in the reconstruction of a public, intersubjective temporal structure that is richer than either Kant's disjunction or Heidegger's concept of the authentic time of isolated authentic *Dasein*. It is the temporal structure of linguistically mediated (ontological) cooperation between language-users who, owing to the temporality of their cooperation, are able to be authentic persons. Such a concept of public temporality is suggested, in several variations, by the term "narrativity". The structure of the narrated – as well as the structure of the practice of (cooperative) narration – mediates between the biographical horizon of personal authenticity and the intersubjectively normative dimension of the world of action, in which no one lives or judges alone.[64] Here, however, I can provide little more than vague suggestions.

It was nonetheless possible to show at least that the conception of *Dasein* as "the Being that ought to Be" can contribute to practical philosophy only if *Dasein*'s Being can both bear and be borne by intersubjective responsibility.

Translated from the German by Joel Anderson

NOTES AND REFERENCES

1. The expression "*Denkweg*" often signals a style of exegesis of Heidegger hampered by veneration. In my view, however, it properly indicates the defensible position that the expression "*Kehre*" often belies, in a rather cavalier fashion, the systematic continuities in Heidegger's work. This continuity leads me to employ the expression "*Denkweg*"; the dangers involved in giving Heidegger this rhetorical licence (in exchange for the demand for intelligible language and intersubjectively criticizable terminology) lead me to leave this expression in quote marks.

2. Gerold Prauss, "Heidegger und die praktische Philosophie", Annemarie Gethmann Siefert and Otto Pöggeler (eds), in *Heidegger und die praktische Philosophie*, Frankfurt: Suhrkamp, 1988, pp. 177–191.

3. With regard to this analysis of the hermeneutically reinterpreted, quasi-transcendental status of the understanding of Being as the groundwork "that

precedes all ontic experience and indicates the bases [Gründe] for its possibility and that also underpins other parts of philosophy such as ethics [!], anthropology, and the philosophy of history", see Klaus Düsing, "Selbstbewußtseinsmodelle, Apperzeption und Zeitbewußtsein in Heideggers Auseinandersetzung mit Kant", in Bad Homburger Forum für Philosophie (ed.) *Zeiterfahrung und Personalität,* Frankfurt: Suhrkamp, 1992, pp. 89–123; at p. 118.

4. In *Being and Time,* (trans. John Maccquarrie and Edward Robinson, New York: Harper & Row, 1962; German: *Sein und Zeit,* Tuebingen: Niemeyer, 1984, 1927, the difference between natural causality and freedom of action is already introduced as an ontic distinction, on which the ontological dimension of the central [*tragenden*] understanding or explication of Being is based.

5. "For as soon as *logos* in the sense of statement assumes the rule over Being, the moment Being is experienced and conceived as *ousia,* already-thereness, the distinction between is and ought [*Sein und Sollen*] is in preparation" (Heidegger, *An Introduction to Metaphysics,* trans. Ralph Manheim, Garden City, NY: Anchor Books, 1961, p. 163, translation modified; German: *Gesamtausgabe,* vol. 40: *Einführung in die Metaphysik,* ed. Friedrich-Wilhelm von Herrmann, Frankfurt: Klostermann, 1983, p. 149). The limits of this characterization of basic philosophical convictions becomes evident at the point at which Heidegger paraphrases his account of the characterization of this false step in the history of Being and makes clear that the meaning of "*ousia*" covers only idealistic positions, that is (with regard to "ought"), initially only the philosophy of value: "'ought' is opposed to 'is' [*Sein*] as soon as the latter defines itself as idea" (ibid., p. 165; German, p. 151). In connection with the philosophy of value, see p. 166f. (German, p. 152).

6. Karl-Otto Apel, "Sinnkonstitution und Geltungsrechtfertigung. Heidegger und das Problem der Transzendentalphilosophie", in Bad Homburger Forum für Philosophie (ed.), *Innen- und Außenansichten,* Frankfurt: Suhrkamp, 1989, pp. 131–176.

7. Is there "one" concept of Being? This question is raised by – among others – Günther Figal, *Martin Heidegger. Phänomenologie der Freiheit,* Munich: Athenäum, 1988, p. 14; and Ernst Tugendhat, *Selbstbewußtsein und Selbstbestimmung,* Frankfurt: Suhrkamp, 1979, p. 167. Apparently, the entire ontological project depends on this question. What remains undecided, however, is whether it is not the case that the justification for the distinction between alternative senses of "Being" can be traced back to a unitary foundation in the genesis of this justification. In that case, the ontological question as to the meaning of Being would have to be understood as a question about the unity of the (linguistic) presuppositions for the distinctions between various modes of givenness [*Gegebenheitsweisen*] of the meaning of "Being".

8. Here it suffices to recall Richard Rorty, *Contingency, Irony, and Solidarity,* Cambridge: Cambridge University Press, 1989, on Heidegger, esp. pp. 96–122.

9. That would involve accepting the presupposition that the fundamental level is the level at which the differences among modes of "givenness" are explicated and therefore that a difference such as the one between "is" and "ought" is, in principle, contingent.

10. See Mark Okrent, *Heidegger's Pragmatism*, Ithaca, NY: Cornell University Press, 1988, esp. Parts One and Two, pp. 17–74; Richard Rorty, "Heidegger, Contingency, and Pragmatism", in *Essays on Heidegger and Others*, Cambridge: Cambridge University Press, 1991, pp. 27–50; Carl Friedrich Gethmann, "Heideggers Konzeption des Handelns in Sein und Zeit", in Siefert and Pöggeler (eds), *Heidegger und die praktische Philosophie*, op. cit., pp. 140–177, at p. 143f. Against this, see, for example, Hubert L. Dreyfus's detailed interpretation of Heidegger's notion of intentionality (which considers Being-in-the-world to be the original mode), which gives rise to the separation between subject and object as well as of action and contemplative knowing, in *Being-in-the-World: A Commentary on Heidegger's "Being and Time", Division 1*, Cambridge, MA: MIT Press, 1991. Dreyfus discusses the distinction between action (which presupposes a subject–object distinction) and activity, without referring explicitly to the parallels with (for example) the pragmatism of Dewey; see, here, p. 57f.
11. This despite all protestations, for example, that the analysis of the "they" [*das Man*] is not pejorative in character, whether they come from Heidegger himself (*Being and Time*, p. 168; *Sein und Zeit*, p. 130) or from interpreters ranging from the lenient to the sympathetic (e.g. Figal, *Martin Heidegger*, op. cit., p. 153).
12. Figal, *Martin Heidegger*, op. cit., pp. 31ff.
13. In his own terminology, Heidegger defines the care structure as "ahead-of-itself – Being-already-in (a world) as Being-alongside (entities encountered within-the-world)" (*Being and Time*, p. 364; *Sein und Zeit*, p. 317).
14. Cf. the discussion of the distinction between causes and motives, with reference to Heidegger and Donald Davidson, in Figal, *Martin Heidegger*, op. cit., pp. 127ff., where it becomes clear that the problem of distinguishing between causes and motives can be viewed as an issue of the compatibility of different vocabularies. Figal is rightly concerned to show that Heidegger's concept of freedom succumbs to this difficulty by making the ontological dimension of freedom of action the basis for the distinction between natural causality and the causality of freedom (Kant). This is why, although I say here that Heidegger employs this derivative difference, this is not intended to mean that it remains impenetrable [*unhinter-gehbar*] for the ontological perspective. It simply becomes clear that the ontological dimension of the pre-understanding draws on a concept of action that (in the language of derivative difference) possesses a normative component from the outset.
15. Heidegger, *The Basic Problems of Phenomenology*, (Bloomington: Indiana University Press, 1982) p. 137f.; *Die Grundprobleme der Metaphysik* (Frankfurt: Vittorio Klostermann, 1975), p. 195.
16. Cf. Heidegger, *Der Satz vom Grund*, Pfullingen: Neske, 1954, p. 29
17. Although the concept of a person and the expression "*Dasein*" do not overlap perfectly, they are related in such a way that *Dasein* can be understood as the mode of being a person. On the relationship between these concepts, see John Haugeland, "Heidegger and the Concept of a Person", *Nous* 16:1, 1982, pp. 15–24.
18. Heidegger, *Basic Problems*, p. 137; *Grundprobleme*, p. 194.
19. Heidegger, *Basic Problems*, p. 138; *Grundprobleme*, p. 195.

20. Heidegger, *Kant and the Problem of Metaphysics*, 4th edn, enlarged, trans. Richard Taft, Bloomington: Indiana University Press, 1990; German: *Gesamtausgabe*, vol. 3: *Kant und das Problem der Metaphysik*, ed. Friedrich-Wilhelm von Herrmann, Frankfurt: Klostermann, 1991. A brief version of the same is to be found in *Being and Time*, 64, p. 366 [*Sein und Zeit*, p. 318].

21. Kant, *Critique of Practical Reason*, trans. L.W. Beck (New York: Macmillan, 1956) p. ... [*Kritik der praktischen Veruunft* (Hamburg: Felix Meiner, 1974) 102]

22. Heidegger, *Basic Problems*, p. 135; *Grundprobleme*, p. 192.

23. Heidegger, *Basic Problems*, p. 135f.; *Grundprobleme*, p. 192.

24. Heidegger, *Basic Problems*, p. 137; *Grundprobleme*, p. 194.

25. On this distinction, see Isaiah Berlin, "Two Concepts of Liberty", in his *Four Concepts of Liberty*, Oxford: Oxford University Press, 1969, pp. 118–172; Charles Taylor, "What's Wrong with Negative Liberty?" in his *Philosophical Papers*, vol. 2: *Philosophy and the Human Sciences*, Cambridge: Cambridge University Press, 1985, pp. 211–229; and Maeve Cooke, "Negative Freiheit? Zum Problem eines postmetaphysischen Freiheitsbegriffes", in C. Menke and M. Seel (eds), *Zur Verteidigung der Vernunft gegen ihre Liebhaber und Verächter. Festschrift für Albrecht Wellmer*, Frankfurt: Suhrkamp, 1993, pp. 300–333.

26. *Basic Problems* p. 146; *Grundprobleme*, p. 207.

27. *Basic Problems*, p. 145; *Grundprobleme*, p. 207.

28. On the function of the concept of freedom as a "cornerstone" of the entire critique of reason, without which the idea of the unconditional would remain empty and would threaten to plunge the whole system into an "abyss of skepticism", see Kant, *Critique of Practical Reason*, p. 3 [Akademie-Edition, p. 3].

29. Kant, *Critique of Practical Reason*, p. 97f.; Akademie-Edition, p. 94;

30. On Heidegger's temporal interpretation, in this connection, of the productive faculty of the imagination (whose function gets interpreted, in one stroke, as both ontological and having the form of *Dasein*) as the mediator between formal universal concepts and vivid concretization, see Heidegger, *Kant and the Problem of Metaphysics*, and Apel, "Sinnkonstitution," op. cit., p. 145. According to Apel, Heidegger's strategy is "exposed" by the fact that Heidegger's attempt to correct Kant fails to consider the role of the productive faculty of the imagination in the second edition of the *Critique of Pure Reason*. This reveals the "violence" (Heidegger on Heidegger, in the book on Kant) with which Heidegger tries to reduce transcendental synthesis to a matter of pure vividness [*Anschaulichkeit*]. Klaus Düsing makes the same argument in "Selbstbewußtseinsmodelle", op. cit., p. 98: "in the second edition of the *Critique of Pure Reason*, Kant considers the activity of the transcendental imagination, namely, the construction figural synthesis, to be nothing other than the exercise of self-affection. In this context, the imagination loses the self-sufficient meaning that it still had in the first edition of the first Critique as an original, more intermediate faculty, which is supposed to mediate between sensuous intuition, on the one hand, and the understanding, on the other (see A 124). This trichotomy of faculties of knowledge was not convergent with the doctrine of two sources of knowledge: sensibility and understanding." Correct as these observations are, in order to undermine Heidegger's argument one would first have to demonstrate the justification for Kant's self-

corrections. And even then, it would have to be decided whether the claim against Heidegger's considerations amounts to anything more than a "merely philological" criticism. The central presupposition, however, with which Heidegger's interpretation stands or falls, is the assumption that "intuition constitutes the authentic essence of knowledge and that, despite the reciprocity of the relationship between intuiting and thinking, [intuition] does possess authentic importance" (Heidegger, *Kant and the Problem of Metaphysics*, p. 16; German edn, p. 23.)

31. G. W. F. Hegel, *Elements of the Philosophy of Right*, ed. Allen W. Wood and trans. by H. B. Nisbet, Cambridge: Cambridge University Press, 1991, Comment on 29, p. 58.

32. Hegel, *Elements of the Philosophy of Right*, Part Three, Section 2 A, '189–208, pp. 227–239.

33. *Being and Time*, p. 75; *Sein und Zeit*, p. 49.

34. *Being and Time*, p. 152; *Sein und Zeit*, p. 116.

35. *Being and Time*, 26, p. 156; *Sein und Zeit*, p. 120.

36. *Being and Time*, 26, p. 154f.; *Sein und Zeit*, p. 118f.

37. *Being and Time*, 26, p. 156; *Sein und Zeit*, p. 120.

38. Ibid.

39. On the question of world-disclosure in both everyday life and the already explicated form of the world in which *Dasein* is thrown, see my "Die kommunikative Erschließung der subjektiven Welt", *Deutsche Zeitschrift für Philosophie* 41:3, 1993, pp. 543ff.

40. The choice of the term "ontological division of labour" is not arbitrary. This is intended to suggest Hilary Putnam's talk of "linguistic division of labor" (see Putnam, *Representation and Reality*, Massachusetts: MIT Press, 1988, pp. 22ff, especially, p. 25: "Language is a form of cooperative activity, not an essentially individualistic activity.") There are two interconnected motives for this. First, Putnam's theory of meaning uses this expression to stress that "meanings aren't in the head", i.e. that the conditions for the intelligibility of linguistic expressions cannot be reconstructed "*ego*-logically" or "psychologically". Applied to Heidegger, this means that a singular *Dasein* alone cannot be conceived of as the originary instance of the interpretation of the meaning of Being. Second, this division of labour is linguistic: herein lies the suggestion that, contrary to Heidegger's strategy, a reinterpretation of the ontological perspective would have to understand linguistic intersubjectivity not as the product of an originary ontological achievement but rather as its medium and its precondition. This is a crucial point, but one that I do not have the space to develop fully here.

41. And the motive for this obligation would not be the egocentric interest in the cooperation of others, because the formation of an interest of that sort presupposes the cooperation imposed upon us, in virtue of our identity. That is, after all, why this cooperation is called "primordial".

42. *Being and Time*, p. 157; *Sein und Zeit*, p. 121.

43. *Being and Time*, p. 158; *Sein und Zeit*, p. 122.

44. *Being and Time*, p. 159; *Sein und Zeit*, p. 122.

45. *Being and Time*, p. 160; *Sein und Zeit*, p. 123.

46. *Being and Time*, pp. 161, 162; *Sein und Zeit*, p. 125.

47. *Being and Time*, p. 163; *Sein und Zeit*, p. 125.

48. See, for example, Dolf Sternberger, *Über den Tod*, Frankfurt: Suhrkamp, 1981; Karl Löwith, "Martin Heidegger und Franz Rosenzweig. Ein Nachtrag zu *Sein und Zeit*", in idem, *Heidegger. Denker in dürftiger Zeit*, Stuttgart: Metzler, 1984, pp. 72–102; and Paul Ludwig Landsberg, *Die Erfahrung des Todes*, Frankfurt: Suhrkamp, 1973.

49. *Being and Time*, p. 164; *Sein und Zeit*, p. 127.

50. *Being and Time*, p. 165; *Sein und Zeit*, p. 127.

51. *Being and Time*, p. 167; *Sein und Zeit*, p. 129: "The Self of everyday *Dasein* is the *they-self*, which we distinguish from the *authentic Self* – that is, from the Self which has been taken hold of in its own way [*eigens ergriffen*]."

52. Jürgen Habermas formulates this principle of self-legislation in terms of a theory of communicative action as follows: "The idea of self-legislation by citizens demands . . . that those who, as addressees, are subject to the law can also consider themselves to be authors of the law" (*Faktizität und Geltung: Beiträge zur Diskurstheorie des Rechts und des demokratischen Reschtstaats*, Frankfurt: Suhrkamp, 1992, p. 153).

53. Hegel, *Elements of the Philosophy of Right*, op. cit., "Addition" to 29; p. 58.

54. *Being and Time*, p. 436; *Sein und Zeit*, p. 384.

55. Barbara Merker, *Selbsttäuschung und Selbsterkenntnis*, Frankfurt: Suhrkamp, 1988, pp. 167ff., esp. p. 192. With regard to the leap into authenticity, which springs from uncontrollable experiences rather than reflection (or dialogue), see B. Merker, "Konversion statt Reflexion, eine Grundfigur der Philosophie Martin Heideggers", in Bad Homburger Forum für Philosophie (ed.), *Innen- und Außenansichten*, op. cit., pp. 228ff.

56. Here one can identify the anti-formalist contribution of an analysis of Being-in-the-world supplemented by a concept of cooperation. In the language of an analysis of "world", the interpretation of the relationship between cooperating existences would avoid, from the outset, a cognitivism that condemns "state-of-mind" [*Befindlichkeit*] (that is, *inter alia*, the affective dimension, including "inclinations" and thus the motivating power of empathetic relations between agents) as rationally insufficient determining grounds of moral judgement, thereby denying even its motivational force a systematic role. With regard to the formalistic and cognitivistic devaluation of the importance of empathy and other morally relevant emotions, such as respect for the law, see Arne Johan Vetlesen, *Perception, Empathy, and Judgment: An Inquiry into the Preconditions of Moral Performance*, University Park, PA: Penn State University Press, 1994.

57. Heidegger, *Kant and the Problem of Metaphysics*, pp. 33, 70, 129ff.; German edn, pp. 50, 103, 188ff.

58. *Being and Time*, pp. 385ff.; *Sein und Zeit*, pp. 336ff.

59. *Being and Time*, pp. 389ff.; *Sein und Zeit*, pp. 339ff.

60. With regard to "*Verfallenheit*" in connection with its temporal relation, see Thomä, *Die Zeit des Selbst und die Zeit danach*, Frankfurt: Suhrkamp, 1990, pp. 291ff. On the identification of authentic and primordial time, see Margot Fleischer, *Die Zeitanalysen in Heideggers "Sein und Zeit". Aporien, Probleme und ein*

Ausblick, Würzburg: Koenigshausen und Neumann, 1991.

61. *Being and Time*, p. 398; *Sein und Zeit*, p. 347.

62. *Being and Time*, p. 400; *Sein und Zeit*, p. 349.

63. In *Basic Problems of Phenomenology*, Heidegger had clearly distinguished "temporality" [*Temporalität*], as ontologically relevant primordial time, from *Dasein's* authentic time (p. 228f; *Grundprobleme*, p. 323f.). See again, Fleischer, *Die Zeitanalysen in Heideggers "Sein und Zeit"*, op. cit., p. 39.

64. Despite the possibility of drawing on contemporary discussions of narrativity, this project of providing a "surpassing" in terms of a theory of time faces many hurdles. Here, I can do justice to neither these hurdles nor the importance of the concept of narrativity. As a result, the following references to works that treat the connection between narrativity, personal authenticity, and ethical validity can do no more than suggest the sort of approach to be taken: Paul Ricoeur, *Oneself as Another*, trans. Kathleen Blamey, Chicago: University of Chicago Press, 1992, especially the "Fifth Study: Personal Identity and Narrative Identity" and the "Eighth Study: The Self and the Moral Norm"; Charles Taylor, *Sources of the Self*, Cambridge, MA: Harvard University Press, 1989, esp. Part 1, ch. 2: "The Self in Moral Space"; Alasdair MacIntyre, *After Virtue*, Notre Dame, IN: University of Notre Dame Press, 1981, ch. 13: "The Virtues, the Unity of Human Life, and the Concept of a Tradition", esp. pp. 191ff.; and Jürgen Habermas, *The Theory of Communicative Action*, vol. 2, trans. Thomas McCarthy, Cambridge, MA: Beacon Press, 1987, pp. 136ff.

Chapter 13

Morality Begins at Home
— or: Can there be a
Levinasian Macro-Ethics?

Zygmunt Bauman

Levinas' moral world stretches between I and the Other. It is this space which Levinas visits again and again throughout his ethical writings, exploring it with an uncanny determination and patience. It is inside this space that he finds the birthplace of ethics and all the food the ethical self needs take to stay alive: the silent challenge of the Other and my dedicated yet selfless responsibility. This is a *vast* space, as far as ethics goes: large enough to accommodate the ethical self in full flight, scaling the highest peaks of saintliness, and all the underwater reefs of moral life, the traps that must be avoided by the self on its way to ethical life – to the assumption of uneasy responsibllity for its responsibility. But this is a *narrow*, tightly circumscribed space as far as the human-being-in-the-world goes. It has room for no more than two actors. The moral drama is always played at the moral party of two: "The Other" or "The Face" are generic names, but in every moral encounter these names stand for just *one*, only one being – one Another, *one* Face; neither name may appear in the plural without losing its ethical status, moral significance. This leaves aside most of the things that fill the daily life of every human: pursuit of survival and self-aggrandizement, rational consideration of ends and means, calculation of gains and losses, pleasure-seeking, power, politics, economics . . . Above all, entering this moral space means taking time off from daily business, leaving outside its mundane rules and conventions. At the moral party of two, I and the Other arrive derobed from our social trappings, stripped of status, social distinctions, handicaps, positions, or roles, neither rich nor poor, high or lowly, mighty or disempowered – reduced to the bare esentiality of our common humanity.

The moral self constituted inside such a space cannot but feel uncomfortable the moment the moral party of two is broken into by the Third.

But can it survive such an intrusion? Does it not rather remind one of the deep-water fish which bursts when drawn out of its element and brought to the surface, its inner pressure no longer bearable in the rarefied atmosphere of the "average" and "normal"?

It is not just the moral self which feels uncomfortable. So does its painter – Levinas himself. No better proof of his discomfort is needed than the obsessive, almost compulsive urgency with which he returns in his late writings and interviews to the "problem of the Third" and the possibility of salvaging the validity of his life-long description of the ethical relationship in the "presence of the Third party" – that is, under the conditions of ordinary mundane life. There is a remarkable similarity between this late Levinasian effort to bring back what he struggled, with such astonishing zeal and success, to exclude and the ageing Husserl's attempts to return to intersubjectivity from the transcendental subjectivity he spent his life purifying of all "inter-bound" contaminations – never to anybody's, and least of all his own, satisfaction. We know what followed Husserl's eager, yet inconclusive attempts: Heidegger's decision to cut the Gordian knot rather than to try in vain to untie it, his bold proclamation that *Sein* is ursprünglich *Mitsein*, "Being-with", and thus the understanding of Being and all its works cannot but start from this *Mitsein* (intersubjective, Husserl would say) condition. But this was the kind of solution to Husserl's troubles which all but invalidated, made null and void the significance of Husserl's "purifying" effort for the understanding of understanding. The question is: is it necesary to cut the Gordian knot also in the case of Levinasian ethics? Can the ethics, born and grown in the greenhouse of the twosome encounter, withstand the assault by the Third party? And – more to the point – can the moral capacity made to the measure of the responsibility for the Other as the Face be strong enough, or potent enough, or vigorous enough to carry an entirely different burden of responsibility for the "Other as such", the Other without Face?

Before the strange, inhospitable to ethics, world that includes the Third turned into his major, obsessive preoccupation, Levinas visited it but briefly and gingerly, without much curiosity or enthusiasm and seldom on his own initiative not prompted by impatient interviewers. And once visiting it, he trod the ground hesitantly, as one tends to do in an unfamiliar landscape one suspects of being full of unspeakable, and above all unreadable, dangers. He did not stop long enough to count the trees in the forest. And his travel reports show that he felt out of his element there: premonitions of threats prevail over all other impressions.

In *Le Moi et la Totalité* (1954) Levinas signals an essential discontinuity between the self's relation to the Other, made fully out of respect for the Other's freedom and integrity, and the relation towards the "concept of the human being", so extended that it falls under the spell of impersonal reason. In that second case, the case of *totality*, the Other – now transformed into the Third – is "a free being to whom I may do harm by violating his liberty".[1] "Totality", sadly concludes Levinas, "cannot constitute itself without injustice".[2] What is more, someone must ask me to account for my action, before I become aware of injustice done and visualize the possibility of justice. Very much in the Husserlian spirit, Levinas suggests that "justice does not result from the normal play of injustices. It comes from the outside, 'through the door', from beyond the mêlée – it appears as a principle external to history".[3] It comes in defiance of the "theories of justice which are forged in the course of social struggles, in which moral ideas express the needs of one society or one class"; it appeals to the "ideal of justice", which requires that all needs – all of them, after all, but relative – are abandoned on "approach to the absolute". Justice comes, therefore, not out of history, but as a judgement pronounced on history: "Human is the world in which it is possible to judge history" – which, in turn, is the world of "rationalisn". In relation to daily charity and cruelty, those dual works of the self struggling toward responsible morality, justice able to conquer the inborn injustice of social totality may arrive only as *Deus ex machina*. Reason, first expelled from the primal moral scene, is called back from exile to take care of humanity which the morality of the self is too slender and finespun to carry.

Almost 30 years later, in *La Souffrance inutile* (1982), the last motif is repeated: "Interhumanity in the proper sense lies in one's non-indifference towards the others, one's reponsibility for the others, but before the reciprocity of such responsibility is inscribed into the impersonal law." For this reason, "the interhuman perspective may survive, but may be also lost in the political order of the City or in the Law which establishes mutual obligations of the citizens". There are – so it seems – two mutually independent, perhaps even unconnected orders, political and ethical.

Political order – whether pre- or post-ethical – which inaugurates the "social contract" is neither the sufficient condition nor the necessary outcome of ethics. In the ethical position "I" is distinct from the citizen and from that individual who, in his natural selfishness, precedes all order, yet from whom political philosophy, from Hobbes on, tried to derive – or derived – the social and political order of the City.

This philosophical strategy is declared mistaken and therefore vain; but what is there to replace it, given the separation and, indeed, virtual absence of communication between the two orders?

In the same year (1982) an interview with Levinas appeared under the title *Philosophie, Justice et Amour*. Pressed by the questions put to him by R. Fornet and A. Gómez, Levinas allows for a certain mutual dependency between the political and the ethical order. Without the order of justice, says Levinas here, there would be no limit to my responsibility and thus cohabitation with Others as generalized citizens would not be possible. But – he insists immediately – "only departing from my relation to the Face, from me in front of the Other, one may speak of the State's legitimacy or illegitimacy". The principle of justice does not come after all, contrary to what he suggested 30 years before, from a cause "external to ethics", from reason; it is the ethics that now claims the right to pass judgment on the politically construed justice, that demands obedience of the state to its own, ethical, rules. And then, in response to the straightforward question, "Do you think that such a (just) state is possible?", comes the equally straightforward answer: "Yes, an agreement between the ethics and the State is possible. The just State will be the work of just people and the saints, rather than of propaganda and preaching ... Charity is impossible without justice, but justice without charity is deformed."

De l'unicité appeared in 1986. Here, an attempt is made to represent the difference between the ethical and the "formal", the legal, in a systematic way – focusing the story on the radical dissolution of the uniqueness of the ethical Other in the commonality/similarity of the Individual as citizen. This dissolution – the loss of uniqueness – is a foregone conclusion since the appearance of "the Third" – other than the one close to me (*mon prochain*), but at the same time close to the one close to me and moreover close to me in his own right – an "also close". Now there are "they". They, those various others, do things to each other, may harm each other, make each other suffer. "This is the hour of justice." The uniqueness of the Other, incomparable when constituted by moral responsibility, won't help much now; one needs to appeal to a force one could do without before, to Reason – which allows, first, to "compare the incomparable", and, second, to "impose a measure upon the extravagance of the infinite generosity of the 'for the Other'". And yet this recourse to Reason feels necessary precisely thanks to the memory of the "uniqueness" of the Other, which was originally experienced in the ethical relationship; it is because each of the "multiple others" is unique in her challenge to my responsibility, in her claim on my "being for", that it "postulates judgement and thus objectivity, objectivation, thematisation, synthesis. One needs arbitrating institutions and political power that sustains them". Justice requires the foundation of the State. In this lies the necessity of the reduction of human uniqueness to the particularity of a human individual, to the condition of the citizen." That latter particularity reduces, impoverishes, dissolves, waters down the splendour of ethically formed uniqueness; but without that already-ethically-experienced uniqueness it would be itself inconceivable, it would never come to pass . . .

Justice is in many ways disloyal to its ethical origins, unable to preserve its heritage in all its inner richness – but it cannot forget its origins without ceasing to be itself, justice. "It cannot abandon that uniqueness to political history, which finds itself subjected to the determinism of power, reason of the State and seduction of the totalitarian temptations." It must, instead, measure itself over and over again by the standards of original uniqueness, however unattainable such standards may be among the multiplicity of citizens. Hence the indelible trait of all justice is its dissatisfaction with itself: "Justice means constant revision of justice, expectation of a better justice." Justice, one may say, must exist perpetually in a condition of *noch nicht geworden*, setting itself standards higher than those already practised.

The same themes return at length in the extensive conversations with François Poirié. In the presence of the Third, says Levinas, "we leave what I call the order of ethics, or the order of saintliness or the order of mercy, or the order of love, or the order of charity – where the other human concerns me regardless the place he occupies in the multitude of humans, and even regardless our shared quality of individuals of the human species; he concerns me as one close to me, as the first to come. He is unique." Beyond this order stretches the realm of choice, proportion, judgement – and comparison. Comparison entails already the first act of violence: defiance of uniqueness. This violence cannot be avoided, since among the multiplicity of others certain divisions (assignment to classes, to categories) are necessary – they are "justified divisions". Ethics demands, one may say, certain self-limitation; so that the ethical demand may be fulfilled, certain sacred axioms of ethics must be sacrificed. The liberal state, says Levinas, the state grounded on the principle of human rights, is the implementation, and conspicuous manifestation, of that contradiction. Its function is nothing less than to "limit the original mercy from which justice originated". But "the internal contradiction" of the liberal state finds its expression in perceiving, "beyond and above all justice already incorporated in the regime, a justice more just . . . Justice in the liberal state is never definitive." "Justice is awaken by charity – such charity which is before justice but also after it." "Concern with human rights is not the function of the State. It is a non-state institution inside the State – an appeal to humanity which the State has not accomplished yet." Concern with human rights is an appeal to the "surplus of charity"; one might say, to something larger than any letter of Law, than anything that the state has done so far. State-administered justice is born of charity gestated and groomed within the primary ethical situation; yet justice may be administered only if it never stops being prompted by its original *spiritus movens*, if it knows of itself as of a never-ending chase of a forever elusive goal – the re-creation among the individuals/citizens of the uniqueness of the Other as Face . . . If it knows that it *cannot* "match the kindness which gave it birth and keeps it alive" – but that it cannot ever *stop trying* to do just that.

Just what can one learn from Levinas' exploration of the "world of the Third", the "world of the multiplicity of others" – the social world? One can learn, to put it in the nutshell, that this world of the social is, simultaneously, the legitimate offspring and a distortion of the moral world. The idea of justice is conceived at the moment of encounter between the experience of uniqueness (as given in the moral responsibility for the Other) and the experience of multiplicity of others (as given in social life). It cannot be conceived in any other circumstances, it needs both parents and to both it is genetically related, even if the genes, though being complementary, contain also contradictory genetic messages.

If not for the memory of uniqueness of the Face, there would be no idea of generalized, "impersonal" justice. And this is the case in spite of the fact that impersonality means the defiance and the denial of personhood – of the selfsame value which is to be cherished and groomed and defended and preserved in moral relationship (moral responsibility is taken up in the name of exactly such a preservation). Thus, paradoxically, morality is the school of justice – even if the category of justice is alien to it and within the moral relationship redundant (justice comes into its own together with comparison, but there is nothing to compare when the Other is encountered as unique). The "primal scene" of ethics is thereby also the primal, ancestral scene of social justice.

Another paradox: justice becomes necessary when moral impulse, quite self-sufficient inside the moral party of two, is found to be a poor guide once it ventures beyond the boundaries of that party. The infinity of the moral responsibility, the unlimitedness (even the silence!) of moral demand simply cannot be sustained when "the Other" appears in the plural (one may say that there is an inverse ratio between the infinity of "Being for" and the infinity of the Others). But it is that moral impulse which makes justice necessary: it resorts to justice in the name of self-preservation, though while doing it it risks being cut down, trimmed, maimed, or watered down. In the *Dialogue sur le penser-à-l'Autre* (1987) the interviewer asked Levinas:

> As far as I am an ethical subject, I am responsible for everything in everybody; my responsibility is infinite. Is it not so that such a situation is unlivable for me, and for the other, whom I risk to terrorise with my ethical voluntarism? Does it not follow that ethics is impotent in its will to do good?

To which Levinas gave the following answer:

> I do not know whether such a situation is unlivable. Certainly, such a situation is not what one would call agreeable, pleasant to live with, but it is good. What is extremely important – and I can assert this without being myself a saint, and without pretending to be a saint – is to be able to say that a human truly deserving that name, in its European sense, derived from the Greeks and the Bible, is a human being who considers saintliness the ultimate value, an unassailable value.

This value is not surrendered once the stern, uncompromising ethical requirement of "being-for" is replaced by a somewhat diluted and less stressful code of justice. It remains what it was – the ultimate value, reserving to itself the right to invigilate, monitor, and censure all deals entered into in the name of justice. Constant tension and never qualmed suspicion rules in the relationship between ethics and the just state, its never-industrious-enough plenipotentiary. Ethics is not a derivative of the State; the ethical authority does not derive from the State powers to legis-late and to enforce the Law. It precedes the state, it is the sole source of

MORALITY BEGINS AT HOME 225

the state's legitimacy and the ultimate judge of that legitimacy. The state, one might say, is justifiable only as a vehicle or instrument of ethics.

Levinas' view of the ethical origins of justice and the state itself as an instrument of justice (and, obliquely, of the ethics itself) can be interpreted as a phenomenological insight into the meaning of justice – or as a non-neutral (indeed, per-locutionary in the Austinian sense) "etiological myth", setting the stage for the subordination of the state to ethical principles and subjecting it to the ethical criteria of evaluation, as well as setting the limits to the state's freedom of ethical manoeuvre. It can hardly be seen, though, as a comprehensive account of the complex and convoluted process through which ethical responsibility for the Other comes (or does not come, as the case may be) to be implemented on a generalized scale through the works of the state and its institution. It certainly goes a long way towards explaining the growing concern with the plight of the "generalized Other" – the far-away Other, the Other distant in space and time; but it says little about the ways and means through which that concern may bring practical effects, and even less about the reasons for such effects falling so saliently short of needs and expectations, or not being visible at all.

Levinas' writings offer rich inspiration for the analysis of the endemic aporia of moral responsibility. They offer nothing comparable for the scrutiny of the aporetic nature of justice. They do not confront the possibility that – just as in the case of assuming moral responsibility for the Other – the work of the institutions which Levinas wishes to be dedicated to the promotion of justice may have consequences detrimental to the moral values. Neither do they allow for the possibility that such detrimental consequences may be more than just a side-effect of mistakes and neglect, being rooted instead in the very way such institutions can – must – operate to remain viable.

Quite a few insights into the latter issue can be found in the work of another great ethical philosopher of our times – Hans Jonas. Unlike Levinas, Jonas puts our present moral quandary in historical perspective, representing it as an event in time, rather than an extemporal, metaphysical predicament. According to Jonas, for the greater part of human history the gap between "micro" and "macro" ethics did not present a problem; the short reach of the moral drive was not fraught with terminal dangers for the simple reason that the consequences of human deeds (given the technologically determined scale of human action) were equally limited. What has happened in quite recent times is the tremendous growth of the possible consequentiality of human acts unmatched by a similar expansion of human moral capacity. What we can do now may have effects on distant lands and distant generations; effects as profound and radical as they are unpredictable, transcending the power of the always time-bound and place-bound human imagination, and morally uncontrollable, stepping far beyond the issues with which human moral capacity had got used to coping. Yet the awareness of responsibility for all this did not make much progress. Quite the contrary: the same development which put in the hands of human kind powers, tools, and weapons of unprecedented magnitude, requiring close normative regulation, "eroded the foundations from which norms could be derived; it has destroyed the very idea of norm as such". Both departures are the work of science which suffers no boundary to what humans can do, but neither takes gladly the argument that not all that could be done should be done; the ability to do something is, for science and for technology (its executive arm), all the reason ever needed for doing it, come what may. New powers need new ethics, and need it badly – as a matter of our collective life and death. But the new powers undermine the very possibility of satisfying that need, by denying in theory and in practice the right of ethical consideration to interfere with, let alone to arrest, their own endless and self-propelling growth.

This blind tendency must be reversed, Jonas demands. New ethics must be called into being, one made to the measure of new human powers; a sort of new categorical imperative – like "Act so that the effects of your action are compatible with the permanence of genuine human life". This is not easy though. First, violating such an imperative Mark 2, unlike in the case of the original Kantian version, entails no rational contradiction, and thus is deprived of the sole *ratio* to which the logic of science would accord a self-imposing and unquestionable authority. Second, it is notoriously difficult, nay impossible, to know for sure which deeds of technoscience are, and which are not, "compatible with the permanence of genuine human life" – at least not before the damage, often irreparable, has been done. Even in the unlikely event of the new categorical imperative having been awarded normative authority, the vexing question of its application would still remain open: how to argue convincingly that a controversial development should be stopped, if its effects cannot be measured in advance with such a degree of precision, with that near-algorithmic certainty, that scientific reason would be inclined to respect? If a truly algorithmic calculation of the looming dangers is not on the cards, Jonas suggests, we should settle for its second-best substitute, "*heuristics* of fear": to try our best to visualize the most awesome and the most durable among the consequences of given technological action. Above all, we need to apply the "principle of uncertainty": "The prophecy of doom is to be given greater heed than the prophecy of bliss." We need, one could say, an ethics of systematic pessimism, so that we may err, if at all, solely on the side of caution.

Kant's trust in the grip of ethical law rested on the conviction that there are arguments of reason which every reasonable person, being a reasonable person, must accept; the passage from ethical law to ethical action led through rational thought, and to smooth the passage one needed only to take care of the non-contradictory rationality of the law, counting for the rest on the endemic rational faculties of moral actors. In this respect, Jonas stays faithful to Kant – though he is the first to admit that nothing as uncontroversial as Kant's categorical imperative (that is, no principle which cannot be violated without violating simultaneously the logical law of contradiction) can be articulated in relation to the new challenge to human ethical faculties. For Jonas, as for Kant, the crux of the issue is the capacity of the legislative reason; and the promotion, as well as the eventual universality, of ethical conduct is ultimately a philosophical problem and the task of the philosophers. For Jonas, as for Kant, the fate of ethics is fully and truly in the hands of Reason and its *alter ego* – *un*reason. In this scheme of things there is no room left for the possibility that reason may, even if only on occasion, militate against what is, in its name, promoted as ethical principles.

In other words, there is no room left for the logic of human interests and the logic of social institutions – those organized interests whose function is, in practice if not by design, to make the by-passing of ethical restrictions feasible and ethical considerations irrelevant to the action. Neither is there room left for the otherwise trivial sociological observation that for the arguments to be accepted they need to accord with interests in addition to (or instead of) being rationally flawless. There is no room either for another equally trivial phenomenon of "unanticipated consequences" of human action – of deeds bringing results left out of account, or unthought of at the time the action was undertaken. Nor is there room for the relatively simple guess that when interests are many and at odds with each other, any hope that a certain set of principles will eventually prevail and will be universally obeyed must seek support in a sober analysis of social and political forces capable of securing its victory.

I suggest that a mixture of all those factors – overlooked or ignored and left out of account in Jonas' search for the new ethics – can be blamed for the present plight of the world, in which growing awareness of the dangers ahead goes hand in hand with growing impotence to prevent them or to alleviate the gravity of their impact. In theory, we seem to know better and better that if catastrophe is to be averted the currently unruly forces must be kept in check and controlled by factors other than endemically disperse and diffuse, as well as short-sighted, interests. In practice, however, the consequences of human actions rebound with a blind, elemental force reminiscent more of earthquakes, floods, and tornadoes than of the model of rational and self-monitored behaviour. As Danièle Sallenave has recently reminded us, Jean-Paul Sartre could aver, just a few decades ago, that "there are no such things as natural disasters"; but today natural disasters have turned into the prototype and model of all the miseries that afflict the world, and one could as well reverse Sartre's statement and say that "there are none other than natural catastrophes". It is not just the dramatic changes in the degree of livability of our natural habitat (pollution of air and water, global warming, ozone holes, acid rain, salination or dessication of the soil, etc.), but also the thoroughly human aspects of global conditions (wars, demographic explosions, mass migrations and displacements, social exclusion of large categories of the population) that come unannounced, catch us unawares, and seem utterly oblivious to the anguished cries for help and to the most frantic efforts to design, let alone to provide, remedies.

Obviously, these are not results one can account for following Jonas' ethical strategy. The dearth of ethical knowledge and understanding can hardly be blamed for what is happening. No one except lunatic fringes certified as lunatic fringes would seriously aver that it is good and beneficial to pollute the atmosphere, to pierce the ozone layer, or for that matter to wage wars, to overpopulate the land, or to make people into homeless vagabonds. Yet all this happens despite its consensual, well-nigh universal and vociferous condemnation. Some factors other than ethical ignorance must be at work if the grinding, systemic consistency of the global damage more than matches the cohesion of ethical indignation. One may sensibly surmise that those other factors are entrenched in such aspects of social reality as either are left unaffected by ethical philosophy, or are able successfully to withstand or by-pass its pressures; or, better still, render ethical demands inaudible. Among such factors, the increasingly deregulated market forces, exempt from all effective political control and guided solely by the pressures of competitiveness, must be awarded pride of place. The sheer size of the main players in the global markets far exceeds today the interfering capacity of most, if not all, elected state governments – those forces amenable, at least in principle, to ethical persuasion. General Motors had in 1992 an annual turnover of USD132.4 billion, Exxon of 155.7 billion, Royal Dutch/Shell of 99.6 billion, against a gross national product of USD123.5 billion of Denmark, 112.9 billion of Norway, 83.8 billion of Poland, and 33.5 billion of Egypt. The five biggest "non-national" companies had a joint turnover just twice as big as the GDP of the whole of sub-Saharan Africa.

This is what Jonas' problem is about: the globally disastrous long-distance and long-term effects of the growing human potential to do things and re-make the world. This is undoubtedly one of the crucial problems with which any macro-ethical reasoning must come to grips. But it is not the only problem; moreover, it is not the one with which Levinas was concerned in the first place. For Levinas, the macro-ethical extension of moral responsibility for the Other reaches further than the defence against shared dangers. His postulates addressed to macro-ethics are therefore more demanding yet than everything which Jonas' "heuristics of fear" may require. Let us recall that for Levinas the macro equivalent of moral responsibility is nothing less than *justice* – a quality of human existence which obviously needs the prevention of global disasters as its preliminary condition, but on no account can be reduced to it, and which need not be provided for and satisfied even if that prevention was somehow made effective.

Unlike disasters which can be *universally* recognized as detrimental and undesirable because they hit at *random* and pay no heed to earned or inherited privileges, justice is a notoriously *contentious* issue. Rarely has human ingenuity and imagination been stretched as much and as painfully as when devising the arguments meant to depict as "justice being done" the state of affairs which some other people considered unjust and thus a legitimate reason for rebellion. One can sensibly expect that in a divided society, and above all in a modern society, which is – simultaneously! – sharply unequal *and* dedicated to the promotion of equality as a supreme value, the contents of justice will forever remain a matter of controversy (Levinas admitted as much, though from a somewhat different angle, when pointing out that the fate of just society is to remain forever dissatisfied with the level of justice achieved). Above all, agreement about when to assume that the postulate of justice has been satisfied, if such agreement were at all attainable, would hardly be reached through philosophical argument alone – appealing as it must to extraterritorial and extemporal joint human essence, while neglecting on the whole the time- and space-bound social, cultural, and political circumstances gestating the experience of injustice.

We know from the thorough and perceptive historical analysis conducted by Barrington Moore Jr that, although "the masses" (more generally, the non-philosophical part of the population) have no, or at best a vague idea of the abstract notion of "justice as such", they tend to recognize unerringly the case of *injustice*. In opposition to what the logic of the vocabulary suggests, "injustice" is the "positive" notion, whereas "justice" is the "negative" one; it is *injustice* that seems to be the prime notion of popular ethics, "justice" being the marked, a derivative, unit in the opposition. Justice makes sense here solely as the enemy (and postulated conqueror) of injustice, the latter being the sole "datum" given in experience; justice means redemption, recuperation of losses, making good the damage, compensation for ills suffered – repairing the distortion caused by the act of *injustice*. In the light of Barrington Moore Jr's findings, it is difficult to say under what conditions the popular perception of the human condition as just and proper will tend to grow, and it is doubtful whether such a growth, if it occurs, will be subject to any ascertainable and generalizable rules. On the other hand, one can reasonably assume that perception of the state of affairs as *unjust* will tend to spread and deepen together with the intensification of the hardships already condemned as unjust and the appearance of new hardships not experienced before (whatever the starting point used to be and however well or badly it fared from the point of view of any abstract models of justice).

If this is the case, then the past three or four decades have done little to enhance the perception of the world as "just". Quite the contrary: virtually all indices of welfare and quality of life point towards growing inequality and, indeed, rampant polarization both on the global scale and inside almost every social political unit: rapid enrichment at one pole is made all the more salient and offensive by rapid impoverishment on the other. The visibility of the process, and the likelihood of its condemnation as unjust, have been further increased by the fact that during the same period, between 1960 and 1992, literacy in the world grew from 46 per cent to 69 per cent and the length of life-expectancy from 46.2 to 63 years. The first factor, coupled with the formidable spread of worldwide communications (which made poverty, once a local plight and local "problem" into a question of "relative deprivation"), must have facilitated competent comparisons of jarringly unequal life standards, while the second factor must to a large degree have arrested the "natural solutions" to the "problems" of extreme deprivation and poverty among the "surplus" or "supernumerary", that is "economically redundant", section of the population.

And the degree of polarization (and therefore also of relative deprivation) has in these three decades broken all recorded and remembered records. In 1960, the top fifth of the world population was 30 times richer than the bottom fifth; in 1991 it was 61 times richer. Nothing points to the likelihood in the foreseeable future of this widening of the gap to be slowed down or stopped, let alone reversed. In 1991, the top fifth of the world enjoyed 84.7 percent of the world's gross product, 84.2 percent of global trade and 85.0 percent of internal investment, against, respectively. 1.4 percent, 0.9 percent, and 0.9 percent, of the bottom fifth. The top fifth consumed 70 percent of world energy, 75 percent of metals, and 85 percent of timber. On the other hand, the debt of the economically weak countries of the Third World, more or less stable at around USD200 billion in 1970, has grown tenfold since then and is today fast approaching the mind-boggling figure of USD2000 billion.

This picture of rapidly growing inequality on the global scale is replicated inside virtually every single "national society". The gap between the rich and the poor, whether measured on the scale of global markets or on a much smaller scale of whatever passes for "national economies" (but is increasingly little more than administratively circumscribed units of computations), is becoming unbridgeable, and the prevailing feeling is that the rich are likely to become richer still, but the poor will most certainly grow poorer. That feeling is likely to be reforged, at the receiving end, into the experience of a wrong having been done, of unfairness and injustice. It does not follow, though, that it will necessarily trigger a desire for collective vindication of wrongs. The shared plight may well be interpreted as an aggregate of individual mishaps, caused by personal indolence or inadequacy – and feed non-cumulative efforts of personal exit from misery and a dream of individual good luck.

That last probability is enhanced by the widely evident tendency to overlay the division between rich and poor by another division – that between the seduced and oppressed. While the rich (presumed satisfied) enjoy a high degree of personal freedom of choice, responding keenly and joyfully to the growing range of attractive market offers, it is all too easy to redefine those who do not respond in the way expected of proper (seductible) consumers as people unfit to put their freedom of choice to good use – people who are, in the last account, unfit to be free. Moreover, the poor of today (those hopelessly flawed consumers, immune to market blandishments and unlikely to contribute to the supply-clearing demand, however alluring that supply may be) are of no evident use to consumer-oriented markets, and increasingly also to state governments, acting more and more as local bailiffs and sheriffs on behalf of extraterritorial finance and commerce. The poor of today are no longer "exploited people" producing a surplus product later to be transformed into capital; nor are they the "reserve army of labour", expected to be reintegrated into that capital-producing process at the next economic upturn. Economically speaking (and today politically elected governments also speak in the language of economy), they are fully and truly *redundant*, useless, disposable – and there is no "rational reason" for their continuing presence. The sole *rational* response to that presence is the systematic effort to exclude them from "normal" society, that is, the society which reproduces itself through the play of consumer supply and consumer choice, mediated by allurement and seduction.

Short of being physically disposed of (pressure for such a "solution" is manifested most conspicuously in the populist slogans demanding the deportation of foreigners, that "drain on our resources", and closing the borders to migrants, *a priori* defined as parasites and spongers, not creators of wealth), they need to be isolated, neutralized, and disempowered, so that the likelihood of their massive, yet individually experienced, miseries and humiliations being condensed into collective (let alone effective) protest is further diminished, ideally reduced to naught. Such results are sought through the two-pronged strategy of the criminalization of poverty and the brutalization of the poor.

Criminalization seems to be emerging as the consumer society's prime substitute for fast-disappearing welfare state provisions. The welfare state, that response to the poverty problem at the time when the poor were the "reserve army of labour" and were expected to be groomed back into the productive process, is in the changed conditions no longer "economically justifiable" and is increasingly seen as a "luxury we cannot afford". The "problem" of the poor is recast as a question of law and order, and social funds once earmarked for the rehabilitation of people temporarily out of work (in economic terms, the re-commodification of labour) are pumped into the construction and technological up-dating of prisons and other punitive/surveillance outfits. The switch is most pronounced in the USA, where the prison population tripled between 1980 and 1993, reaching 1 012 851 in June 1994 (the average growth was more than 65 000 a year). The poorest, black part of the "underclass" constitutes roughly half of those sentenced to one year of imprisonment and more, and the systematic increase in expenditure on police and prisons goes hand in hand with systematic cuts in welfare funds and entitlements. Some observers suggest that massive incarceration, spine-chilling stories of lengthening death-row queues, and a systematic and deliberate deterioration in prison conditions (the progressive and widely advertised dehumanization of prisoners) are deployed as the principal means of "terrorization" of the underclass, now presented to public opinion as – purely, simply, and unambiguously – the enemy number one of public safety and a drain on public resources. One may guess at another function, however – a deterrent to the possible rebellion of the well-off against the tensions endemic to consumer life; the horrors of the alternative to the "free consumer" life render palatable and endurable even the most vexing stresses for which that life is notorious. Europe is as yet far behind the United States, but a similar trend, albeit on a much diminished scale, is in evidence. According to statistics provided by the Council of Europe, between 1983 and 1992 the prison population grew by more than 50 percent in Greece, Spain, Portugal, and the Netherlands, and by between 20 and 50 percent in France, Switzerland, Ireland, and Sweden; everywhere the trend was upwards.

Policing, and thereby obliquely criminalizing, the "global poor" – that is, the areas of the world afflicted with, or allocated to, the endemic poverty – is another necessary accompaniment of growing inequality, confronting the rich part of the world with a no less urgent, yet much more complex task. Police operations, military expeditions, long-term "pacification" of troublesome areas are costly affairs, which well-off taxpayers are the less willing to finance the more distant from home, and therefore less relevant to their own well-being, they appear to be. The task of keeping the "global poor" at bay is thus the most suitable case for the deregulation, privatization, and commercialization of punitive and surveillance activity that is still applied only half-heartedly and gingerly in the domestic prison system. No excessive ingenuity is needed to move the task altogether from the "debit" to the "credit" side of the budget: supplying local chiefs and warlords of distant lands with sophisticated weapons may bring the double profit of financial gains and such a brutalization of life as is guaranteed to all but paralyse the protest potential of the poor. The endless, increasingly devastating and ever less ideologically motivated (or in any other way "cause-oriented", for that matter) civil (or simply gang) wars are from the rich countries' point of view utterly effective, cheap, and often profitable forms of policing and "pacifying" the global poor. Beamed to millions of TV screens for everybody to watch, they provide a vivid testimony of the savagery of the poor and the self-inflicted character of their misery, as well as convincing arguments for the pointlessness of aid, let alone any substantial redistribution of wealth.

Brutalization of the poor (not necessarily deliberately induced, but eagerly embraced once it appears, keenly transformed into a "public concern number one", and beefed up and magnified by constantly spurred media attention) may also be seen as serving the task of policing the domestic scene. Made into the outcasts of the thriving society of seduced consumers, transformed into an underclass without a present or prospective place in society, and deprived of the legally recognized tokens of access to the goods hailed as having the highest value in the good life, the poor tend to resort to drugs, those poor man's (and illegal) substitutes for the rich man's (and legal) tools of consumer ecstasy. They also on occasion initiate the politically neglected "redistribution of wealth", attacking the nearest-to-hand private possessions and thus supplying the guardians of law and order with the most welcome statistical proof of the close link between being a ghetto-dweller and being a criminal, keenly used (the way all self-fulfilling prophecies normally are) in support of the criminalization of poverty. From time to time the outcasts of consumer society assume the role of its Luddites – going on the rampage, demolishing and burning down shops, those outposts of consumerism scattered on the hostile, not-yet-conquered, perhaps unconquerable territory; committing acts which are immediately re-presented as riots and thus further proof, if further proof were needed, that the question of the underclass is – first and foremost, perhaps even solely – a problem of law and order.

To conclude: the situation of a large part of the present-day population, whether located in the areas of the globe afflicted with endemic poverty or residing within the relatively well-off societies boasting high GNP and high "average" levels of consumption, is not just "comparatively bad", but also rapidly – and thus palpably – deteriorating. Under such conditions, one would expect a widespread feeling of *injustice*, with a potential to condense into a mass protest movement, if not an open rebellion against the system. The fact that this does not happen testifies perhaps to the effectiveness of the combined strategies of exclusion, criminalization, and brutalization of potentially "problematic" strata.

This, however, is not the problem most relevant to our main topic: the question of "macro-ethics" as essentially one of justice as the extension of the responsibility for the Other that is induced and trained inside the "moral party of two". Even if the experience of growing deprivation did lead to an effective protest of and by the poor, this would be, by and large, the case of a forceful *vindication* of claims, maybe a case of redistribution of inequalities – not necessarily heralding the rule of ethical principles in the world of economy and politics and unlikely to promote the cause of "ethical politics". If justice is to be understood, as Levinas wants, as stretching out and generalizing the narrowly applied and selective responsibility for the singular or singled out Other, then, like that responsibility, it needs to arise not from the demands of the Other, but from the moral impulse and concern of the moral self which assumes the responsibility for justice being done. *Demanding* is not by itself a moral act (only its recognition may be); awarding the right to demand, and even more the anticipation of a yet-unspoken-demand, is. Moral responsibilities are asymmetrical and non-reciprocal.

The *ethical* question, therefore, is not so much whether the new deprived and disprivileged stand up and are counted fighting for justice – which they can understand only as rectification of the injustice done to them – as whether the well-off and by the same token privileged, the new "contented majority" of J. K. Galbraith, rise above their singular or group interests and consider themselves responsible for the humanity of the Others, the less fortunate. Whether, in other words, they are ready to endorse, in thought and in deed, and before they are forced to do so and not out of the fear of being forced, such principles of justice as could not be satisfied unless the Others are awarded the same degree of practical, positive freedom they have been enjoying themselves.

The proposition that being ready to do exactly that is the condition *sine qua non* of such justice as may be properly considered the "macro" equivalent of a "micro" moral stance is a philosophical one. Whether the contented majority is likely to do it, however, is a sociological and political question. More to the point: the factors which facilitate and the factors which hamper the chances of taking up responsibility for admittedly weaker and less outspoken Others (precisely *because* of their weakness and inaudibility) is not an issue which can be unpacked theoretically by philosophical analysis or resolved practically by the normative/persuasive efforts of philosophers.

It goes without saying that the problem of justice cannot be so much as posited unless there is already in place a democratic regime of tolerance which guarantees, in its constitution and political practice, "human rights" – that is, the right to retain one's identity and uniqueness without risking persecution. This tolerance is a necessary condition of all justice; the point is, though, that it is not its *sufficient* condition. By itself, the democratic regime does not promote (let alone guarantee) the transformation of tolerance into *solidarity* – that is, the recognition of other people's misery and sufferings as one's own responsibility, and the alleviation and eventually the removal of misery as one's own task. More often than not, given the present shape of political mechanisms, democratic regimes translate tolerance as callousness and indifference.

Most democratic political systems are moving today from the parliamentary or party rule model towards the model of "opinion poll rule", where the composition of political platforms and decision-making on controversial issues are guided by the advance consideration of the relative popularity of the intended move and careful calculation of anticipated electoral gains and losses – the number of votes a given measure may attract and the number of electors it may repel. As has been noted by political scientists, this attitude leads in practice to the rule of the "median voter" principle: no measure is likely to be undertaken by the government of a country if it is not seen as being "in the interest" of at least half the voters plus one. With the demise of the welfare state as all-inclusive, universal entitlement to collective insurance, and its replacement with a model of administered charity for the minority who fail the "means test" (that is, are certified as "sub-normal") – the chance of the "median voter" approving of larger welfare provision (now experienced first and foremost as an increased burden of taxation) has shrunk radically. Hence the growing electoral approval for the demotion of the welfare state and for leaving the impecunious and the destitute to their own (non-existent or inadequate) resources. Under present conditions, it is not very hard, and certainly not fanciful, to imagine the majority of voters giving their democratic approval to the total and permanent removal of people dependent on the state-administered redistribution of resources from the list of public concerns.

Democracy is also a necessary condition of free public discussion of issues – and particularly of the issue of social justice and the ethical quality of public affairs. Without democracy, with its freedom of expression and open controversy, it is difficult to envisage a serious consideration of the shape of the good society, of the overall ends which political decision-making should promote and the principles by which its effects ought to be critically assessed, or mature public awareness of the risks ahead and the chances of their prevention. And yet, once more, one finds that, being a necessary condition of public awareness, democracy is not the sufficient condition of the public action that such awareness would demand. Again and again one finds a growing gap, indeed a contradiction, between values promoted in the public discussion and those whose cause is served by political practice. Aversion to war, loathing of cruelty, abhorrence of massacre, rape, and looting are today almost universal – yet wars and genocides on an ever-growing scale are made possible by the saturation of present and prospective warring factions with modern weapons, whose production and sale are keenly promoted by politicians and supported by their voters in the name of the national balance of payments and defence of jobs. Pictures of famine and destitution arouse universal alarm and anger – yet the destruction of the economic self-sufficiency of the afflicted peoples in the name of free trade, open markets and favourable trade balances can count on the wide support of democratic electorates. The progressive depletion of world resources and associated mortgaging of the life conditions of future generations are unanimously bewailed and protested against – yet politicians promising increased "economic growth", that is, a larger-yet consumption of non-renewable resources, can invariably count on electoral success.

Two books have appeared recently in France by François Thual and

Bertrand Badie, which trace the contradictions of contemporary politics and the resulting impossibility of meeting the ends which enjoy widespread, perhaps even universal, approval with the principle of *territoriality* – the principle which was taken originally for the major tool in the modern struggle for the rule of law and order, but proved to be a major source of contemporary world disorder. The authors point to the present practical impotence of states, which however remain to this day the only sites and agencies for the articulation and execution of laws; devoid of all real executive power, not self-sufficient, and unsustainable militarily, economically, or culturally, those "weak states", "quasi-states", often "imported states" nevertheless claim territorial sovereignty – capitalizing on identity wars and appealing to, or rather whipping up, dormant tribal instincts. It might be seen that the kind of sovereignty which relies on tribal sentiments alone is a natural enemy of tolerance and civilized norms of cohabitation. But the territorial fragmentation of legislative and policing power with which it is intimately associated is also a major obstacle to effective control over the forces that truly matter, which are all, or almost all, global and extraterritorial in character.

Thual's and Badie's arguments carry a lot of conviction. And yet their analysis seems to stop short of unravelling the full complexity of the present plight. Contrary to what the authors suggest, the territorial principle of political organization does not stem from tribal instincts alone, natural or contrived, and its relation to the processes of economic and cultural globalization is not simply one of the "spoke in the wheel" kind. In fact, there seems to be an intimate kinship, mutual conditioning, and reciprocal reinforcement between "globalization" and "territorialization". Global finance, trade, and information industry depend for their liberty of movement and unconstrained freedom to pursue their ends on the political fragmentation of the world scene. They have all, one might say, developed vested interests in "weak states" – that is, in such states as are *weak* but nevertheless remain *states*. Such states can be easily reduced to the (useful) role of local police stations, securing the modicum of order required for the conduct of business, but need not be feared as effective brakes on the global companies' freedom. It is not difficult to see that the replacement of territorial "weak states" by some sort of global legislative and policing powers would be detrimental to the extraterritorial companies' interests. And so it is easy to suspect that, far from being at war with each other, political "tribalization" and economic "globalization" are close allies and fellow conspirators. What they conspire against are the chances of justice being done and being seen to be done; but also the chances that neighbourhood responsibilities will swell, stretch, and eventually grow into a consistent concern for global justice – and result in a politics effectively guided by ethical principles.

Immersed as we are in the "primal scene of morality", in times that favour (though not necessarily guarantee) the "re-moralization" of primary human relations and the facing up to the question of responsibility for the Other (a responsibility which comes to the surface also in the act of its denial and abandonment), we cannot help becoming increasingly morally sensitive, and, as Levinas suggested, are also prone to set ourselves ethical goals that reach beyond the narrow sphere of the "moral party of two" – into the world ruled by the principles of justice rather than by personal responsibility. It seems, however, that the social institutions which could conceivably serve as the vehicles of that extended ethical sensitivity in fact bar its translation into the practical progress of justice. The road from the "primal moral scene" to macroethics leads through political action. But is there any kind of political action in sight which may prove adequate to this task?

In a recent article, Richard Rorty singles out "movement politics" as one dominant, and preferred, form of political action in modern times.

> Membership in a movement requires the ability to see particular campaigns for particular goals as parts of something much bigger. This bigger thing is the course of human events described as a process of maturation . . . [P]olitics is no longer just politics, but rather the matrix out of which will emerge something like Paul's "new being in Christ" or Mao's "new socialist man" – the mature stage of humanity, the one which will put aside current childishness . . .
>
> This kind of politics assumes that things must be changed utterly, so that a new kind of beauty may be born.

To this "movement politics" Rorty opposes "campaign politics", which disposes of the idea of "maturation", "growing rationality", and "forward movement of history", without which movement politics would have had no legitimacy and would have been unable to accord sense to any of its undertakings. "Campaigns for such goals as the unionization of migrant workers in the American Southwest, or banning big trucks from the Alps, or the overthrow (by votes or by force) of a corrupt government, or legal recognition of gay marriage, can stand on their own feet." The turn away from movements and toward campaigns, Rorty suggests, is a turn away from the transcendental question "What are the conditions of possibility of this historical movement?" to the pragmatic question "What are the causal conditions of replacing this present actuality with a better future actuality?" ... The intellectuals of our century have been distracted from campaigns by the need to "put events in perspective," and by the urge to organize movements around something out of sight, something located at the impossibly distant end of this perspective. But this has made the best the enemy of the better.

It is better to concentrate on the better than on chasing the best, implies Rorty. The alternative, as we know now only too well, never managed to reach the best while it did manage to sacrifice a lot of the better into the bargain. Campaign politics looks attractive precisely as a substitution for the discredited movement politics, notorious for neglecting the real present for the sake of an imaginary future, only to neglect again today's future the moment it stops being imaginary. As a replacement for movement politics, campaign politics indeed has advantages that can hardly be dismissed; it may bring a lot of succour and genuine improvement here and there, now and then, to these or those people. Whether it will improve on the "totality" and drag mankind as a whole to a radically better condition is another matter. But doing this was neither its intention nor its promise. Its advantages over the alternative are thus indubitable. Its own virtues though – yet untried – are open to questioning.

What Rorty proposes here is a fragmented politics made to the measure of the fragmented world and fragmented human existence. His proposition squares and chimes well with the life-experience of many people with scattered, diffuse, and always partial – fragmented – worries; with American experience better than with Serbian or Croatian, with American Midwest better than with American Southeast, with American Midwest academics better than with American Midwest unemployed and ghetto-dwellers. It also fits well the fleeting and flitting attention of the era of shrunk space and flattened time – the kind of attention notorious for its inability to concentrate, to stay put, to cling to any object for longer than the attraction of novelty lasts; an attention that uses itself up before it consumes its object and shifts perpetually in search of new attractions, acquiring in the process remarkable skating and gliding skills but shunning all deep diving and digging.

Choosing political strategies means also taking sides in political/social divisions. Fragmented politics, a politics in which campaigns do not cumulate into movements and do not count the overall improvement of life among their ends, must look flawless – and, above all, as the sole politics needed – to those whose worries are fragmented, do not cumulate into an experience of injustice, and do not sum up into the desire to change the rules of the game or the world in which the game is played. There are many such people; as Galbraith suggested, they constitute the "contented majority", at least inside the "contented minority" of well-to-do countries. Is not Rorty's proposition addressed primarily to them? Does not Rorty's proposition tell them what they wish to hear: that there is not much point in worrying about the justice of the world, in assuming responsibility for the unfreedom and prospectless life of those whose worries are not as scattered, unfocused, and peripheral as our own? That these "big issues" of justice are best served when split and fragmented just like their own problems are, and never confronted in their genuine or imaginary entirety, as the question of "something being wrong with that world we all share"? And, above all, that those "big issues" have nothing to do with the fragmentariness of our own affluent worries, and with our decision to settle for "campaigns" instead of "movements"?

These are perhaps the reasons Rorty's proposition rings true and proper to us, its intended addressees. They are unlikely to be received as good news by many others, who may well spy a Pontius Pilate gesture in this recipe for "deconstructing" the big issue (which we have decided that we can do nothing about) into a series of little ones (which we think we can do something about without sacrificing the big and little comforts we like so much about our life). This clash of perspectives and ensuing perceptions is, however, once more an essentially *political*, rather than ethical, issue. More directly relevant to our subject-matter on the other hand is the question of the *ethical* ramifications of Rorty's proposition. More particularly – what does it augur for the feasibility of the Levinasian passage from micro- to macro-ethics, from the self's responsibility for the Face to commonly administered justice?

To invoke Bakhtin's famous analysis of the function of the "carnival" in reasserting norms through the periodic yet strictly controlled visualization of their reversal, we may say that there is a pronounced tendency in the affluent part of the world to relegate charity, compassion, and brotherly sentiments (which according to Levinas underlie our desire for justice) to carnival events – thereby reasserting, legitimizing, and "normalizing" their absence from quotidianity. Moral impulses aroused by the sight of human misery are safely channelled into sporadic outbursts of charity in the form of Live Aid, Comic Aid, or money collections for the most recent wave of refugees. Justice turns into a festive, holiday event; this helps to placate the moral conscience and to make bearable the absence of justice during working days. Lack of justice becomes the norm and the daily routine.

These seem to be valid objections and well-grounded suspicions. What they suggest is that Rorty's project of "campaign politics" is unlikely to serve the cause of justice better than the "movement politics" it is proposed to replace. Instead of smoothing the road from personal morality to public justice, for which movement politics is notorious, it substitutes new dangers for the old ones. The cause of justice, one could say, is not "safe in its hands". And yet such caveats do not invalidate Rorty's proposal. They would amount to the round condemnation of campaign politics only if the set of assumptions which sustained and validated movement politics were retained; if it was believed that the lifting of moral sentiments to the level of public justice has not been accomplished "as yet" to full satisfaction solely because the right, reliable, and fully effective lever has not been found, but that a perfect crane to do the lifting job without fail can be construed and constructed, that designing it is but a matter of time and that historical time "runs towards" its construction. The point is, though, that those beliefs are ever more difficult to be seriously entertained. For all that we know today, history does not seem to run towards "just society", and all attempts to force it to run in this direction tend to add new injusticies to the ones they are bent on repairing. It seems more and more likely that justice is a movement, rather than a goal or any describable "end state"; that it manifests itself in the acts of spotting and fighting injustices – acts which do not necessarily add up to a linear process with a direction; and that its trademark is a perpetual self-deprecation and dissatisfaction with what has been achieved. Justice means always wanting more of itself.

And so it looks as if we need to reconcile ourselves to less than perfect, less than "100 percent effective" means. But it looks too as if such reconciliation is not necessarily bad news for the prospects of justice; it may well be, on the contrary, more akin to the nature of justice – and thus, in the last account, better serve its cause. Rorty's proposal offers just what is needed: the salutary irony that pierces the veil of humourless, unctuous solemnity of "alternative world" movements – but irony that itself is treated seriously, like all fate should be, if one wants to live it consciously, as a vocation. The weaknesses of campaigns politics are simultaneously its strength. It is important not to entertain illusions and to know that partial, specific improvements are indeed partial and specific; that they settle problems, and do not resolve issues; that none of the improvements is likely to conclude the history of "humanity's long march to justice" and bring the progress to its victorious end; that every improvement will leave justice as wanting and as unsatisfied as it was before, as pressing for further effort, and as militating against all slow-down and let-up. Only when we know all this is the desire for justice likely to be immune to the most awesome of dangers – that of self-contentment and of a conscience once and for all cleaned and clear.

In this crucial respect the realm of justice does not differ from the realm of moral responsibility; it retains all the essential features fully formed already at the "primal moral scene". Both realms are kingdoms of ambivalence; both are conspicuously short of patented solutions, cures free of side-effects, and moves free of risks; both need that uncertainty, inconclusiveness, underdetermination, and ambivalence to keep the moral impulse and the desire for justice forever alive, vigilant, and – in their less than perfect, limited way – effective. Both have everything to gain and nothing to lose from knowing of their endemic and incurable ambivalence and refraining from an (in the end, suicidal) anti-ambivalence crusade. And so it is in its never-conclusive, never truly satisfactory, chronically imperfect form, in its state of perpetual self-indignation, that justice seems best to answer Levinas' description of it as the projection of moral sentiments upon the wide screen of society.

Both morality and justice (or, as some would prefer, micro- and macro-ethics) are true to their name only as open-ended conditions and projects aware of their open-endedness. They are linked by this similarity much as they are linked genetically. Let me repeat that the primal moral scene, the moral party of two, is the breeding ground of all responsibility for the Other and the training ground for all the ambivalence that the assumption of that responsibility necessarily contains. This being the case, it seems plausible that the key to a problem as large as social justice lies in a problem as (ostensibly) small scale as the primal moral act of taking up responsibility for the Other nearby, within reach – for the Other as Face. It is here that moral sensitivity is born and gains strength, until it grows strong enough to carry the burden of responsibility for any instance of human suffering and misery, whatever the legal rules or empirical investigations may say about their causal links and "objective" allocation of guilt.

NOTES AND REFERENCES

1. Emmanuel Levinas, *Le Moi et la totalité*, 1954.
2. Ibid.
3. Emmanuel Levinas, *La Souffrance inutile*, 1982.
4. Ibid.
5. *Philosophie, Justice et Amour*, 1982.
6. Emmanuel Levinas, *De l'unicité*, 1986.
7. François Poirié, *Emmanuel Lévinas: Qui êtes-vous?* Lyon: Éditions la Manufacture, 1987.
8. Emmanuel Levinas, *L'Autre, utopie et justice*, 1988.
9. *Dialogue sur le penser-à-l'Autre*, 1987.
10. Hans Jonas, *The Imperative of Responsibility*, Chicago: University of Chicago Press, 1984.
11. Danièle Sallenave, "L'Alibi de la compassion", *Le Monde Diplomatique*, July 1995.
12. *United Nations Programme for Development*, 1994.
13. François Thual, *Les Conflits identitaires*, Ellipses/Iris, ; Bertrand Badie, *La Fin des territoires*, Fayard.
14. All Badie's expressions.
15. Richard Rorty, "Movements and campaigns", *Dissent*, Winter 1995.
16. Ibid.

Contributors

ASBJØRN AARNES is professor emeritus of French at the University of Oslo. He has translated works by Descartes, Kafka, and Levinas, and he has published numerous books and articles on Continental literature, art, and philosophy.

ZYGMUNT BAUMAN is professor emeritus of sociology at the University of Leeds. He has published more than twenty books, including *Modernity and the Holocaust* (1989), *Modernity and Ambivalence* (1991), and *Postmodern Ethics* (1993).

R. S. DOWNIE is professor of moral philosophy at the University of Glasgow. Recent books include *The Making of a Doctor* (1992) and *The Healing Arts* (1994).

ALASTAIR HANNAY is professor of philosophy at the University of Oslo. He is the editor of *Inquiry*. In addition to translations of Kierkegaard, he has published *Kierkegaard* (1982, rev. ed. 1991) and *Human Consciousness* (1990).

HARALD JODALEN is associate professor of medicine at the University of Oslo and associate editor of *The Journal of the Norwegian Medical Association*.

EMMANUEL LEVINAS (1906-1995) was director at École Normale Israélite Orientale in Paris and professor of philosophy at the Sorbonne. His principal works in ethics are *Totality and Infinity* (1961) and *Otherwise Than Being or Beyond Essence* (1974). He has also written extensively on phenomenology and the philosophy of religion.

KNUD E. LØGSTRUP (1905–1981) was professor of theology at the University of Aarhus. Among his many books are *The Ethical Demand* (1956), *Norm and Spontaneity* (1972), and *Metaphysics I-IV* (1976ff.).

MARTHA C. NUSSBAUM is Ernst Freund Professor of Law and Ethics at the Law School, the University of Chicago. She has published many books and articles on ethics, besides co-editing a number of anthologies. Among her recent books are *Love's Knowledge* (1990) and *The Therapy of Desire* (1994).

JOACHIM RENN is a research fellow at the University of Erlangen, where he is helping prepare the collected works of Alfred Schütz for publication. He has published *Existentielle und kommunikative Zeit* (1997) and articles on hermeneutics and the philosophy of language.

ARNE JOHAN VETLESEN is associate professor of philosophy at the University of Oslo. He is the editor of the *Norwegian Journal of Philosophy*. He has published *Perception, Empathy, and Judgements* (1994) and four books on ethics in Norwegian.

Index

ECCL XII xii